Imperial Immigrants

Imperial Immigrants

Scottish Settlers in the
Upper Ottawa Valley, 1815–1840

MICHAEL E. VANCE

DUNDURN
TORONTO

Editor: Jane Gibson
Copy Editor: Cheryl Hawley
Design: Jesse Hooper
Printer: Webcom

Library and Archives Canada Cataloguing in Publication

Vance, Michael E. (Michael Easton), 1959-
    Imperial immigrants : Scottish settlers of the Upper Ottawa Valley, 1815-1840 / by Michael Vance.

Includes bibliographical references and index.
Issued also in electronic formats.
ISBN 978-1-55488-756-9

    1. Scots--Ottawa River Valley (Québec and Ont.)--History--19th century. 2. Ottawa River Valley (Québec and Ont.)--Emigration and immigration--History--19th century. 3. Scotland--Emigration and immigration--History--19th century. I. Title.

FC2779.S3V36 2012   971.38004'9163   C2012-900101-5

1 2 3 4 5   16 15 14 13 12

We acknowledge the support of the **Canada Council for the Arts** and the **Ontario Arts Council** for our publishing program. We also acknowledge the financial support of the **Government of Canada** through the **Canada Book Fund and Livres Canada Books**, and the **Government of Ontario** through the **Ontario Book Publishing Tax Credit** and the **Ontario Media Development Corporation**.

Care has been taken to trace the ownership of copyright material used in this book. The author and the publisher welcome any information enabling them to rectify any references or credits in subsequent editions.

J. Kirk Howard, President

Printed and bound in Canada.
www.dundurn.com

Dundurn	Gazelle Book Services Limited	Dundurn
3 Church Street, Suite 500	White Cross Mills	2250 Military Road
Toronto, Ontario, Canada	High Town, Lancaster, England	Tonawanda, NY
M5E 1M2	LA1 4XS	U.S.A. 14150

For my immigrant parents — Maggie and Easton

CONTENTS

LIST OF MAPS & TABLES

ABBREVIATIONS

AO: Archives of Ontario, Toronto

Con.: Concession Line

DCB: Dictionary of Canadian Biography

DNB: Oxford Dictionary of National Biography

LAC: Library and Archives Canada, Ottawa

NAS: National Archives of Scotland, Edinburgh

NA(UK): National Archives (United Kingdom), Kew, England

PCA: Presbyterian Church in Canada, Archives and Records Office, Toronto

QUA: Queen's University Archives, Kingston, Ontario

SBA: Scottish Business Archive, University of Glasgow

UCA: United Church of Canada Archives, Toronto

W.S.: Writer to the Signet

ACKNOWLEDGEMENTS

This book began life as a series of lectures that I gave to the Ontario Genealogical Society at their Migration Mosaic Seminar held in Ottawa in May 2000. The enthusiastic reception received from that very knowledgeable group encouraged me to consider making my research available to a wider audience. This plan received the keen support of Barry Penhale and Jane Gibson at Natural Heritage Books/Dundurn Press. Indeed, without their encouragement this book would never have been completed. There have been many challenges that had to be overcome, and I am grateful to Jane Gibson as editor for helping me navigate these difficulties.

Historical research of any kind relies on a great many institutions and individuals in order to be successful. I have benefitted enormously from the generous assistance provided by the staff at Library and Archives Canada in Ottawa, the Archives of Ontario, the National Archives in Edinburgh, and the National Archives at Kew Gardens in London.

While it would be impossible to acknowledge all those who have given me invaluable assistance, I would like to particularly thank several individuals. Barbara J. Griffith very generously shared with me her own research on the Scottish community in North Sherbrooke Township, and Karen Smith, Killam Library, Dalhousie University, gave invaluable assistance with the selection of images for this book. Emma Garden worked very patiently with me on the maps and I am very thankful for her attention to detail. Dr. Renée Hulan also carefully read over the entire manuscript in draft form and her suggestions are gratefully incorporated into this final version. I am indebted to her in ways far too numerous to mention here.

Finally, I wish to acknowledge the grant support that I have received over the years from the Faculty of Graduate Studies and Research at Saint Mary's University. That support allowed me to make the numerous trips needed to track down sources at various archives in Ontario and the United Kingdom.

It remains to be said, that while I have benefitted from the assistance provided by others, any errors or omissions in the following text are my sole responsibility.

Michael E. Vance
Halifax, Nova Scotia

Legend

Country
Border ....
Border

REGIONS

Communities

ORKNEY

Thurso

LEWIS
Stornoway

HARRIS

NORTH UIST

Elgin

Inverness

SKYE

GLENELG

SOUTH UIST

KNOYDART

Aberdeen

Fort William

BRAEDALBANE

Dundee

Perth

ARGYLL   Stirling

Alloa

Leith

Greenock   Edinburgh

Paisley   Glasgow   Dalkeith

Kilmarnock

Irvine   Lanark

Campbeltown   Ayr

Moffat

Dumfries

Stanraer

0   80 km

Carlisle

Cartographer: Emma Garden, August 2011. Base map modified from: T.C. Smout, A History of the Scottish People (London: W. Collins, 1969).

Map of Scotland

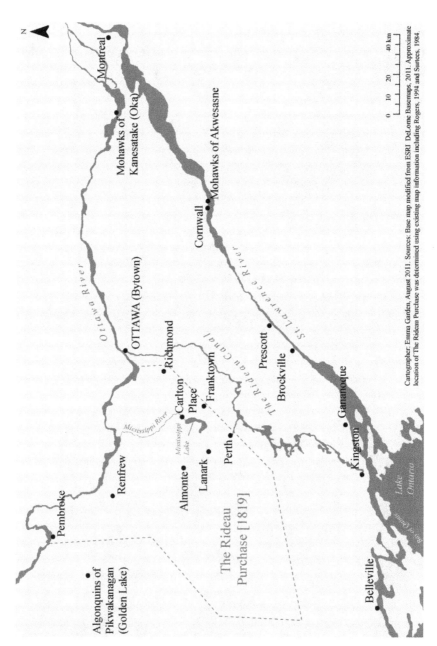

Ottawa Valley Region

Cartographer: Emma Garden, August 2011. Sources: Base map modified from ESRI DeLorme Basemaps, 2011. Approximate location of The Rideau Purchase was determined using existing map information including Rogers, 1994 and Surtees, 1984.

0   10   20   40 km

PREFACE

It has been twenty years since I first wrote about the Scots who settled in the Ottawa Valley in the early nineteenth century. At that time, I was trying to understand what conditions had prompted the British government to assist the nearly four thousand Scots, who had participated in the government schemes, to emigrate to Upper Canada, and why these individuals had chosen to leave their homeland. I concluded that while some of these Scots were small tenant farmers who had experienced considerable hardship brought about by large-scale reorganization of agriculture on Highland estates, the vast majority of the emigrants were people from the urban Lowlands in and around the vicinity of Glasgow who had greatly suffered in the economic depression that followed the Napoleonic Wars. I also discovered that these Lowland emigrants were skilled artisans who had petitioned government for assistance to emigrate by forming societies similar to artisan groups that had earlier demanded the reform of Parliament. One group of Scottish artisans had seen political change in the homeland as a solution to their postwar hardships, while the other viewed emigration as the best way to improve their lives, even though the two groups shared similar attitudes toward authority. I subsequently followed up on this initial research with an attempt to show how the Scottish experience of these Upper Canadian immigrants influenced the demand for political reform in the colony.

Much of that earlier research is included in this book, but in turning to the subject once more I have been prompted to ask new questions about this remarkable group of emigrants. Reflecting on one image in particular, *A First Settlement*, by the London-born illustrator William Henry Bartlett, led me to the central theme of this book — the relationship between Scottish emigration and British Imperialism. Bartlett's much reproduced engraving, drawn for Nathaniel Parker Willis's *Canadian Scenery* and first published in 1842, is one of the few contemporary illustrations that we have of bush life in the first days of settlement. It shows the young pioneer family beside their outdoor kitchen with a recently killed deer and surrounded by dark forest. A few stumps indicate where the logs for the house, still under construction, were obtained.

In evoking the rough conditions associated with pioneering, *A First Settlement* has understandably been a popular illustration, but Bartlett's *Wigwam in the Forest* frontispiece for Willis's *Canadian Scenery* is not as widely known. The overwhelming presence of the woods in both engravings and the attention to the construction of the dwellings in each reflects Bartlett's early training as an architectural artist, but it was the image of the First Nations family and not the settlers that was chosen to be the lead illustration for Willis's volume. Seen in their original context,

The settlers depicted in Bartlett's A First Settlement, *which appears near the end of Nathaniel Willis' second volume, are ill at ease in the forest. The casually strewn deer carcass and the bewildered expressions of the family members are in marked contrast with the tranquil scene represented in* Wigwam in the Forest. *From* Canadian Scenery, *vol. II.*

Courtesy of Killam Library, Dalhousie University.

Bartlett's illustrations remind us that the British reading public was well aware that the land being settled in Upper Canada was already inhabited, but they also demonstrate that both the "Indians" and the "Pioneers" were exotic subjects when viewed by an observer from the homeland.

Indeed, Bartlett's career was based on travelling to far-off lands, sketching what he saw, and publishing the results of his labour in order to satisfy a growing taste for the exotic. He began closer to home with illustrations of architectural ruins found throughout the British Isles before making several trips to North America and ended his career providing engravings for his own books on the Middle East. The frontispiece illustration from one of those later works, *Walks about the City*

William Henry Bartlett's sympathetic portrayal of the First Nations group in Wigwam in the Forest, *the frontispiece of* Canadian Scenery, *was echoed in his other representations of indigenous peoples. From Nathaniel P. Willis,* Canadian Scenery Illustrated *Vol. I (London: Nathaniel Parker, 1842).*

and Environs of Jerusalem, shows the same interest in family groups and domestic dwellings that is found in Bartlett's engravings for *Canadian Scenery* as it depicts a Jewish family at home. For Bartlett, then, the pioneer settler family represented in *A First Settlement* was yet another exotic subject to be recorded for a home audience, but scholars of imperialism have suggested that such images were themselves part of the process of colonization. In this view, drawing and mapping are essential preconditions for possessing. As a London-born and based artist, Bartlett, whether he was aware of it or not, could be seen as an agent for nineteenth-century British Imperial expansion.[1]

The Scottish settlers that came to the Ottawa Valley were part of this expansion of empire and this book re-examines them from this perspective. Fortunately, these settlers have been well-documented since they drew the attention of local chroniclers almost from the start. Among them were Reverend William Bell, the first Presbyterian clergyman in Perth, Ontario, who discusses the Scots settlers in his 1822 cautionary guide *Hints to Emigrants*, and Andrew Haydon, the Liberal senator whose 1925 book, *Pioneer Sketches of the District of Bathurst*, was the first to incorporate a detailed account of the assisted-emigration scheme into a history of the upper Ottawa Valley.

More recently, highly informative community histories by Glenn J. Lockwood, Jean S. McGill, Howard M. Brown, and Carol Bennett have provided valuable details on the early history of the region. While this book frequently draws on these publications, it seeks not to retell the story of Scottish settlement, but rather to explore the extent to which Scots in the region may have reflected the broad character of contemporary British Imperialism.

The chapters that follow introduce topics in a chronological fashion — starting with an introduction to the postwar settlement schemes and ending with a chapter that examines how this period has been recalled. At the same time, each chapter introduces the reader to a specific type of historical evidence related to a broader theme. The first chapter looks at the role of the Colonial Office in promoting the settlement of the region by examining closely a document associated with the "Rideau Purchase" — a Native "land surrender" that ostensibly removed the

Upper Ottawa Valley from First Nations control. The chapter then explores the further role London played in selecting and surveying the land and emphasizes the importance of imperial military strategy in all aspects of the original planning.

Chapter Two explores the role of the state in encouraging and settling the earliest Scottish emigrants who arrived in the region. The early appearance in the settlement of former soldiers with extensive imperial campaign experience is highlighted through an analysis of one such soldier's service record. Other official government sources, such as the Colonial Office papers and the Upper Canadian land records, are also examined in order to illustrate the pervasive influence of the British state in bringing Scots to the settlements.

The third chapter focuses on the tenants from the Breadalbane estate in Perthshire, who successfully petitioned the Colonial Office to provide them with assistance to become colonists in Upper Canada in 1818. The tension created on the estate by the desire to preserve ancient practices and yet embrace the opportunities presented by Britain's imperial expansion is reflected in the history of a single artefact, the Crozier of St. Fillan, which was brought from Breadalbane to Beckwith Township by its hereditary keeper, only to be repatriated to Scotland decades later. The largest number of Scots to receive assistance from the imperial government to settle in Upper Canada, however, belonged to emigration societies, which began forming in the Lowland industrial communities in and around Glasgow in 1819. Petitions produced by these groups persuaded the imperial government of the need to offer further assistance.

Chapter Four examines the context for one such document produced in Paisley. Most signatories were weavers, a group known for involvement in agitation for political reform and demands for greater levels of poor relief. This tradition of collective action was maintained by emigrant society members who settled in Lanark County. The focus on life in Upper Canada continues in Chapter Five, which explores the political and religious attitudes that the Scottish immigrants brought with them to the new settlement. Early newspapers highlight the prominent role that Scots played in promoting both the conservative and reform positions in the political life of the settlement, reflecting divisions that were already apparent in the imperial homeland. Despite these divisions, the kirk session records indicate that the churches founded by Scottish settlers were deeply conservative in their daily functioning and played a central role in maintaining order in the new settlement.

Because women's behaviour was of particular concern to church elders, Chapter Six explores their role in early colonial life in greater detail through the window provided by emigrant correspondence. Letters are among the very few surviving sources that provide insight into women's lives, and those sent to and from Upper Canada reveal that, despite patriarchal assumptions about women's secondary status, female labour was vital for putting into practice the imperial settlement plans for the Ottawa Valley.

The closing chapter examines the way in which the migration of these imperial immigrants was remembered by themselves and by the community they helped create. Recollections, in the form of personal journals or newspaper articles, reveal that the attempt to shape the memory of this experience started almost as soon as settlers reached their destination, and became increasingly evident toward the end of the nineteenth century as the last of the original emigrants reached the end of their lives. The recalling of journeys from "Auld Scotland" tended to reinforce the image, created by the renaming of the region at the beginning of the century, that the settlement had largely been achieved by Scots. Thus, these recollections tended to exclude other immigrants from the British Isles, but also to confirm the erasure of the memory of the original inhabitants whose dispossession had been initiated by the British state and completed by settlers from the imperial homeland.

Chapter One

LAND AND EMPIRE

Among the early nineteenth-century papers of the Indian Department, held in Ottawa, is a proposal to increase the trade goods provided to the "Chiefs of the Mississauga tribes of Bay of Quinty and Kingston" in return for the surrender of land "commonly called the Rideau purchase."[1] The land in question, approximately 2.7 million acres, lay between Nepean Township to the east, the Ottawa River to the north, and what was then known as the Midland District to the west. The southern boundary was formed by the northern extent of the Eastern District townships that stretched from the St. Lawrence River shoreline to Burgess, Elmsley, Montague, and Marlborough.

The initial negotiations with the Mississauga, as the British called the Ojibwa peoples residing on the north shore of Lake Ontario, had started in May 1819 at a council in Kingston, and, while the provisional agreement concluded at that time was approved by the British Treasury, there were delays in implementing the "annual presents." The proposed increase in goods, submitted a year later and endorsed by all of the leading members of the Indian Department, including the superintendent general, Sir John Johnson, and the deputy superintendent for Upper Canada, William Claus, appears to have been aimed at encouraging the Mississauga to confirm their surrender. The increase was approved in London with the condition that payment would be made to no more than 257 individuals, the number who had originally claimed ownership of the land. A final treaty concluded on November 28, 1822, was duly endorsed by fourteen Native leaders, including Nawacamigo, Papewan (Papiwom), Antenewayway, and Wabakeek (Wobukeek), all of whom "not knowing how to write" signed with their totems.[2]

The inclusion of over three hundred point blankets in the list of goods to be provided annually reflects the importance of the fur trade in establishing the protocol for such negotiations between the First Nations in Upper Canada and representatives of the imperial government. The blankets had been introduced by the Hudson's Bay Company as part of their trading practices, with the distinctive points on each woollen blanket reflecting their relative weight. In addition to being prized for their practical qualities, the blankets quickly became prestigious items across North America, and their inclusion in the list reflects the legacy of this earlier exchange. Other items, such as the three hundred pairs of silver ear bobs and the 144 looking glasses, would also have been prized for their prestige value. As would be the silver brooches, particularly if they were Scottish heart brooches, which were introduced by the North West Company and traded extensively among First Nations in eastern Canada. The thirty-one pairs of silver arm bands and three laced hats were similar status items, but most of the goods had a more practical value.

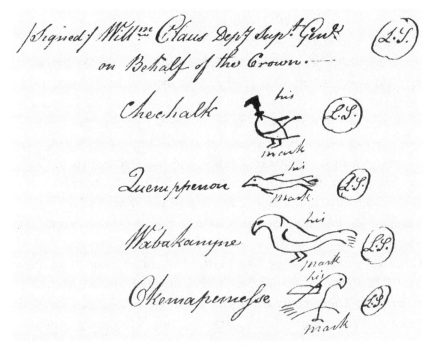

A scribe's rendering of the totem signatures of Mississauga leaders, Chechlak, Quenippenon, Wabakanyne, *and* Okemapenesse, *on the Colonial Office copy of the treaty that purportedly surrendered the land for Etobicoke Township, Home District, in 1805.*

Courtesy of the National Archives(UK), CO 42/340 ff.41-4.

Most of the fabrics, "Flannel, Caddis, Broad Cloth, Molton, Stroud, Bath Coating," and even the "Irish Linen," were durable and could withstand heavy use. This was particularly true of "Osnaburg," a coarse material originally crafted in Osnabruck, but, starting in the eighteenth century, made in large quantities in the east of Scotland and often exported to clothe slaves in the West Indies and the American colonies.[3] Other items such as kettles, knives, and sewing needles had obvious domestic utility, while the inclusion of fish lines and hooks, guns, and gunpowder, as well as hunter's pipes and tobacco, reflected the manner in which the Ojibwa used the land. While some agriculture was practised with the planting of corn, beans, and squash, the lands away from the shores of the Great Lakes were largely exploited for their supply of fish and game or the harvesting of wild rice. Settlement was usually confined to river basins, with the interior lakes and rivers being visited on a seasonal basis.

The land ceded in the Rideau Purchase contained the Mississippi waterway that linked the interior lands to the Ottawa River, but the Ojibwa on the shores of Lake Ontario were not the first to take advantage of the route.[4] Artefacts found by the early settlers and later collectors, particularly in the environs of Dalhousie Lake, indicate that at least as early as the Laurentian Archaic period (5000–1000 B.C.) indigenous peoples had been residing in the area. In addition, pictographs found at Lake Mazinaw are among the evidence placing the Algonquin in the area well before European contact, and seventeenth-century records of the French regime, as well as local oral tradition, indicate that a series of violent conflicts had occurred in the upper Ottawa Valley between the Algonquin and the southern Iroquois over the control of the lucrative Kichi Sibi (Ottawa River) trade route.

The importance of this route also drew the northern Huron into the region, and they too fought their southern Iroquoian brethren. Nevertheless, by the end of the seventeenth century, it was the Ojibwa who had wrestled control of most of what would become southern Ontario from the Iroquois — although the Mohawk communities of Akwesasne and Kanesatake remained on the upper Saint Lawrence. By the time the Rideau Purchase negotiations were unfolding, however,

Algonquin peoples of the upper Ottawa Valley were still occupying the land being ceded at Kingston. Indeed, in the opening decades of the nineteenth century, Algonquins residing in the watersheds of the Rideau, Mississippi, and Tay Rivers continued to trade and summer camp at Kanasatake on the confluence of the St. Lawrence and Ottawa Rivers in Quebec. Some of the descendants of these people now live on the Pikwakanagan (Golden Lake) Reserve in the upper northwest of the Ottawa Valley. They have highlighted the exclusion of the Algonquin from treaties like the Rideau Purchase as part of their comprehensive land claim launched in 1991.[5]

In recent years there has been a renewed interest across Canada in the early land surrenders as First Nations have reasserted their treaty rights. Much of the debate has focused on the subsequent encroachment on reserved Native land and the failure to honour the terms of the original treaties. There has also been a parallel discussion that highlights the contrasting understandings of the nature of the agreements — members

Stump Lake on the Mississippi was part of the traditional waterway used by First Nations peoples. As late as the 1890s, travellers were still using the route in a seasonal round of journeying that often reached as far as Oka at the confluence of the Ottawa and Saint Lawrence rivers.

Photo by M. Vance.

of the non-Native society tend to think of treaties as the foundation for their individual property rights, whereas members of Native societies think of treaties as mutual agreements on how to live together. The 1820 proposal to augment the trade goods given in return for the surrender of the Rideau Purchase, however, also illustrates how such agreements were part of a complex process that involved representatives of the First Nations, crown agents in the colonies, and the imperial administration in London. While the imperial capital dictated the general terms for negotiating the surrenders, local representatives were required to finalize the arrangements, and back and forth communication from the colony to the imperial capital often caused considerable delay. Nevertheless, both colonial and imperial authorities agreed that such agreements had to be in place in order for any settlement to be considered legitimate. The document also makes it clear that considerable effort was made to secure the Rideau Purchase, and the fact that London readily agreed to the proposed increase emphasizes the importance of the region for British strategists. In the aftermath of the War of 1812, authorities in both the imperial capital and in Upper Canada were preoccupied with securing the colony from any future American attack, and controlling the upper Ottawa Valley had become a central element in postwar defensive planning. As a consequence, members of the British military would play a key role in naming, surveying, and laying out roads in the region even before the final agreement had been reached with the Mississauga in Kingston.

The documents produced as part of the Rideau Purchase negotiations between 1819 and 1822 reflected an imperial policy that had been in existence for over half a century. In the aftermath of the Seven Years War, the imperial government found that leaving the negotiation of land purchases from indigenous peoples in the hands of colonists had created a great deal of tension on the colonial frontier in North America. During the Pontiac War of 1763–66, the violent clashes that erupted across the Ohio Valley were suppressed by units of the regular British Army, at considerable expense to the home government. In response, the Royal Proclamation of 1763 sought to deal with this particular problem by prohibiting settlement west of a line stretching from Quebec to Florida along the Appalachian Mountains.

Individuals were denied the right to purchase any territory in the region from the indigenous peoples, and any settlers already west of the line were required to leave. The 1763 Proclamation further stated that the British Crown had sovereignty over the entire region west of the line, but that the land was still in possession of the Native peoples who inhabited it. Finally, the document stipulated that any future land purchases would be undertaken by the British Crown, whose representatives would meet in public councils with representatives of the First Nations whose lands were to be taken. Once a formal purchase had been concluded, the Crown would sell or grant the acquired lands to individual settlers. These new regulations, while causing a great deal of resentment in the Thirteen Colonies, were designed to eliminate unscrupulous methods of trading and avoid competing claims to land among settlers. Nevertheless, as the Rideau Purchase documents indicate, in practice, the Crown purchases followed the earlier agreements of both colonists and fur traders by exchanging trade goods in return for access to Native land.[6]

Although the Saint Lawrence Valley east of the Ottawa River had been excluded from the 1763 Proclamation, the new regulations were applied to Upper Canada, but it was not until the arrival of the Loyalists in the aftermath of the American Revolution that land surrenders were negotiated to any great extent in the colony. Initially, the governor-in-chief of British North America, Frederick Haldimand, only intended to settle Britain's Mohawk "Indian allies," who had lost their lands to the newly created United States, but pressure from other Loyalist refugees in Quebec resulted in plans to also accommodate them on lands along the upper Saint Lawrence and the north shore of Lake Ontario. The superintendent general of Indian affairs, Sir John Johnson, who had himself lost a 200,000-acre estate in the Mohawk Valley, approached the Mississauga in the Bay of Quinte region, and, when it was clear that they would be prepared to negotiate, he placed Captain William Redford Crawford in charge of convening the council.

In October 1783, parties representing the Ojibwa and Iroquois in the region met at Carleton Island. No official record of the proceedings or subsequent surrender document has survived, yet Crawford reported that in return for some guns, powder, and ball for winter hunting, twelve

laced hats, and enough red cloth for twelve coats, the Mississauga had
agreed to sell all the land from the Gananoque River to the Trent River
"in the Bay of Quinte within eight leagues of the bottom of the said Bay
including all the islands, extending back from the lake so far as a man
can travel in a day." [7] He also reported that a Chief Mynass had agreed
to sell all the territory between the Gananoque River and the Toniato
(Jones) Creek, from the St. Lawrence to the Ottawa River, in return for
yearly supplies of clothing for his family. In 1784, Sir John Johnson and
representatives of the Indian Department also reached agreements with
the Iroquois for the surrender of most of the remaining riverfront of the
upper St. Lawrence from Toniato Creek to Lake St. Francis. [8]

The vague nature of these "purchases" left a great deal of room for
interpretation. While the extent of the lands along the river and lake
frontage was relatively clear, the depth of the inland territory was open
for debate. In the short term, it was the lands along the water that were
surveyed and settled first, but townships were laid out further inland.
Maps of the region produced in the opening decades of the nineteenth
century reveal the extent of the surrenders as interpreted by the colonial authorities. Townships had been laid out three deep between Trent
River and Leeds Township in Crawford's purchase from the Mississauga
and also in the land between Landsdowne and Elizabeth townships in
the territory ceded by Mynass. Aside from the strip of land reserved for
the St. Regis Mohawk, the remaining river frontage was entirely laid out
in townships from the St. Lawrence to the Ottawa River. Since most of
the Loyalists who were awarded lands in the interior townships tended
to hold on to them for speculative purposes, rather than clear the land,
there was little need to establish the exact interior extent of the Crawford
Purchases until there was renewed interest in the region at the end of
the Napoleonic Wars. Not until plans to settle soldiers and emigrants on
lands above the Rideau River were well underway did it occur to colonial authorities that the land might not have been surrendered under
the terms of the Proclamation Act. In the winter of 1816, Lieutenant
Governor Francis Gore hastily requested that the Indian Department
begin negotiations for what would become Bathurst, Drummond, and
Beckwith townships in the Eastern District. [9]

These annotations on the 1817 map of Upper Canada indicate some confusion in London as to the precise location of the military depots. All the same, the incorrect placement of the Richmond on the Rideau was a reflection of that river's importance for imperial strategic planning.

Courtesy of the National Archives(UK) ref: CO 700/CANADA 77.

The confused interpretation of land surrenders in the Upper Ottawa Valley in the immediate postwar period is illustrated by a printed map in the Colonial Office records of Upper Canada in 1817, upon which Bathurst, Drummond, Beckwith, and Goulbourn townships, along with the military depots of Perth and Richmond, have been added in by hand — probably the work of Lieutenant-Colonel Robert Pilkington of the Woolwich Arsenal in London, who also signed the document. Although he mistakenly located Richmond depot in Oxford Township, with the stroke of a pen, Pilkington extended the Crawford Purchases in the area from three to four townships deep.[10]

While this appears to have been sufficient for military authorities in the capital at the time, it became clear that further expansion of settlement in the region would, as Gore had believed, require a new agreement. Indeed, there is evidence that even earlier First Nations groups in the interior lands were offering resistance to surveying crews as they tried to mark out new townships.[11] It had become evident to the indigenous peoples of the region that unlike previous agreements, which had allowed for the construction of military forts or fur-trading posts, these new treaties had brought in large numbers of settlers who were permanently transforming a great deal of land into farms. As a consequence, when the Mississauga of the Bay of Quinte and Kingston were asked for further land surrenders in 1819, they were determined to obtain greater concessions — as the proposed 1820 increase in trade goods indicates.

After 1815, land surrenders were no longer obtained by a single payment of trade goods, as Captain Crawford had negotiated, but by the annual gifts like those stipulated in the Rideau Purchase documents. The Ojibwa also tried to ensure that, in exchange for permitting settlement on their traditional lands, the colonists would respect their fishing grounds and seasonal hunting territory. The accounts of several early settlers indicate that indigenous peoples continued to hunt and fish along the Upper Ottawa Valley waterways long after the Crawford and Rideau Purchases were concluded. Reverend William Bell, shortly after arriving in Perth, reported having several encounters with hunting parties as well as his own attempt at employing Native technology. When the clergyman tried to cross the Mississippi by canoe, only to end up in the water, he reported that "a camp of Indians close by ... laughed and clapped their hands in high glee." But as late as 1824, in noting that indigenous peoples were still inhabiting the islands in Mississippi Lake and hunting on its northern shore, Reverend Bell understood that they were "... far from being pleased with the encroachments our settlers are making on their territories."[12] What is not clear from the early accounts is the origin of the peoples that settlers like Bell encountered, but it is likely that they were members of the Algonquin First Nation who were still regularly using the Mississippi waterways.[13]

Whether or not Sir John Johnson and other members of the Indian Department were aware that Algonquin peoples were also residing in the Upper Ottawa Valley has not been determined, but it certainly would have been more convenient to negotiate with the Ojibwa living near the administrative centre of Kingston than to travel into the woods in search of other peoples who might have a claim to the region. Since the original land surrenders designed to accommodate the Loyalists in eastern Upper Canada were made with the Ojibwa and Iroquois on the Bay of Quinte and the upper Saint Lawrence, it would have seemed logical to seek to extend those treaties with the original groups. Indeed, many colonial officials may have viewed the Rideau Purchase merely as a clarification of the original Crawford treaties.

What is not clear in the official colonial records and surviving settler accounts is if the Bay of Quinte Mississauga also continued to exploit the waterways of the upper Ottawa Valley after their negotiations were concluded. If not, the annual "presents" that they obtained in Kingston would have provided them with the means to trade with others who continued to exploit the region's resources in the traditional manner even if they had ceased to do so themselves. While the Indian Department documents indicate that nearly three hundred people benefited directly from the Rideau Purchase, no attempt was made to count the number of other Ojibwa, Iroquois, or Algonquin people who continued to live in the upper Ottawa Valley. Recent estimates, however, suggest that the number of indigenous people residing in the region would have been in the hundreds — in marked contrast to the thousands of emigrants who would pour in once the imperial government had made its settlement a priority.[14]

St. Regis village was one of the first Loyalist settlements built along the upper Saint Lawrence River. Bartlett's sketch of the Mohawk community shows a number of figures who appear to be wearing the type of trade blankets that feature so prominently in agreements like the Rideau Purchase. From Canadian Scenery, Vol. I, 107.

The idea of settling disbanded soldiers and assisted emigrants in Upper Canada in order to strengthen the defences of the colony appears to have originated with Henry Bathurst, the third Lord Bathurst, who was a dominant figure in early nineteenth-century British political life. A member of the English landed elite, the Eton-educated Bathurst began his career in 1783 as the member of Parliament for Cirencester and early on held prominent positions in the government, including lord of the Admiralty, lord of the Treasury, and commissioner of the Board of Control. After entering the House of Lords, in 1794, he would also serve three prime ministers as master of the mint. His longest tenure would be as the secretary of state for war and the colonies in Lord Liverpool's government. The position had been created in 1794, with the intention of providing a central administration to deal with imperial matters beyond those involving Ireland and India, and, by 1830, what became known as the Colonial Office still only had a staff of ten. Nevertheless, Lord Bathurst and his office were able to exert a dramatic influence over both the conduct of the Napoleonic Wars and on the postwar British colonial policy. Early in his tenure as colonial secretary, Bathurst demonstrated a keen interest in strategic matters and was credited by many with providing the Duke of Wellington with critical support during his campaign in the Iberian Peninsula. Military conditions first drew his attention to Canada.[15]

Only a year after his appointment, and in the midst of the War of 1812, Lord Bathurst wrote to Sir George Prevost, the governor-in-chief and commander of the forces in British North America, suggesting that in the aftermath of the Battle of Queenston Heights and the American attack on York (later Toronto) that it might be wise to offer Highlanders in Caithness and Sutherland grants of land and free passages for themselves and their families "for the present defence and future protection of Upper Canada."[16] Sir Gordon Drummond, the lieutenant governor and commander of the British forces in Upper Canada, was enthusiastic about the proposal. Drummond had broad military experience, having begun his remarkable career as an ensign and ending it as a lieutenant-general while serving the army in the Netherlands, Egypt, and the West Indies as well as North America. In Drummond's view, if Lord Bathurst's plan were adopted "the ranks of the militia will be filled with a brave and hardy race of men whose desertion to the enemy would not be apprehended."[17]

The proposal had come at a difficult juncture in the War of 1812 when Drummond was desperate for men and resources. As a member of a well-established landed Perthshire family, he may have been inclined toward the proposal to supply Highland reinforcements. Drummond's comments were, nevertheless, echoed by others. Colonel Edward Baynes, who served in the Glengarry Light Infantry regiment raised among Highland Loyalist settlers in the colony, argued that the Americans who had arrived in Upper Canada after the initial Loyalist migrations, particularly in the Eastern District, had proven reluctant or disloyal subjects during the war. According to Baynes, if the invaders had not been checked by the "loyal Scottish settlers" of Glengarry and Stormont "it would have been impracticable to have preserved communication with the Upper Province, and this intercourse once interrupted, it would have been impossible for the Upper Province to long sustained itself."[18]

As a former Glengarry officer, Baynes' comments may have been a bit self-serving, but his analysis touched on the strategic concerns that Lord Bathurst had hoped to address with his proposal, specifically preventing Upper Canada from falling into the hands of the United States while ensuring that any new settlers remained loyal to Britain. The first group that had come to mind in order to achieve these goals were Scottish Highlanders. The eighteenth century had witnessed a remarkable integration of Highland soldiers into the British Army, and, while they had fought on both sides of the American Revolution, the overwhelming majority supported the British cause as they did again during the War of 1812. In both the Scottish Highlands and in the colonies, the reward expected for such military service was access to land. That these expectations were often realized can account, in part, for the disproportionate presence of Highlanders in the British Army — particularly in regiments serving in the overseas empire.[19] As secretary of state for war and the colonies, Lord Bathurst was well aware of the importance of Highland service in North America, but elsewhere in the empire others were also suggesting that the permanent settlement of emigrants from the north of Scotland would help to secure British possession.

In 1812, after a brutal campaign against the indigenous amaXhosa peoples on the eastern frontier of the Cape Colony, the commander of the Cape Regiment, Lieutenant-Colonel John Graham, who had arrived in southern Africa with the 93rd Sutherland Highlanders, suggested that the settlement of five hundred Highlanders from the estate where the 93rd had been raised would be an ideal way to secure the frontier. Colonial authorities in the Cape, who also saw British settlement as key to retaining possession of the colony, reinforced Graham's suggestion with their own request for settlers sent to Bathurst in 1813, the same year that the colonial secretary approached Governor Prevost with his proposal for Upper Canada.[20]

While the British forces had once again relied on their "Indian allies" during the War of 1812, unlike southern Africa, the relatively small number of indigenous people present in Upper Canada did not present an organized military threat — as the supply of firearms to the Mississauga as part of the Rideau Purchase clearly indicates.[21] But in both colonies, British settlement was seen as the key to counterbalancing a potentially disloyal settler population — the Boers in the Cape and the Americans in Upper Canada.

Of the two groups, the Americans caused Bathurst the greatest concern. The colonial secretary had become convinced that they posed a serious military threat. After the war, when his proposal to settle Scots in Upper Canada was finally acted upon, he instructed the governors in British North America to refuse to provide land grants to American citizens and do their utmost to prevent their settlement in the colonies. Even before the formal end of hostilities, Bathurst had decided to further address the perceived threat by expanding his settlement scheme to include regular army troops stationed in the colony. In 1814 he had written to Prevost, stating that the governor was authorized to offer to "a certain proportion" of troops, particularly those with families, free land grants in Upper Canada, and that the government would pay the expense of transporting their families to the colony if they were still residing in Britain. He made his intentions clear by adding that "[s]ettlers of this description ... may be established with great advantage along the Frontier ... in the Districts most open to Invasion."[22] In addition, by including ex-servicemen in his free land grant scheme, Bathurst was able to hand over the responsibility for overseeing the settlement of both the emigrants and former soldiers to the military and, indeed, the Colonial Office offer was later extended to other veterans wishing to settle in Upper Canada.[23]

The colonial secretary also hoped that a successful assisted emigration to Upper Canada in 1815 would encourage other British emigrants to choose to settle in British North America, instead of the United States where they had largely gone prior to the war. For Bathurst, redirecting emigrants away from a potential enemy was as important as securing the colonies.[23] Since the Colonial Office expected that once the war was over the lion's share of emigrants were likely to come from Ireland and Scotland, as they had before the conflict, plans were made in the spring of 1815 to recruit two thousand emigrants from each country, as well as a smaller number from England.

The London architect and illustrator Thomas Allom had been raised in a working-class household and this may account for his rather unsentimental representation of the Highland soldiers stationed at Stirling Castle. The women depicted in the scene could be washerwomen or coal carriers and others like them may well have entertained the idea of accompanying a soldier to the colonies in order to escape such ill-paid work. From William Beattie, Scotland Illustrated *(London: George Virtue, 1838) Vol. I, 171.*

In order to ensure that the emigrants would not depart for the United States upon arrival, each potential emigrant had to provide a £16 deposit for each male member of the family over the age of seventeen and two guineas for each married woman. The emigrants would, in return, receive a free passage and hundred-acre land grant as well as six months rations from the military stores. In order to control costs, the Colonial Office planned to send the emigrants to Canada on the transport ships that would be returning with British regular troops that had defended the colonies. Delays in ratifying the peace agreement with the United States meant that in the end the scheme was only advertised in Scotland, in March. Bathurst suspended it entirely in April, when Napoleon returned from his exile in Elba and the war was renewed on the continent. In that short time, over seventy Scottish families from the Highlands and the Lowlands had already accepted the government's terms, in addition to a few others from England. The Colonial Office agreed to honour these agreements, and between July and August 699 emigrants left Glasgow onboard transport ships headed for Quebec.[24]

The extra expense caused by the various delays meant that Bathurst was not keen to revive the assisted-emigration scheme after 1815, but he was still committed to directing emigrants away from the United States to destinations within the Empire, and, as a consequence, his office agreed to further unadvertised assistance to a party of over three hundred emigrants from the Breadalbane estate in Perthshire, as well as to 170 others from Cloghjordan, Tipperary, and nearly a hundred from Alston, Cumberland. All three groups left for Upper Canada in 1818, but by that time it had become clear that the effort to redirect emigrants to British North America was having an effect and Bathurst did not plan to offer any further government assistance.

A dramatic rise in unemployment and radical activity in Lowland Scotland, however, resulted in considerable political pressure to renew the scheme. At first, attempts were made to recruit settlers for the Cape of Good Hope, where the governor, Lord Charles Somerset, was still looking for British settlers to secure the eastern frontier. A small party of Scots did participate in the 1819 assisted emigration to the Cape, but the renewal of assisted emigration to Upper Canada in 1820 produced a much more enthusiastic response. Between 1820 and 1821 over two-and-a-half thousand, primarily Lowland, Scots took advantage of the scheme. Two further assisted emigrations, involving over two thousand emigrants from Cork, took place in 1823 and 1825 before the Colonial Office finally stopped providing assistance to emigrate to Upper Canada.[25]

While these settlement schemes had clearly originated in London, the decision to locate the settlers in the upper Ottawa Valley was determined through an exchange between the colonial military leadership and Lord Bathurst, in which Lieutenant-General Drummond would play a central role. As commander of the forces in Upper Canada, Drummond was keenly aware of the vulnerability of the St. Lawrence frontier with the United States, and agreed with Colonel Baynes that had the Americans captured the upper St. Lawrence, the lines of communication would have been cut with Lower Canada, and Upper Canada may have been lost. Fear that the conflict might restart at any moment prompted Governor Prevost, in the early winter of 1815, to instruct Drummond to examine alternative routes between Montreal and Kingston.

After consulting with his fellow officers, Drummond reported that the Ottawa and Rideau Rivers appeared to offer the best inland route, and he ordered a new survey made of each waterway. By the following autumn Bathurst was communicating directly with Drummond, stating that the government was "deeply impressed with the importance of carrying into execution the works necessary for the improvement of the Water Communication between the Upper and Lower Province,"[26] and asking for an estimate for rendering the Ottawa and Rideau Rivers navigable. A detailed survey of the route was undertaken by the Royal Engineers during the spring of 1816, and the report they provided outlined ambitious plans for what would become the Rideau Canal, which after many delays finally began construction in 1827. Although the military canal was still only a proposal in 1815, it had an immediate impact on Bathurst's settlement scheme since his plan to create a settlement of loyal settlers and former soldiers could be directed toward this undeveloped but vitally important route. It was left to Drummond to find a specific location for the settlers that suited these new imperial strategic concerns.[27]

In the spring of 1815, Lieutenant-General Drummond was made commander-in-chief and administrator of Lower Canada, and he maintained responsibility for Lord Bathurst's scheme through the newly created Military Settling Department that was under his command. The department was to oversee all aspects of the settlement scheme, with the exception of the actual surveying of the land grants and the issuing of land patents, which remained in control of the Upper Canadian civilian authorities. Earlier in the year, while he had still been responsible for the administration of Upper Canada, Drummond had asked the surveyor general of Upper Canada, Thomas Ridout, to identify all of the land in Upper Canada purchased from the First Nations that was still available for settlement, including the Crown Reserves that Lord Bathurst had contemplated using for the scheme.

Ridout reported that land was available in the western part of the colony near Lake St. Clair, and also between Lake Simcoe and Georgian Bay, where the settlers could be located together, as Bathurst clearly

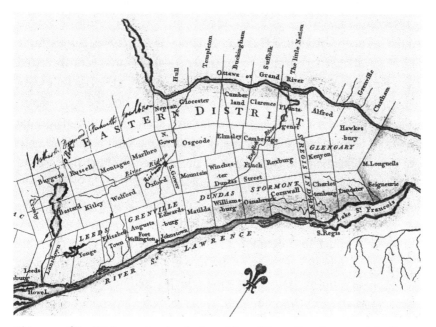

This copy of the 1817 map showing the townships of Upper Canada was originally kept in the Woolwich Arsenal in London.

intended, but that only scattered lots were available in the Eastern District. These lots, representing 300,000 acres, were turned over to the Military Settling Department and some former soldiers were located on them, but, given the strategy envisioned by the colonial secretary and the military, Drummond was opposed to dispersed settlement. Instead, he proposed placing the settlers south of the Rideau in Oxford Township where they could be supplied from Fort Wellington (Prescott) on the St. Lawrence. Drummond believed that those already owning land in the township could be compensated with land elsewhere. Although his Oxford Township proposal was rejected, Drummond continued to argue for compensation for existing landowners in order to make way for settlement along the strategic Ottawa-Rideau route and proposed the townships of Alfred and Plantagenet on the Ottawa River as an alternate destination.[28]

While Drummond's selections remained sparsely settled, the Loyalists were deeply resentful of his proposal to reallocate lands originally surveyed for their use and were especially displeased with the use of reserved lands, previously denied to them, for the scheme. The lieutenant governor of Upper Canada, Sir Francis Gore, was sympathetic and ensured that Drummond's proposed reallocations were thwarted when he returned to Upper Canada in September 1815. The following February, Gore, who had been on leave in Britain during the war, offered instead to create a new range of townships above the Rideau for the accommodation of the soldiers and emigrants. Bathurst had planned to award good farmland to the settlers in order to ensure that they would remain on their locations, but Gore had identified marginal land near the Canadian Shield. Nevertheless, his proposal placated the Loyalists and allowed for the compact settlement envisioned by the colonial secretary. The fact that demobilized soldiers and more than six hundred assisted emigrants from Scotland were anxiously awaiting their allocation of land at various locations in the colony also encouraged Drummond and the Colonial Office to agree to Gore's new townships. Once his plan was adopted, the lieutenant governor immediately called for the negotiations that would ultimately result in the Rideau Purchase from the Mississauga.[29]

Gore had played a critical role in locating Bathurst's settlement in the Upper Ottawa Valley, but the Military Settlement Department was responsible for creating the infrastructure that would make it possible to locate settlers in the region. Drummond and his successors oversaw the establishment of three depots that the military supplied with the required rations and equipment while the settlers began clearing the land. All three were located on tributaries of the Rideau and Mississippi Rivers as part of the overall strategic plan, but they had to be reached by new roads since the construction of the planned canal was years away. The department oversaw the blazing of a trail from the Rideau River to the first depot at Perth on the Pike River, renamed the Tay, followed by the construction of a "rude" overland route to Brockville. This road would be extended north to the Lanark depot, on the banks of the Clyde, in order to accommodate the assisted emigrants who arrived from Lowland Scotland in 1820 and 1821. Prior to that, the Richmond depot, established on the Jock River in summer 1818, had been connected by a path to the Ottawa River and was also linked by road to Perth the following autumn.

Although they were often no more than crude tracks, these first roads provided the two routes, the first via Brockville on the St. Lawrence and the second via Richmond landing on the Ottawa River opposite Hull, that allowed settlers to reach the district. In addition, the stores established in the depots by the Military Settlement Department ensured that settlers would not starve while they attempted to carve out farms from the forests. These depots were so vital to the entire project that they remained under military control until 1822, when the last of the settlers who had arrived under the assisted emigration and veteran settlement scheme were finally located.[30]

Prior to the work supervised by the military, Bathurst's settlement had existed only on maps. The first, showing the new townships above the Rideau, was provided by Gore when he asked the Indian Department to begin negotiating for the land in the winter of 1816, and two years later Lieutenant-Colonel Pilkington was adding them to his map of Upper Canada in London. As many scholars have pointed out, this map-making was an essential element in asserting imperial control and the renaming of the land was a critical step in acquiring it.[31] In the Upper

Ottawa Valley, the process had started with the mapping and naming of townships in the lands identified in the Crawford treaties and would continue well after the Rideau Purchase was finalized.

The names, recorded first on paper before any soldier, settler, or surveyor visited the region, illustrate the deliberate linking of the region to the wider British Empire. Gore had initially proposed three townships, naming them Bathurst, after the colonial secretary, Drummond, for the commander-in-chief in Lower Canada, and Beckwith, the surname of the quartermaster general for the army in British North America. Major General Sir Sydney Beckwith already had a distinguished career in imperial service, having fought in India, Denmark, Hanover, and Spain, before he arrived in British North America to take on the vital task of ensuring supplies for the army during the War of 1812. To these well-known representatives of the imperial government and the British military, a fourth name, representing the Colonial Office itself, was added when Goulbourn Township was created in 1818. Henry Goulburn, whose personal wealth was based upon an inherited slave-holding plantation in Jamaica, served as Bathurst's undersecretary from

By placing Highland soldiers in the foreground of his view of Kingston harbour, William Henry Bartlett reinforced the point made by the colonial secretary that the security of Upper Canada depended upon the presence of imperial soldiers. From Canadian Scenery, *Vol. II, 50.*

Courtesy of Killam Library, Dalhousie University.

1812 to 1821. He had the responsibility of supervising the government-assisted emigrations and dealing with the thousands of queries that flooded into his office from those seeking aid to settle in the colonies, but, unlike the others at the time the townships were named, Goulburn was hardly a well-known figure beyond government circles.[32]

The earlier townships that sat below these new postwar creations had also been given names with imperial associations. Elmsley Township, first surveyed in 1794, had a local affiliation, having first been named after the administrator of Upper Canada, Peter Russell, and then changed to honour his most vociferous critic, John Elmsley, the chief justice of the colony. Montague Township, which had been surveyed in the same year, was named after Admiral Sir George Montague, who had played a leading role in the British naval war effort during the American revolution.[33] North and South Sherbrooke were named after the former governor-in-chief of British North America, Sir John Coape Sherbrooke, who had served as an army officer for over thirty years, and, as the colony's lieutenant governor, had organized the defence of Nova Scotia during the War of 1812. Dalhousie and Ramsay were named after the Scottish nobleman Sir George Ramsay, the ninth Earl of Dalhousie, who, like Sherbrooke, had become governor-in-chief in 1820 after having served as lieutenant governor of Nova Scotia — a position he gained as a consequence of his military service during the Napoleonic Wars. He would end his career as commander-in-chief of the British forces in India.[34]

Similarly, the Richmond depot was named in 1818 after Charles Lennox, the fourth Duke of Richmond and then governor-in-chief, who also had an extensive military career in which he saw action against in the French in the West Indies and Gibraltar before he came to British North America. A colourful figure who had fought a duel with the Duke of York and done much to encourage field sports in both his homeland and in British North America, Lennox died suddenly in 1819 while visiting the settlement that bore his name, but he was further recognized in the district when Lavant Township was named after the river that ran beside Goodwood House, the Duke of Richmond's home in Sussex.

In a similar manner, Colonel Francis Cockburn was paid tribute by Franktown, the name given to the village in Beckwith where he had established a government store. The name of the first military depot in the district may have also been a subtle tribute to Sir Gordon Drummond, since his family resided near Perth in the Scottish home-land, but this is far from certain. The name does not appear on Gore's map indicating the lands to be purchased from the Mississauga, since the site had not yet been selected, and the name was not used until after work had begun on the depot storehouse in March 1816. In early April, correspondence from the depot was headed Township No. 2, Pike River, but by the middle of the month the superintendent, Alexander McDonell, who was from the western Highlands of Scotland, was head-ing his correspondence to the lieutenant governor's secretary with Perth-on-Tay. He also began issuing printed location tickets to settlers that were also headed Perth, Upper Canada.[35]

While natives of Perthshire were among the assisted emigrants and demobilized soldiers who were located on their land grants by the Perth depot, the surviving evidence does not suggest that this played a direct role in the naming of the settlement. The naming of the Lanark depot and township in 1819 was, however, a direct response to the impending arrival of the assisted emigrants drawn from the environs of Glasgow in Lanarkshire and Renfrewshire. Glasgow itself may have been com-memorated in the late 1820s when Morphy Falls, the largest town in Beckwith, was renamed Carleton Place after a street in that Scottish city. The first name recognized an original Irish settler, but the Scots who came to dominate the commercial and manufacturing businesses in the town chose instead to associate themselves with a prosperous neigh-bourhood inhabited by the business elite of Glasgow.[36]

As settlers began to move into the townships, other names appeared — such as McDonald's and Watson's Corners in Dalhousie and Armstrong's Corners in Drummond — that identified specific Scottish emigrants or others that commemorated specific locations in Scotland, such as Glentay in Bathurst and Kilmarnock on the Rideau River. The renaming was also applied to natural features like the Tay and Clyde Rivers, and, as a consequence, maps of the district would not only reflect the wider British imperial world, but also give the region, particularly in what would become Lanark County, a distinctively Scottish appearance.

Thomas Allom's image of field workers harvesting grain outside of Perth captures its dramatic setting on the edge of the Scottish Highlands. This landscape was utterly different from the flat, forested tract in the Upper Ottawa Valley named after the Scottish town by imperial authorities. From Scotland Illustrated, *Vol. II, 21.*

Courtesy of Killam Library, Dalhousie University.

Mapping and naming had initiated the process of British resettlement of the Rideau Purchase, but in order for settlers to acquire specific locations, the townships first had to be surveyed and subdivided into lots. The imperial government had laid down the regulations for this process in 1791, stating that inland townships had to be ten miles square and laid out in lots of two hundred acres. What was desired was a division of the land into rational grids, where an orderly society could be established. It was a vision that came straight out of the Enlightenment, the European intellectual movement that emphasized the application of reason to all branches of human activity, and its expression can be clearly seen on the blank maps of Lanark County produced for the Colonial Office. A precise grid, divided by twelve concession lines and twenty-seven lot numbers, was arbitrarily superimposed over the landscape, paying little attention to physical features and none to the Native people's understanding of the region.[37]

Making the orderly vision a reality proved difficult. In Beckwith Township, for example, the precise lines of the Colonial Office map do not match the patchwork of irregular lots now evident in aerial photographs. While the intent was to follow the imperial regulations, surveyors found that difficult terrain and faulty equipment greatly hampered their efforts. This was compounded by the haste with which the early surveys were undertaken. As soon as the Perth depot was established, the settlers arrived looking to take up their land, but the delay in selecting the location of the settlement meant that surveying had only begun. There were also disputes over which government, the colonial or the imperial, should pay the costs involved, and this caused further confusion. In order to accelerate the process, the surveyor general hired additional surveyors, but this also created problems as the lines laid out by each crew did not always correspond to each other.[38]

Ruben Sherwood, the son of one of the first Loyalist settlers in Leeds County, who had served as Captain of the Guides during the War of 1812, was the first surveyor in the district. He knew the region well, having surveyed Burgess Township just prior to the war, and his advice had been sought by Drummond on the proposed Ottawa-Rideau route as well as on the location of the military settlement. Sherwood's field diary provides insight into the difficulties that the surveyors experienced and how they went about their task. His crews had to deal with dense woods, swampy ground, broken chains, and changing requirements from the Military Settlement Office. In addition, while some of the former soldiers and assisted emigrants worked on the crews for the wages, many abandoned the difficult work — particularly during the harsh winter months. Sherwood was himself criticized by the settlement superintendent for his own frequent absences from the survey parties. In one letter of complaint, Alexander McDonell stated that Sherwood had stopped surveying Drummond Township and had instead "gone up the river in a canoe with an Indian" for an unknown purpose.[39]

What the superintendent had failed to acknowledge, but what Sherwood knew from his work with Native guides during the war, was that local indigenous knowledge was vital. From the first land surrenders, members of First Nations worked with survey crews when their seasonal rounds allowed, but would leave to hunt, fish, and gather at the appropriate times in their annual cycle, causing some surveyors to complain about their work ethic. The diary of William Fortune, who had surveyed Montague Township in 1794 with a segregated crew, divided along Native and non-Native lines, was full of disparaging remarks about the "Indians," but it also makes it clear that they were responsible for keeping the party on the correct course down the Rideau.[40] Indeed, the indigenous crew members provided them with invaluable detailed knowledge of the land. Ironically, the indigenous surveyors were assisting the final step of a series of processes directed by the imperial authorities that would result in their own dispossession.

While not all First Nations in the upper Ottawa Valley had been party to the Rideau Purchase or to the Crawford treaties, these agreements had initiated a virtual erasure of the indigenous presence in the upper Ottawa Valley. Native peoples continued to reside in the area and continued to hunt and fish along its waterways in the traditional manner, but by the 1820s only a handful of place names were left on the maps of the region indicating that there had been any previous occupation of the land. Intriguingly, the most notable of those that survived was "Mississippi," a corruption of the indigenous name for the waterway that had drawn both the First Nations and the imperial government to the region.[41] Instead, the land had been reimagined with imperial associations that made it a natural destination for British settlers, and while these individuals would be drawn from all over the British Isles, the use of specific Scottish names was meant to suggest the particular suitability of the region for immigrants from that part of the imperial homeland.

Chapter Two

EARLY SETTLEMENT AND THE IMPERIAL STATE

During the French Wars (1793–1815), Britain and its colonies experienced a mass mobilization that was without parallel until the World Wars of the twentieth century. Indeed, by 1814 the number of men serving overseas in the British regular army had reached over 200,000. In Scotland, which had a disproportionately high number of men in the armed forces, the unprecedented recruitment drive had ensured that almost every community had supplied men to serve both at home and abroad. For policy-makers in London, settling some of these former soldiers in the Ottawa Valley not only offered an apparent solution to the vulnerability of Upper Canada, but also had the added benefit of reducing the number of disbanded veterans who were returning to the British Isles and joining the growing number of unemployed produced by the postwar depression that was already underway.[1]

The presence of a woman and child in William Henry Bartlett's representation of Highland soldiers at Edinburgh Castle reflects the artist's interest in domestic scenes and the fact that many wives followed their husbands to their postings both at home and abroad.

From *Scotland Illustrated*, Vol. I, 90. *Courtesy of Killam Library, Dalhousie University.*

Simon Gray, a former sergeant in the 4th Royal Veteran Battalion, was one of the men who took advantage of the Colonial Office offer, settling with his wife on a lot near the newly established military depot at Perth, Upper Canada, in the summer of 1817. Since the surviving records merely identify the men, little is revealed about Mrs. Gray or the other women who accompanied their husband soldiers. This male bias is particularly evident in the records of the imperial army and, as a consequence, the reconstruction of the early settlement history of the Rideau Purchase tends to lead to the activities of prominent male figures. Nevertheless, the military records allow for a detailed understanding of the careers of rank-and-file soldiers like Simon Gray — if not their wives.[2]

Like those of a great many veterans of the French Wars, Simon Gray's discharge papers survive among the War Office records in London and these provide a useful illustration of the imperial experience that the military settlers brought with them to the pioneer settlement.[3] Gray had been a career soldier having served an astounding forty-five of his sixty-one years in three different army corps. As a boy in Inverness he had joined the 68th Durham Light Infantry during a recruiting drive just prior to the American Revolution. He had risen through the ranks from drummer to sergeant while the regiment had served in Ireland during the American war, and in Gibraltar and the West Indies during the French Wars. Britain had tried to take advantage of the turmoil created by the French Revolution to expand its possessions among the sugar islands of the Caribbean, particularly in Haiti where Toussaint L'Ouverture had led a successful slave revolution. The lack of success against L'Ouverture put the British forces on the defensive and in 1795, while the 68th was engaged in suppressing a slave revolt on Grenada, Gray was wounded in his right hand and leg.[4] He was discharged from the Durham Light Infantry on September 24, 1803, but the next day he joined the Royal Newfoundland Regiment, which had been authorized to recruit soldiers for North American service after the collapse of the Peace of Amiens, the 1802 treaty that had briefly halted conflict with France. Finally, after serving almost nine years with the Royal Newfoundland Regiment, Gray transferred to the 4th Royal Veteran Battalion that had been raised in British North America to protect the colonies during the War of 1812.[5]

Simon Gray's discharge papers also indicate that despite his successful military career he had no obvious civilian skills as his trade is listed as labourer, and, more significantly, that he was illiterate since he signed his papers with a cross. The War Office records, however, also indicate that despite his labouring origins and lack of literacy, Gray was able to make calculated strategic transfers between army corps at key moments in his career. Indeed, his transfer from the 68th in 1803 had allowed him to escape the disease-prone garrisons of the West Indies, where his former regiment lost 1,588 of its 2,330 men from 1801 and 1806 while stationed at St. Lucia.[6]

Gray's decision to join the Royal Newfoundland Regiment was likely made on the basis of information obtained from other soldiers regarding the more favourable conditions in North American service. His decision to remain in Quebec after the 4th Royal Veteran Battalion was disbanded was probably encouraged by his encounters with other soldiers arriving from the British Isles with tales of deteriorating

One of the earliest stone buildings in Perth, Ontario, this residence on Mill Street, built in 1829, is indicative of the military investment that enabled the town's residents to be among the first to replace their log homes.

Photo by M. Vance.

conditions in the homeland.[7] As his discharge papers indicate, Gray was also aware that he was entitled to a veteran's pension and his application was endorsed, as required of all applicants, by his commanding officer Lieutenant-Colonel William MacPherson, who "highly recommended" him. Other War Office records indicate that Gray's application as an "out-pensioner" of the British Army's Chelsea Hospital was successful and that the former sergeant received a pension of 2s 10d. a day — which undoubtedly contributed to his success as an Upper Canadian settler. By 1822, Simon Gray had acquired freehold of his two hundred-acre land grants in the Ottawa Valley after successfully completing the settlement duties.[8]

The importance of military settlers for securing the early settlement in the Ottawa Valley has been well-recognized, but little use has been made of the War Office records for understanding the experiences of individual soldiers like Simon Gray.[9] Indeed, it has recently been suggested that British Army service and pension records are a largely untapped source for both the social history of the British Isles and the history of emigration within the British Empire. One analysis of a sample of Scottish rank-and-file soldiers in the early nineteenth-century military pension records does suggest that most veterans returned to Britain after the end of hostilities and that their pensions assisted them in making a relatively smooth transition back into civilian life in Scotland. This appears to have been particularly true of veterans who had an artisanal skill before enlistment and who were able to use their pension as a supplement to family income.[10]

As Gray's case indicates, however, provisions to pay pensions to veterans overseas were not made by Chelsea Hospital until 1816, and this may have encouraged some soldiers to return to or remain in Scotland. Nevertheless, while those veterans who chose to reside in the colonies may have represented a minority of soldiers demobilized after the Napoleonic Wars, they made a dramatic impact on the new settlements. As the Colonial Office had intended, the demobilized soldiers gave the early Ottawa Valley townships a decidedly military and imperial character. Their individual experiences and personal connections had been shaped by service in the imperial army and their very presence in the settlement was a direct consequence of a policy designed by officials in London. The imperial state remained heavily involved in selecting immigrants for the settlement when the offer of free land was extended to Scottish civilians with the assisted emigrations of 1815. Indeed, John Campbell, the Edinburgh lawyer selected by the Colonial Office to oversee the scheme in Scotland, had personal connections to both the military and the empire. Taken together, the War Office, Colonial Office, and Upper Canadian land-settlement records demonstrate the dominance of veterans in the early years of the settlement and the central role played by the imperial state in establishing Scots in the Ottawa Valley. What is less discernable, but equally important, are the fragmentary records that reveal the role that rank-and-file soldiers like Simon Gray played in encouraging further emigration to Upper Canada, among veterans like themselves and from the communities where they originated.

Since imperial strategic considerations led to the Rideau Purchase it is hardly surprising that the military men played a key role in the early days of the settlement. Scottish officers were particularly prominent in the military depots, which became the earliest towns in the Upper Ottawa Valley. The officer in charge of the Perth depot, Alexander McDonell of Collachie, was a former assistant paymaster general and colonel in the Upper Canadian Militia, as well as a veteran of the Revolutionary War. As an emigrant from the Glengarry estate, McDonell's personal history reflected both Britain's military activities in North America and the emigration history of the Scottish Highlands. His family had left Scotland, as part of a general exodus of tacksmen from Glengarry, on board the *Pearl* in 1773, and settled in the Mohawk Valley in what would become upstate New York.[11]

When conflict broke out between colonial and imperial armies, the fifteen-year-old McDonell joined Sir John Johnson's forces. During the conflict he would also serve in the Royal Highland Regiment and Butler's Rangers, rising to the rank of lieutenant. After the war the McDonell family was among the Loyalists who arrived in Quebec, but, in 1792, Alexander moved to Upper Canada with General Simcoe, who appointed him the first sheriff of the Home District, the administrative district that encompassed the town of York, modern-day Toronto. He also represented the newly established Glengarry County in the Upper Canadian Legislature and served as the body's speaker from 1804–08.

In 1805, McDonell, who by this time had resigned his sheriffdom, took on the added responsibility of supervising Lord Selkirk's Argyllshire settlement at Baldoon on the shores of Lake St. Clair. When war broke out again in 1812, McDonell joined the Upper Canadian Militia, but he was captured at Niagara-on-the-Lake the following year and spent the remainder of the conflict as a prisoner of war in Lancaster, Pennsylvania. After his release, he was recommended by Lieutenant Governor Francis Gore for the position of superintendent of the Department of Settlers. The appointment was likely intended as a reward for his military service, but McDonell's previous experience with the Baldoon settlers also made him a likely candidate for the position.[12]

In addition to McDonell himself, military officers with Glengarry connections were highly visible in the early settlement and at the Perth depot. The superintendent's assistant based in Cornwall, Lieutenant Angus McDonell, was not only a veteran of the Glengarry Light Infantry Regiment, which had been raised in Canada for the War of 1812, but was also the a nephew of Father Alexander McDonell, the man who earlier had been instrumental in raising the Glengarry Fencibles in Scotland and had arranged for the emigration of several of their number to Upper Canada in 1803. Father McDonell had demonstrated that the British Army could rely on the loyalty of Highland Catholic soldiers, both at home and in North America, and parlayed this into further rights for his co-religionists in Upper Canada, which include a Bishopric for himself in Kingston. But, in the short term, the appointment of Alexander and Angus McDonell helped facilitate the settlement of large numbers of men from the Glengarry Light Infantry in the townships surrounding Perth, and ensured that the regiment's officers would dominate the early life of the town.[13]

Roderick Matheson, the paymaster of the regiment whose substantial former residence now houses the Perth Museum, used his half pay income to establish a successful general store after he was granted a lot in town in July 1816. In addition, his land grants in the surrounding townships served as the foundation for a career in land speculation. His rise to prominence was also reflected in a series of local appointments

— major in the militia, justice of the peace, commissioner on the Court of Requests, member of the Legislative Council, and one of the first senators to be named after Confederation.

While Matheson was able to establish himself among the elite of the community, early detractors commonly referred to him as the "drummer" in order to highlight his relatively humble origins and deflate his pretensions.[14] Indeed, as the slur suggested, Matheson's early personal history demonstrates the possibilities for social advancement that an imperial military career could offer some Scots. He was born in Ross-shire, but his father had died while he was a boy attending school in Inverness. His elder brother, Farquhar, who was serving in the British Army, brought him to Lower Canada in 1805 at age twelve. After completing his schooling in Lower Canada, Roderick Matheson joined the Canadian Fencibles, but without family support it is unlikely that either he or his brother would have been able to purchase a commission, and he may indeed have joined as a drummer. When he transferred to the Glengarry Light Infantry, Matheson joined as a non-commissioned ensign, the lowest officer rank in the army, but in 1813, partly as a consequence of his battlefield experience in New York, he was promoted to the rank of lieutenant before eventually becoming paymaster.[15]

As the military piper in Thomas Allom's engraving suggests, the army was highly visible in Inverness and many Highland regiments were recruited in the town. From Scotland Illustrated, *Vol. II, 41.*

Several of Matheson's friends and business associates also used their regimental experience and connections to establish themselves among the Perth elite. Captain Alexander McMillan, a veteran of the British assault on Oswego who was later wounded at the battle of Cook's Mills, followed a similar career path from the Canadian Fencibles to the Glengarry Light Infantry. After the war he became a significant landowner who held several key offices in Perth, including justice of the peace, registrar of lands and deeds, and colonel in the militia.

Lieutenant William Blair, who also fought at Cook's Mills, had joined the 8th Regiment in Scotland and transferred to the Glengarry Infantry after the 8th was sent to Lower Canada. In 1816 he was granted land in Drummond and Beckwith townships, and subsequently established a brickworks that would not only supply building materials for the Perth district, but would also elevate Blair to one of the leading businessmen in the town. Similarly, Lieutenant Anthony Leslie, who had also served in the 8th Regiment before transferring to the Glengarry Regiment, used his half pay and regimental connections to pursue a successful career as agent for the Commercial Bank of the Midland District in Perth. Leslie had served as paymaster of the regiment and had recommended Matheson as his successor after resigning the position in order to command troops in the field. The two men would continue their association in Perth. While several Glengarry officers returned to Scotland after their wartime service, Leslie took the unusual step of returning to his homeland late in life. Unlike his fellow former Glengarry officers, Leslie and his wife were childless and this may have made retirement in Scotland more appealing and practical.[16]

In addition to the Glengarry veterans, many other Scots who had been officers in other regiments also settled in Perth, including the career soldier Captain William Marshall of the Canadian Fencibles. He would eventually oversee the settlement of government-assisted emigrants who arrived in 1820 and 1821. Perhaps the most influential figure in the pioneer settlement, Aberdeen-born Dr. Alexander Thom had joined the army in 1795 at age nineteen, serving first with the 88th and 35th Regiment of Foot before transferring to the 41st in 1803. While serving with the 35th Regiment, Thom had risen to the rank of surgeon and also served the 41st in that capacity before obtaining the post of staff surgeon for the army in Upper Canada in 1813. While he was with the 35th Thom had served in the Mediterranean, and he had briefly been held captive by the Americans while with the 41st during the War of 1812. This military experience undoubtedly placed him in high esteem among the fellow officers of the Perth settlement, but it was his medical knowledge that was particularly welcome among the early settlers of the community. As early as 1816 he was requesting the appointment of additional physicians to assist with the demand. At the same time, Thom used his army half pay to establish a sawmill and gristmill on the Tay River, making him a leading businessman in early Perth. As a consequence of his status, Thom was asked to serve as a magistrate in 1816 and justice of the peace in 1835, around the time that he briefly served as one of the district's members of Parliament.[17]

Men like Alexander McDonell, Roderick Matheson, and Alexander Thom dominated the town life of early Perth, but many other Scottish officers, although occupying key positions, did not enjoy as high a profile. One of these men was John Watson, a Scottish veteran of the Royal Artillery who replaced Matheson as quartermaster of the Glengarry Light Infantry in 1813, and settled with his wife in Bathurst Township in 1816. Initially he was given the responsibility of issuing stores to settlers from the military depot, and later he served as a magistrate in Perth. Like many former soldiers, Watson would also join the Lanark County Militia, which served to reinforce the social networks among the veterans in the community. Nevertheless, many other Scots, such as Captain George Ferguson of the Canadian Fencibles or Lieutenant James Gray of the 104th Regiment of Foot, do not appear to have sought any public post or participated in the local military units, but concentrated instead on establishing themselves on their land. Officers like Ferguson and Gray were found in all the district's townships where they often became the largest landholders as a consequence of the larger grants awarded to them on the basis of their rank.[18]

The influence of Scottish enlisted men like Simon Gray was also readily apparent in the institutions of the early settlement. Two former sergeants, John Adamson, a veteran of the Glengarry Light Infantry, and Angus Cameron, of the Canadian Fencibles, were among the earliest innkeepers in the region. Adamson's Inn on Craig Street, which still stands as a private residence today, served as Perth's first hotel and a social centre for the local elite. Adamson had received one of the first licences to sell liquor and his hotel quickly became a favourite gathering place for the retired officers in the community. It also had rooms that accommodated balls and political rallies, as well as the town's first Presbyterian church services.

Reverend William Bell, the minister who conducted those services, kept a diary record of Adamson's unhappy domestic life in his diary, which he undoubtedly attributed to the influence of the large quantity of cheap spirits consumed in his establishment. There does indeed appear to have been a number of early deaths in the community brought about by excessive drinking, but Bell had no complaint with Angus Cameron, who ran a similar inn just north of Perth on the banks of the Mississippi, probably because Cameron had served as one of Bell's elders and even supplied him with a horse to make his rounds in the early days of the settlement. Taverns were frequently the first public buildings constructed in pioneer Upper Canadian communities, where they served a vital social function as early community centres. Reverend Bell himself solemnized marriages in Angus Cameron's inn, and the patronage of former officers had provided early support for Adamson and Cameron, but their own British Army pensions had given both men the capital required to start their businesses.[19]

While very few of the privates who made up the majority of the soldier settlers in the region appear to have had the benefit of a military pension, their service in the army had provided them with free land grants. Although many soldiers would later abandon their lots, as late as 1822 they still represented well over half of the settlers in Bathurst and Drummond townships. It has been demonstrated that all types of settler were represented among those who chose to leave the settlement, but in Bathurst and Drummond the poor quality of some of the land grants, rather than a military background, appears to have been the most common factor underlying these departures.[20] Indeed, there are numerous examples of common Scottish soldiers, both single and married, who chose to remain on their grants. Among the single men who successfully completed their settlement duties in Drummond Township were Angus McMillan, Donald McGregor, and William Wilson of the Canadian Fencibles. Collectively they had over twenty-eight years of army service, while Alexander and Charles Duncan of the 104th New Brunswick Fencible Regiment, both with over twelve years service each, were among those who had performed their settlement duties in Bathurst. Married soldiers who remained in the settlement included John Bowie, a veteran with over twenty-one years of service, who had fought in the Peninsular War before being posted to Canada and settling with his wife in Bathurst. David Hogg and Duncan MacKenzie of the Royal Artillery had served over eight years each before they settled with their wives and children in Drummond and Burgess.[21]

Rank-and-file Scottish soldiers who had served with British Army units in North America continued to be given land grants in the settlement well after the initial awards of 1816 and 1817. Donald Gillis of Boliskin, Invernes-shire, and Alexander Cameron of Abernethy, Perthshire, served with the 103rd Regiment that had arrived in Quebec from Ireland in 1812 and settled with their families in Burgess and Bathurst townships in 1818. Ronald McLelland of the 37th, who had served in Spain, and William Robinson of the 70th, who had served in Ireland, received their grants in Beckwith and Bathurst in 1820 and 1821 respectively. The arrival of men like these ensured that former soldiers continued to be highly visible in the community, but there is also evidence that awareness of the settlement spread to soldiers who had not served in the Canadas. James McIntosh, a fifteen-year veteran of the Coldstream Guards, who suffered from ill health due to his service with the regiment in Holland and Spain, not North America, settled with his wife and four children in Bathurst in September 1817. McIntosh, who was born in Elgin, Morayshire, and had first served with the 97th Regiment, was discharged in London in 1814. Rather than return to Scotland, he chose to take his family across the Atlantic and settle in Upper Canada. McIntosh's arrival demonstrated that information about land grants in the settlement were not only circulated among British Army veterans already in North America but had also reached across that Atlantic. Indeed, as late as the 1820s, Robert Forrest, who had settled in Lanark Township, was informing his soldier brother, Samuel, still in Scotland, that as a former staff sergeant he could obtain a free three-hundred-acre land grant in Upper Canada.[22]

Regardless of where they had originated or where they had fought, all of these former soldiers had qualified for land as a consequence of their service in the imperial army. But at the same time that the first soldiers were being placed on lots in and around Perth, government-assisted emigrants from Scotland were also receiving their land grants. While several contemporaries and subsequent historians have made a distinction between the civilian and the military settlers, it has been pointed out that settlers from the Highlands, and the Glengarry estate in particular, dominated the 1815 scheme. Of the nearly seven hundred settlers who left Glasgow with government assistance in 1815, more than half were from the Highlands. Those who left from the Glengarry lands in Glenelg and Knoydart successfully petitioned the colonial authorities to be allowed to settle in Glengarry County, rather than the intended destination above the Rideau River.[23] These emigrants were drawn from the same families that had provided recruits for the British Army, both in Scotland and in North America, and it is very likely that some of them had served as soldiers during the French Wars. In addition, Colonial Office documents relating to the 1815 assisted emigration provide further indications that former soldiers were among the first to express interest in the government scheme.

William Henry Bartlett's sketch of Calton Hill, overlooking Edinburgh's new town, suggests that soldiers were a frequent sight throughout the Scottish capital in the early nineteenth century. From Scotland Illustrated, *Vol. I, frontispiece.*

Courtesy of Killam Library, Dalhousie University.

On March 13, 1815, only two days after receiving official recognition of his appointment as the government agent for Scotland, John Campbell forwarded a list of thirty queries from prospective emigrants to Lord Bathurst. The fourth item on Campbell's list — appearing after questions relating to the choice of destination (Upper or Lower Canada), the deposit required for children over sixteen years of age, and the cost of transportation to the port of embarkation — was a request to clarify whether or not soldiers' pensions would be paid in the colony. Queries 25 and 26 asked if settlers would be provided with firearms or if they were permitted to bring their own in order "to protect themselves from the Enemy, Indians, etc.," strongly suggesting that individuals familiar with the use of weapons were expressing interest in taking advantage of the scheme.[24] In addition, two of the 1815 emigrants who eventually settled in Lanark County, James MacDonald and John MacLeod, are identified in Upper Canadian land records as former soldiers, although only their trades were recorded in the Colonial Office documents.[25] In addition, MacDonald and MacLeod had emigrated from Edinburgh and Glasgow, respectively, indicating that interest in the scheme among former soldiers was found throughout Scotland.

While information may have already been circulating among Scottish veterans about opportunities in Upper Canada, it is clear that John Campbell played an important role in distributing news about the scheme. The Edinburgh lawyer's first act as government agent was to publish the terms of the assisted emigration in as many Scottish newspapers as he could. This was reinforced by the printing of a handbill, which he personally signed and circulated — particularly in Argyllshire, Perthshire, and Inverness-shire where, as he informed Lord Bathurst, he had both "clients and friends." The newspaper advertisements reached the whole literate Scottish audience, and, in Campbell's words, caused "a strong sensation," particularly in Glasgow, but notices also drew inquiries from northern England and as far away as Ireland, where Campbell's advertisement had been reproduced as news in the Dublin *Evening Post*.[26]

Among the military men who saw Campbell's circular was Lieutenant-Colonel Robert Pilkington, at Woolwich Arsenal, the same man who had annotated the War Office map of Upper Canada to reflect the new townships above the Rideau. While Pilkington had written on behalf of several "artificers & labourers" in London who wished to take advantage of the scheme, Campbell noted the lieutenant-colonel's "knowledge of Canada" and asked him to recommend the "most authentic book" on the country. The government agent reported that he had been told in Glasgow, "where they have much connection with Canada," that the entry in Dr. Brewster's *Edinburgh Encyclopaedia* provided the most useful information on the colony and as a result he had copies printed for distribution.[27] While Campbell believed that the entry would answer "a great number of questions" for potential immigrants, Brewster's *Encyclopaedia*, a forerunner of the *Encyclopedia Britannica*, merely provided general information on the history, climate, and trade of the colony. Indeed, the entry's discussion of early violent conflict with First Nations peoples may have actually encouraged some prospective settlers to believe that they required guns for protection. Nevertheless, the materials printed by Campbell enhanced the profile of Upper Canada throughout Scotland as they were circulated widely — both by local clergyman and by Campbell himself during the course of his other professional activities in both the Highlands and the Lowlands.[28]

Recognizing Bathurst's original intention of settling Highlanders in Upper Canada, Archibald Colquhoun, the lord advocate of Scotland, had recommended the appointment of John Campbell as government agent since he had served as "law agent" for several great landowners in the region such as the Earl of Breadalbane and Lord MacDonald of Sleat. His father, John Campbell Sr., had been a prominent member of Edinburgh society by virtue of his position as cashier of the Royal Bank, and he inherited the business relationship that his father had enjoyed with several Highland magnates. In addition, his sister Mary had married the advocate Alexander Campbell, whose son, Sir Duncan, became the first baronet of Barcaldine and her brother's client.[29]

In his recommendation to Bathurst, the lord advocate did not, however, mention that Campbell's family relationships also connected him to North America. His brother, Lieutenant-General Colin Campbell, with whom he shared an estate in the family's ancestral lands in Perthshire, had served in New York during the Revolutionary War, in Nova Scotia in the 1780s, and the West Indies until 1803. While in Nova Scotia, Colin had married the eldest daughter of Colonel Guy Johnston, whose brother Sir John had been instrumental in the foundation of the Loyalist settlements in the Canadas.[30] In making his recommendation, Archibald Colquhoun may not have been aware of this imperial connection or, indeed, of the depth of Campbell's interests in the Scottish Lowlands.

While training for a career in law, Campbell had apprenticed in Glasgow, where he had developed links with many of the firms engaged in transatlantic trade. The marriage of another sister, Margaret, to David Dale also connected him to the rapid industrial development occurring in the region. Dale had used his position as agent for the Royal Bank of Scotland in Glasgow to obtain the capital required to establish his innovative cotton mill at New Lanark, and Campbell heavily invested his Highland clients' money with his brother-in-law, thus linking the Highland pastoral economy with Lowland industry.[31] Campbell also held property in both the Highlands and the Lowlands. In addition to the Perthshire estate that he held with his brother, John Campbell had also inherited Citadel House at Leith from his father. In Edinburgh, where his business office was located at 26 Abercromby Place in the New Town, Campbell owned a house and grounds at Warriston as well as property on Elder Street and James Square. In acquiring these properties, Campbell, like his father before him, was typical of many middle-ranked Highland gentry who pursued a Lowland career in law as a means of advancing their status. But these individuals also encouraged an appetite for urban living and Lowland luxuries among their Highland clients that resulted in financial ruin for many — including Campbell's nephew the baronet of Bracaldine.[32]

While the French Wars were being waged, the great landowners had sought to retain their population for military recruitment, but with the end of hostilities they found that large numbers of small tenants were incapable of providing the revenue required for the lordly lifestyle that most Highland lairds craved. In his reports to Bathurst, Campbell indicated that he spent a good deal of his time persuading Highland lairds that some emigration from their estates would be in their interest and would not lead, as many had feared, to a general depopulation. He found that Highland magnates, who had opposed emigration in the past, were now willing to allow the government agent to recruit on their estates, and Campbell reported that if the emigrant ships had departed from the region, instead of Greenock, hundreds more would have participated in the scheme.[33]

Like many others with Highland connections, Campbell had originally sought to curtail emigration and had lobbied for the 1803 Passenger Act that regulated and restricted the trade. While his attitudes had changed by the time of his appointment, Campbell still believed that the greatest difficulty any emigrant would face was "the wretched and infamous practices that have been followed by those Emigration Crimps, whose unprincipled thirst for gain have led them to such a traffic, at times not much less to be dreaded than the Slave trade." As a consequence, he reported to Bathurst that he was also "anxious" to explain to applicants in Edinburgh and in Glasgow "the terms offered by Government in order to prevent disappointment or misunderstanding." While these meetings also generated a great deal of interest from prospective emigrants, Campbell reported that the required deposit, rather than port of embarkation, had greatly reduced the number of Lowlanders able to participate in the scheme.[34]

As Lord Bathurst had first intended, the majority of emigrants for the 1815 government-assisted emigration had been recruited in the Highlands, but John Campbell's personal and professional connections in both regions of Scotland, as well as his efforts at promoting the scheme, had ensured that awareness of Upper Canada had been raised across the country. Indeed, the Upper Canadian land records reveal that the overwhelming majority of the 1815 emigrants, who settled in what would become Lanark County, originated from the Lowlands.[35] Most of these families were placed close together along the concession dividing the Elmsley and Burgess townships from Drummond and Bathurst. As a consequence, the road quickly became known as the Scotch Line and military authorities continued to place later Scottish arrivals, like Simon Gray, in close proximity to the 1815 settlers.

The concentration of settlement appears to have been a deliberate policy, since military units were also generally located near each other in the new settlement. The land records reveal, for example, that lots near Perth in Drummond and Bathurst Township were largely granted to soldiers and officers of the Glengarry Light Infantry and Canadian

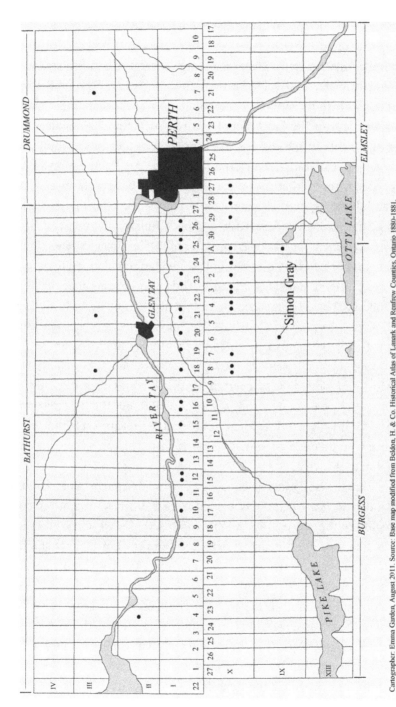

The Scotch Line

Fencibles. It would appear, then, that placing the 1815 emigrants together along the Scotch Line was merely an extension of military practice of settling units together rather than an attempt to create a Scottish enclave.[36]

Shortly after his arrival in Perth on June 24, 1817, Reverend Bell was provided with information on the population of the settlement by the superintendent of the Perth depot. He recorded that 709 soldiers had taken up grants in the district while only 239 other men, whom Bell classified as "emigrants," had done the same. An examination of the land records reveal that more than half of the "emigrants" were from Scotland, but, despite their prominence among the officers, less than a tenth of the soldiers had Scottish origins. Similarly, the wives of Scots soldiers accounted for less than a quarter of the "military" women in the settlement, but nearly two-thirds of the "civilian" children were born in Scotland.[37] The military depot land records also indicate that the Scots who followed the 1815 assisted emigrants had continued to bring their families with them. The *Lord Middleton*, for example, which sailed from Leith with 163 passengers, included three families and three single men who would eventually settle in the Upper Ottawa Valley. (See Table 1)

Most emigrant vessels departed Scotland from Greenock and they were joined by passengers from across Scotland, but there were several that sailed directly from regional ports, and it appears likely that many of those who boarded these vessels came from the immediate vicinity. Family names such as Robson, Sterling, Armstrong, and Scott certainly suggest that the emigrants on board the *Lord Middleton* originated in the Lowlands and provide indirect evidence for continued migration from the region to the upper Ottawa valley after 1815. Most of the emigrant vessels, like the *Lord Middleton*, departed from the Lowlands, but a few left from northern ports. The family names of Lanark County settlers who sailed with the *Morningfield* from Stornoway on the Isle of Lewis were commonly found in the western Highlands (See Table 2). While several of those passengers also brought their families with them, single men made up the majority of those who settled in Lanark County. Three of these *Morningfield* men were among the first settlers of Beckwith Township and provided the genesis of a distinctive Gaelic-speaking community that emerged in that township.[38]

TABLE 1

Lord Middleton Passengers Who Sailed from Leith in May 1817 and Settled in Lanark County.[39]
[**D** = Drummond; **E**=Elmsley; **BR**=Burgess].

Name	Date of Grant	Township, Concession & Lot	Marital Status
Robert Sterling	Aug. 1817	**BR** C8 SW13	single
Adam Robson	Aug. 1817 & Jan. 1820	**D** C1 NE12 **D** C1 NE14	married, 6 children
Neil McFarlane	Aug. 1817	**D** C6 SE8	married, 1 child
Walter Armstrong	Dec. 1817	**E** C3 SW4	single
James Scott	Mar. 1818	**E** C10 NE8	married, 1 child
William Scott	Oct. 1818	**E** C3 NE4	single

TABLE 2

Morningfield Passengers Who Sailed from Stornoway in August 1816 and Settled in Lanark County.[40]
[**D** = Drummond; **B**=Bathurst; **Bk**=Beckwith; **r**=land later regranted].

Name	Date of Grant	Township, Concession & Lot	Marital Status
John Cameron	Oct. 1816	**D** C2 SW14	single
William Fraser	Nov. 1816	**D** C2 NE14 - **r**	single
Donald McLelland	Nov. 1816	**Bk** C7 NE3	single
John McDonald	Nov. 1816	**Bk** C7 SW6	single
Donald Campbell	Nov. 1816	**D** C6 SW3	married
Ronald McDonald	Dec. 1816	**D** C4 NE7	single
Duncan Cameron	Dec. 1816	**B** C7 SW14	married, 1 child
John McMillan	Dec. 1816	**D** C3 SW15	married
Alexander Campbell	Dec. 1816	**Bk** C4 SW9	married, 1 child
John McDonald Sr.	Dec. 1816	**D** C4 NE6 - **r**	married, 5 children
John McDonald Jr.	Dec. 1816	**D** C4 SW9 - **r**	single
Archibald McDonell	Dec. 1816	**D** C5 SW26	single
Archibald McDonald	Dec. 1816	**Bk** C7 SW3	single
Donald McMillan	Jan. 1817	**D** C7 N16	single
Samuel McEchan	Nov. 1816	**Bk** C5 NE6	married, 2 children

Soldier settlers were drawn from across Scotland and their letters home would have encouraged many others to consider following, but despite the Lowland origins of most of the 1815 assisted emigrants, settlers from Perthshire, particularly from the Breadalbane estate, comprised most of the Scottish emigrants who would arrive in Beckwith in 1818. John Campbell's activities had raised the profile of the colony in the district and the participation of several families from the region ensured that news of the settlement would continue to circulate. The settlement of three families from Callander and three from Killin in northeastern Perthshire, in particular, provided considerable encouragement for further emigration from the region. John Ferguson, for example, settled with his large family in Bathurst Township in 1816 and two years later other Ferguson families from Perthshire could be found throughout the settlement, especially in Beckwith.

Further government assistance had made their journey possible, but a letter written in 1823 by Lieutenant Robert Ferguson reflects how family contacts as well as government aid and military connections were supporting emigration after 1815. In trying to persuade his father-in-law to leave Scotland and join his family in Beckwith, Lieutenant Ferguson painted a glowing picture of the settlement extolling its natural features, thriving timber trade, free schools, and "Church of Scotland" minister, but emphasized that there were also plenty of "friends" (i.e., *relatives*) in the settlement. He added that "if you will be convinced to come to America your home is before you."[41] That Robert Ferguson found himself at "home" in Beckwith was due in large part to the imperial army and the imperial state whose agents had directed his fellow soldiers and his Scottish relations to Upper Canada.

Chapter Three

THE BREADALBANE IMMIGRANTS

In a letter of March 12, 1877, addressed to John Stuart, the secretary of the Society of Antiquaries of Scotland, Daniel Wilson,[1] the professor of history and English literature at University College in Toronto triumphantly announced the return of the Crozier of St. Fillan to Scotland.[2] According to Wilson, the early medieval relic had been rescued from "its inevitable fate if much longer abandoned to the contingencies of a Canadian clearing" and would now be safe in the National Museum of Antiquaries in Edinburgh. As a consequence of the artefact's remarkable journey from northern Perthshire to Beckwith Township and then back to Scotland, the crozier, or *Quigrich* as it is known in Gaelic, is now a centrepiece of the Medieval Church gallery at the National Museum of Scotland.

Wilson's involvement in its story also reveals how Upper Canadian colonial institutions were themselves populated by imperial immigrants. A long-time member of the Scottish Society for Antiquaries, Daniel Wilson had made his scholarly reputation with books that had examined the historic buildings of his native Edinburgh and the archaeology of prehistoric Scotland. It was on the basis of this work that he was awarded an honourary LLD from Saint Andrews University, but the opportunity to pursue an academic vocation came from Upper Canada, not Scotland. As with many other immigrant Scottish scholars, Wilson had a long and distinguished career at what would become the University of Toronto, and he became that institution's first president in 1887. He also twice held the position of president of the Canadian Institute, founded to promote scientific study in British North America, and was also one of the founding members of the Royal Society of Canada. In both his own scholarship and in his public service, Wilson did a great deal to encourage serious study of the prehistory of indigenous peoples of North America and to incorporate this knowledge into a broader account of human civilization. Impressed by Wilson's erudition, one British reviewer of his *Prehistoric Man: Researches into the Origin of Civilization in the Old and New World* (1862) wrote that it was hard to believe Wilson had written the book in the "woody depths of Canada." But despite his commitment to North American research, Wilson's role in repatriating the Crozier of St. Fillan demonstrates that he too saw his new home as a remote intellectual outpost of empire.

Wilson had first heard that the *Quigrich* was in Canada while he was in Scotland and he made several attempts to obtain it after he arrived in Toronto in 1853. In his letter to Stuart, he confided that he had feared that the American showman P.T. Barnum would hear of the relic and put it in his exhibition of curiosities. Believing that if the crozier remained in Canada it would necessarily fall victim to such desecration, Wilson tried to raise money from wealthy Scottish immigrants in Canada to purchase the relic. When that failed he considered approaching the British Museum for help. His belief that the colonial owners could not be relied upon to protect their own heritage was analogous to the arguments made by Lord Elgin when he acquired the Parthenon's marble frieze for the British Museum in order to preserve it from supposed Greek neglect.[3]

In the end, Wilson chose not to involve London, since "a relic so thoroughly Scottish in all would be robbed of much of its genuine interest if transferred to the custody of strangers." These associations included a reference to the crozier being with Robert Bruce prior to the Battle of Bannockburn and a royal letter from James III naming the Dewar family of Glendochart as hereditary keepers of the relic. The Dewars had resided in Killin on Loch Tay, and well into the eighteenth century local residents used water passed through the crozier to cure their sick cattle, a practice that apparently continued in Beckwith Township where many immigrants maintained their Highland customs. Wilson reported that Archibald Dewar, although born in Beckwith, recalled that in the early days "the whole home talk, entirely in Gaelic, was of old Scottish memories and traditions; and so, though himself a native of Canada, he was more familiar with Glendochart and Balquidder, than with anything in the New World," though these family recollections were now fading. Wilson's own family had Gaelic origins and the *Quigrich*'s connection to Highland lore, as well as to the Scottish Wars of Independence, added a patriotic dimension to his antiquarian desire to see it returned to the homeland.[4]

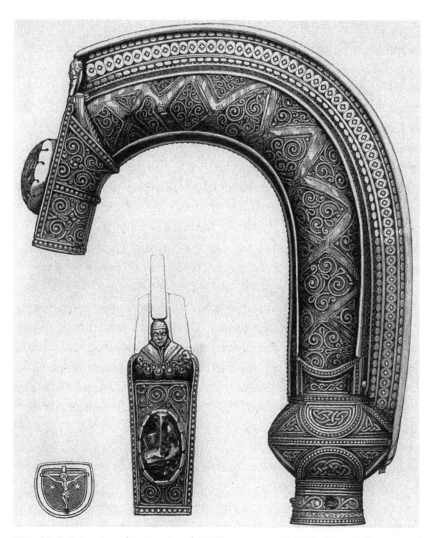

This detailed drawing of the Crozier of St. Fillan accompanied John Stuart's discussion of the artefact in the March 12, 1877, issue of the Proceedings of the Society of Antiquaries of Scotland.

Courtesy of Queen Elizabeth II Library, Memorial University.

Naturally, Daniel Wilson was keen to highlight his own efforts and his account underplayed the Dewar family's role in the returning the relic in their safekeeping. Wilson first learned that the crozier was in Canada when the former Bathurst District MPP Malcolm Cameron wrote to the Society of Antiquaries on behalf of the Dewars in 1852. While the family were asking £420 for the artefact, which Wilson was finally able to obtain for $500, it was not because of impoverished circumstances that they were willing to sell the relic. Alexander Dewar, who was in possession of the crozier at the time of its repatriation, had become a very successful farmer after moving from Beckwith and purchasing more productive land in Plympton Township in Western Ontario. In the deed surrendering the *Quigrich*, Dewar made it clear that he also wished the relic to be preserved for "the use, benefit, and enjoyment of the Scottish nation."[5]

Alexander's father, Archibald Dewar, who brought the Crozier of St. Fillan to Upper Canada, had also enjoyed farming success in Scotland prior to emigrating. Archibald had left Killin on Lochtayside as a young man and managed a sheep farm in Comrie for Campbell of Edinchip. He lost the farm in 1808 when Campbell died, but rented another farm in Glenartney in Strathearn. Although considered a good farmer and an excellent judge of cattle, Archibald Dewar chose to emigrate with the Breadalbane assisted immigrants in 1818 as a consequence of the rapid rise in rents that followed the Napoleonic Wars. That Dewar was able to participate in the scheme by paying the required £10 deposit for each adult male member of his family clearly indicates that he was not a poor landless cottar "cleared" off an estate, but a relatively successful tenant farmer who had been at the forefront of many of the agricultural changes that had been implemented across the Highlands.[6]

The conventional image of Highlanders being forced to emigrate as the consequence of estate changes, made by rapacious lairds bent on increasing their rents by replacing people with sheep, has undergone considerable revision. Many studies now emphasize the fact that the Highlanders who could afford to emigrate were often like the Dewars, individuals who had been responsible for implementing many of the "improving" practices associated with commercial agriculture. Competition among these tenants, which in turn helped to produce the

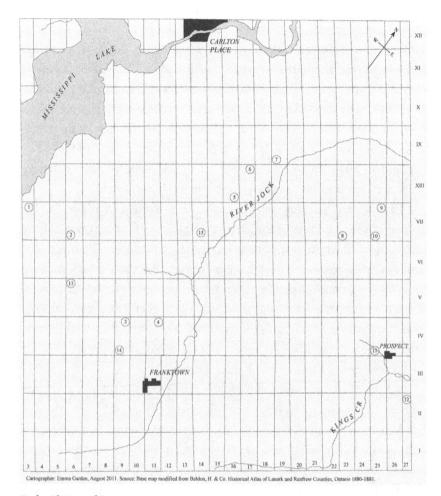

Cartographer: Emma Garden, August 2011. Source: Base map modified from Beldon, H. & Co. Historical Atlas of Lanark and Renfrew Counties, Ontario 1880-1881.

Beckwith Township

1. Donald McLelland
2. John McDonald
3. Jean [née Moir] & Lt. Robert Ferguson
4. Catherin [née McNaughton] & Duncan Campbell
5. James McDairmid
6. John McDairmid & family
7. Janet [née Kennedy] & Alexander Dewar
8. John Dewar

9. Anne [née Comrie] & Malcolm Dewar
10. Margaret [née Ferguson] & Archibald Dewar
11. Daniel McLeod
12. John Robertson & family
13. Ann [née McDonald] & Samuel McE[a]chan
14. Alexander Campbell & family
15. Church of Scotland, Presbyterian Church

dramatic increases in rent, is now seen as equally important for creating the conditions for emigration as were the more well-known, but relatively rare, wholesale "clearances."[7] Nevertheless, Archibald Dewar's decision to take the *Quigrich* with him to Upper Canada was a reflection of the attachment that many Highlanders still had for age-old traditions, even as they adapted to the radical changes taking place in the rural economy. The tension between tradition and change was particularly evident on the fourth Earl of Breadalbane's estate centred on Loch Tay, and in large measure accounts for the decision of several tenant farmers to petition for assistance to settle in Upper Canada.

The Dewars had departed Scotland from Greenock on board the *Curlew*, whose passengers included over twenty other families from Comrie parish, many of whom settled near each other in Beckwith Township. The family names, however, strongly suggest that, like the Dewars, most of the 1818 emigrants had personal connections to Lochtayside, where most of the assisted emigrants originated, and all of them were undoubtedly aware that over a dozen families from northern Perthshire had participated in the 1815 scheme. At least six of these families had settled along the Scotch Line in Elmsley and Bathurst townships.[8]

But the 1815 emigrants were not the first from the region, as former soldiers and tenants had been settling across the Atlantic for decades. The Maritime colonies of British North America were a favoured early destination. In 1778 a hundred men were recruited from the Breadalbane estate to defend the empire in America with the 74th Regiment (Argyll Highlanders), and after the war several of these veterans settled in New Brunswick and Nova Scotia.[9] In addition, the New Brunswick legislature allocated funds, in 1803 and in 1815, to pay for the passages of emigrants from Perthshire and these settlers were found in many of the early agricultural communities in southern New Brunswick. Others, like the Logierait-born merchant Robert Ferguson, were drawn by the timber trade to the northern part of colony, where one community in the Miramichi region was named Breadalbane after the homeland. That these earlier settlers attracted others to the Maritime colonies is reflected by the fact that a small party of the 1818 emigrants, upon arrival in Quebec, broke away from the main group and headed to Cape Breton.

Although they ended up settling on Prince Edward Island.[10]

A handbill in the Breadalbane records advertising for plowmen to work on a gentleman's property in Upper Canada, perhaps Lord Selkirk's at Baldoon, indicate that as early as 1802 word of the colony was circulating in Breadalbane, but it was the 1815 scheme that the petitioners had in mind when they requested assistance to emigrate to Upper Canada early in 1817.[11] The petition from eighty families residing on the north side of the Loch Tay does not appear to have survived, but reportedly stated that the signatories "could no longer live on the estate," and Lord Breadalbane's factor, John McGillewie, expressed his fear that the numbers involved meant that if the petitioners were successful, the area around Morenish would be left "with few or no inhabitants." The factor added that there was a serious problem of defaulting tenants on the estate, particularly on the north side of the loch, and urged Breadalbane to grant his tenants an abatement in rent.[12] John Campbell, as the earl's man of business, wrote to the colonial secretary on his client's behalf arguing that the distress experienced was not unique to the estate but general throughout the Highlands, and that, far from a reckless disregard for his tenantry's welfare, the earl had done his utmost to "improve his lands" with his "extended views of political economy." The fact that during the French Wars the earl had been able to raise three battalions for his Fencible regiment, largely from his own estates, was also cited by Campbell as proof of Breadalbane's belief in the necessity of preserving the Highland population. He concluded that the petition could not be a result of ill-treatment from the proprietor, but was instead the consequence of the favourable reports received from those who had participated in the 1815 assisted emigration and that the petitioners would soon give up their plan when it became known that the earl had agreed to provide an abatement of rents in order to alleviate their distress.[13]

Despite these claims, over thirty families from Lochtayside departed with government assistance for Upper Canada in the summer of 1818. For his own part, Lord Breadalbane believed that he had "sacrificed more than any of his neighbours to retain his population" and refused to interfere. Indeed, he instructed McGilliwie not to provide abatements in rent to any of the tenants who had signed the petition, thus leaving them little choice but to leave.[14] The factor, though initially alarmed at the numbers involved, soon branded the petitioners as malcontents and disreputable characters. In a letter to John Campbell, he wrote that "after inquiring pretty minutely into the emigration list" he had found that a number of the signatories were "young felons" who had no holding on the estate while many of the others could be "well spare[d] out of the country." According to McGillewie, if it were not for the fact that there had been a disastrous crop failure in the autumn of 1816, all of the petitioners would be employed in illicit whisky distillation and "in the ruinous Trade of Smuggling."[15]

The factor believed that Duncan Campbell, a former tenant farmer on the north side of Loch Tay, was responsible for writing the petition and suggested to the earl that he was "one of the worst characters in the country." Like the Dewar family, Campbell and his wife Catherin, along with their three children, John, Elizabeth, and Jannet, were among those who left Scotland onboard the *Curlew* and subsequently settled in Beckwith. Despite McGillewie's characterization, Duncan Campbell appears to have

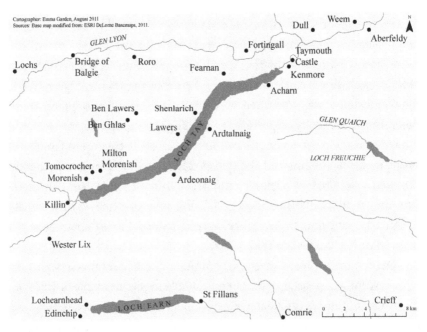

Loch Tay Region

encountered little difficulty in the township. He was among the original members of the township's first Presbyterian congregation when it formed in 1822. By that time he had also been able to perform his settlement duties and obtain freehold to his land grant, despite the fact that his eldest son was only ten years old at the time of the family's emigration.[16]

Like his Beckwith neighbour, Lieutenant Robert Ferguson, Duncan Campbell also had a military background, having served as an officer in the Perthshire militia. There is evidence to suggest that former soldiers were having a particularly difficult time on the Breadalbane estate and were aware that army veterans had been offered land in the Ottawa Valley. After the 1818 emigrants had departed, Hugh McEwen wrote to Earl Bathurst asking if the ex-servicemen on the north side of Loch Tay would be eligible for further government assistance. McEwen alluded to the colonial secretary's "past favour" and stated that if members of the Fencibles, Volunteers, and local Militia were also considered part of the army that many of them would take advantage of "the proposals of government, and emigrate to Upper Canada."[17]

Since levels of military recruitment had been particularly high on the Breadalbane estate, it is likely that most of 1818 emigrants would have known a former soldier, or, like Duncan Campbell, had served themselves. It has been calculated that three out every five farms on the earl's Perthshire lands supplied recruits for the Breadalbane Fencibles between 1793 and 1795, and many of these men subsequently served in regular army units.[18] The earl made it clear that service in the Fencibles was expected, and, at least initially, he went to considerable lengths to reward recruits with land — a time-honoured tradition for Highland military service. The surviving evidence indicates that the earl seems to have favoured soldiers, and families that had supplied soldiers, over those that had not.

Of the thirty-three petitions that arrived in 1799 at his Taymouth Castle residence asking for preference to crofts, ten were marked out by the factor for special attention because the petitioners had either served in the Fencibles or provided a recruit. Even those who offered sons but were refused, such as Duncan Menzies, who claimed to be the first to offer aid when his neighbours were "unwilling to give any," were accorded special attention.[19] Favourable hearing of some of the requests encouraged a spate of such petitions during the first years of the nineteenth century. The vast majority asked for preference for small holdings — crofts, cow holdings. or pendicles — a reflection of the fact that most of the recruits had come from the lower end of the social scale, that is labourers, crofters, tradesmen, or tenants who shared a single farm. Despite the favourable hearing that these initial petitions received, the earl reported that at the time of disbandment one thousand of his men volunteered for general service in Europe, although their previous service had not extended beyond Ireland. Breadalbane suggested that this reflected his men's zeal, but increasingly limited opportunities on the estate must have also played a role.[20]

The predicament experienced by many ex-soldiers was clearly evident in the petition of Duncan Clark, a drill sergeant in the Fencibles. In 1803, after disbandment, Clark had joined the North Killin Volunteers, but found himself unable to attend the daily drill at Morenish because of his reduced circumstances. He claimed that he had "nothing for his own support," and that he was forced to share his father's cow holding. Unless he was provided a salary for his duties as "dreel sergent," Clark argued that he would have to leave the corps and "betake himself of some other employment."[21] Many former soldiers shared Clark's problems in trying to find a place, or employment, on the estate as a consequence of so many returning at the same time and the demands being created on the available land. In addition, the earl's factors were warning him that giving preference to former soldiers was resulting in the removal of some of the best "improving" farmers and undermining the productivity of the estate. Lord Breadalbane had been paid a government bounty for each of his Fencible recruits, but those payments ceased with the regiment's disbandment, and, therefore, there was less economic incentive for the earl to retain his estate's population. As a consequence, former soldiers were increasingly less likely to receive a favourable hearing from either the laird or his factor.[22]

Indeed, as the years progressed it is apparent that the earl became less inclined to grant requests based on previous military service. Peter MacEwen, after serving as a private in various regiments for over twenty-one years, returned in 1813 to his relations at Ardeonaig on the south side of Loch Tay and petitioned the earl for "a House and a piece of land to enable him to settle in his native country." Lord Breadalbane replied that the petitioner's brother had "two Lots in Newton and has Spare houses with which the Petitioner can be accommodated."[23] The earl preferred to settle MacEwen in his tradesman's village beside Kenmore, rather than provide him with land from the farms around Ardeonaig. These lands were set aside for the large tenant farmers, who had become the leading contributors to the estate revenue, and it was not in the earl's interest to subdivide them. Ironically, it had been the absence of large numbers of men in the imperial army that had provided the opportunity to create the large farms in the first place.

The fourth earl was not the first to try to reorganize land holding on Lochtayside since the third earl had surveyed the estate in 1769, and subsequently introduced the first large individually held farms. Nevertheless, practices changed little because subletting of these new holdings was rampant.[24] Not satisfied with the changes instituted by his predecessor, and taking advantage of the absence of so many men in the Fencibles, the fourth earl introduced dramatic new "Arrangements" in 1795. He and his factors had concluded that large sheep farms could afford to pay much higher rent by increasing the production of wool. In order to facilitate this change, smaller holdings that had been farmed communally for generations raising black cattle were eliminated and the land joined together to create new, large "stock" farms.[25] As a consequence, several hundred tenants lost their land. The vast majority of the dispossessed were widows and crofters who had held the small possessions that the new arrangements sought to abolish. In order to compensate those removed for their loss of land, Lord Breadalbane set up crofter "towns" in various parts of his estate. Two of the larger settlements were located at Wester Lix in Glendochart and on his lands south of Loch Tay in Glenquaich.[26]

After the demobilization of the Fencibles in 1802, competition for the land that remained available became intense and was accompanied by a dramatic increase in those failing to meet their rents. The factor believed that the roots of the trouble lay within the Highland character, and, in particular, that local rivalries encouraged fierce competition between tenants that resulted in offers for farms well beyond what the lands could yield in return.[27] The tenants, on the other hand, blamed their misfortunes on the new arrangements. The rationale behind the changes were hard to grasp for many of the earl's tenantry. Crofters in Glenquaich, for example, expressed their deep concern to Lord Breadalbane when they learned that their small holdings were to be used to expand neighbouring farms. As they saw it, such a change would deprive them of "the only means of support they had for the subsistence of their weak and numerous families."[28]

While Glenquaich tenants hinted at the emotional impact of the new leasing arrangements, a shieling hut at Meall Griegh on the south side of Ben Lawers provides physical evidence of the profound transformation that occurred in grazing practices on the estate. Archaeological excavations conducted on the site have uncovered numerous layers indicating the traditional temporary use of the building as a habitation

The ruins of abandoned sheilings are still visible on Ben Lawers. Originally, they were used as summer residences, when entire communities moved up the hill from the north side of Loch Tay with their black cattle. After the introduction of large sheep farms, shepherds used the sheilings for shelter on occasion, but they quickly fell into disrepair.

Photo by M. Vance.

during the summer months, but that form of occupation suddenly ceased and the building was apparently transformed into a dairy.[29] A specific example of how the widespread changes of this kind exerted pressures that led to emigration can be seen in the history of the Roro tenants, who occupied farms on lands belonging to the Earl of Breadalbane on the south side of Glenlyon. (Prior to the reforms of 1795, the tenants of Lawers and Carwhin on the north side of Loch Tay held summer grazings on their side of Ben Lawers, as well as some on the north side shared with the Roro farmers.) In compensation, the Roro people had access to grazings, called the Lochs, on the north side of Glenlyon. The irregular, but nevertheless time-honoured arrangement did not suit the earl's factor, who convinced the earl to give the Lochs to a single tenant, with annual rent of £200, and restrict the Roro tenants to the shielings above them.[30] Even though the tenants on the north side of Loch Tay were also restricted to their own side of Ben Lawers, the Glenlyon tenants were unhappy.

Patrick and Widow Campbell, the tenants of Roroyere, complained of not only being deprived of the pasture at Lochs, but that the tenants of two other farms in the district were, in response, depriving them of other grazing that had been a common pasture "from time or ages past memory." In addition to this affront to tradition, the Campbells claimed that the changes had left them "hemmed in" by the other tenants, and, as a consequence, they found it difficult to meet their obligations to the earl.

The rental returns for the Roro district make it clear that other tenants also found it difficult to meet their new rents, including John McLean the occupant of the new Lochs farm. By 1810, McLean was £221 in arrears and the sum was never collected since, as the factor's ledger book recorded, McLean had "gone to America."[31]

When Duncan Campbell departed the estate for Beckwith Township he also left an irrecoverable debt of over £15 for the Shenlarich farm near Lawers. He had taken the farm with a relative, Donald Campbell, and like John McLean at the Lochs, the Campbells had also been unable to meet the rental required under the new estate leasing arrangements.[32] Rather than pay what he owed, Campbell used his remaining capital to provide the £10 deposit needed to participate in the 1818 government-assisted

To this day, sheep are raised on Roromore farm in Glenlyon. Shearers are often flown into the region on a seasonal basis from New Zealand – another imperial destination favoured by former Breadalbane tenants during the nineteenth century.

Photo by M. Vance.

emigration. Despite John McGilliwie's low opinion of Duncan Campbell, he was not the only tenant who had difficulty meeting the rent for the Shenlarich farm. While estate arrears lists confirm that the Campbells had continual problems, their successors, Donald and John McEwen and Peter Dewar, were also in arrears. Chronic indebtedness was, in fact, a shared experience across the entire extent of the north side of Loch Tay.[33]

There were a large number of multiple tenant farms like Shenlarich on the north side of the loch, and these farms had provided the largest number of family members for the Breadalbane Fencibles. As a group, however, they had also provided the greatest number of hired recruits when family members could not be spared, often at a cost well above the rent for their farm. This could have added to the high levels of debt in the region. Nevertheless, even the largest farm on the north side of the loch, Tomochrocher, was in arrears and the records show that by 1818 the tenants owed over £1,900. Tomochrocher was one of the model establishments of the estate's new sheep-rearing policy and the fact that large "stock" farms like these were suffering was an indication of how serious the situation had become by the time Duncan Campbell drafted the petition to the Prince Regent.[34]

In the month that the petition was sent, the factor wrote to the earl, stating that crop failures were making the situation even worse and that "the tenants ha[d] not what [would] support their families till the next crop." John McGillewie advocated buying seed for the use of the tenantry in order that the lands not "lie waste ... or be sown with seed of such inferior quality that no good Crop can reasonably be expected from it, and of course the tenant, be unable to pay the rent." The earl's first response was to increase the allowance for "improvements" as an alternate solution to the distress. This was very much in keeping with Breadalbane's self image as an improving landlord, which had resulted in rewarding tenants who followed the new estate policies by digging drains, building field walls, and rotating their crops, but such a policy must have appeared ludicrous to an impoverished tenantry facing starvation.[35]

Equally galling would be the fact that, at the same time, work was continuing on the rebuilding of Taymouth Castle. Integral to the earl's vision of how his estate should be transformed was his belief that his residence should adequately reflect his status as the country's leading highland magnate — a position he held by virtue of his vast estates in Perthshire and Argyllshire and the role he played in the House of Lords.[36] The massive reconstruction of the building started early in the 1800s and was not fully completed till his son, the fifth earl, took control of the estate in the 1830s. The extent of Breadalbane's preoccupation with the project can be seen in his insistence that all factor's reports, which were submitted monthly, begin with an account of the "Taymouth Works" — the state of the tenantry was to be discussed at the end of the report, but only if necessary. The huge building, which still stands but has been vacant for many years, was remolded in the Gothic revival style made popular by the Romantic movement. In choosing the Gothic style, the earl was not only demonstrating his enormous wealth, but also his up-to-date sense of taste.[37]

This engraving from a mid-nineteenth century tourist guidebook shows the view from above Taymouth Castle looking west toward Ben Lawers. The scene, complete with hunting party and enthusiastic kilted attendants, is the embodiment of Lord Breadalbane's vision for his estate. From Black's Picturesque Tourist of Scotland *(Edinburgh: Adam & Charles Black, 1861) 288.*

A portrait of the earl, painted by Sir Henry Raeburn and now in the National Galleries of Scotland collection, reflects this desire to be seen as a sophisticated consumer of culture since it shows Breadalbane seated on a *chaise longue* in a modern suit of clothes with a single finger pressed to his temple. A romantic windswept landscape is visible over his right shoulder. Despite being ranked a major-general in the imperial army, Lord Breadalbane chose not to have Raeburn portray him as a Highland warrior in the fashion of the artist's famous contemporaneous portrait of Colonel Alastair McDonnell of Glengarry. This choice can be explained, in part, by the fact that the fourth earl of Breadalbane spent most of his time at his Mayfair London residence and only occasionally visited his Highland estate. Rather than seeing Taymouth Castle as his principal residence, the earl viewed it as a retreat, for a few months of each year, to which important individuals could be brought, entertained, and impressed. Indeed, the fourth earl was among the first to use Highland estates as shooting retreats for the English aristocracy, an activity which became increasingly popular after Queen Victoria began her trips to Balmoral.[38]

In order to ensure game for his hunting parties, Breadalbane created deer parks and planted large areas of woodland along both sides of Loch Tay. The earl's attention to the finest detail of their management is reflected in the full instructions he sent his factor regarding their welfare. Since he believed that "woods and Game suffer very materially by the cutting of Faggots," the tenants were to be allowed only timber that was absolutely necessary. No full-grown trees were to be cut without permission, and, despite his own massive construction project, new tenant building was heavily restricted. The distribution of wood was also regulated and even cart wheels were brought from Perth in order to save the estate timber. At times such jealous protection provoked open conflict between tenants and the estate managers. In 1816 Mr. Malcolm, the wood-keeper in Killin, was attacked by a group of tenants and stabbed by a man named Clark. Although the factor had intended to dismiss Malcolm for previous "misbehaviour" he hoped that the trial of Clark "would Strike more terror into the minds of the people, and I trust would in some degree prevent such outrages in future." Similarly, when Duncan McGibbon, a former soldier, was prosecuted for shooting a roe at Achmore, the factor hoped that it would curtail a rise in poaching.[39]

While the tenants on the north side of Loch Tay were petitioning for assistance to emigrate, the factor, understanding clearly where the earl's priorities lay, reported "that the deer Park is finished and the deer safely removed."[40] Although Lord Breadalbane eventually granted an abatement of rent in order to deal with the economic crisis of 1817, it must have become clear to many of his tenants that neither former service in the Fencibles nor the studious implementation of the earl's new management policies could ensure his attention or support. His insistence on payment of rents, even during periods of crisis, while continuing to enhance Taymouth Castle provoked one of his contemporaries to write, "Lord Breadalbane may build a palace but his sole bears no proportion to it."[41] Certainly, his tenants found that by 1817 arguments for favour based upon past service or time-honoured practice were having little impact on the management of the estate. Nevertheless, the earl was not averse to playing the role of clan chief and frequently surrounded himself with the trappings of Highland culture. He provided a pension to the famous Gaelic bard Duncan ban McIntrye, perhaps in reward for the flattering address the poet had composed to honour him, and when Prince Leopold of Belgium visited Taymouth in 1819, the earl assembled his Fencible veterans in full Highland dress to drill for the honoured guest. The men were accompanied by various pipers who had enjoyed the earl's patronage from an early date. Indeed, the famous players Neil Gow and Malcolm McDonald composed tunes for the earl and McDonald dedicated his second published collection to Breadalbane and his fourth collection to his wife, Mary Turner, an heiress of David Gavin of Langton.[42]

As with many Highland magnates, Lord Breadalbane had been keen to represent himself as a sophisticated, powerful member of the British aristocracy, and he pursued estate management policies that would provide the revenue needed for a grand lordly lifestyle in both the Highlands and in London. At the same time, the raising of the Fencibles during the French Wars and his patronage of Gaelic culture demonstrated that the earl was reluctant to completely abandon the role of Highland chieftan. As a consequence, he did not pursue a policy of wholesale evictions, as had occurred on the Sutherland estate, but his policies nonetheless created the conditions that led many of his tenants to emigrate.[43]

The Earl of Breadalbane's apparently contradictory goal of improving while maintaining tradition was also shared among many of his tenants who chose to seek a new life in the empire. Despite the earl's patronage of their craft, two pipers from Lochtayside, Donald McDougall and Malcolm Fisher, abandoned their farm and left for Glengarry County in 1816. Although their adjustment was undoubtedly aided by the fact that they were emigrating to a community where many still spoke Gaelic, it was nonetheless a dramatic step to take for individuals so intimately connected to Highland musical tradition.[44] In addition to the pipes, Highland cultural practices also appear to have crossed the Atlantic with the Breadalbane emigrants. Hugh Robertson, who settled in Drummond Township and reportedly possessed "second sight," apparently "saw" his land in Upper Canada before he ever left Scotland and foretold the death of another settler who was later crushed by a falling tree at a logging "bee." While it is difficult to corroborate these claims, Robertson's assumption of the role of community "seer" is indicative of a desire to hold on to homeland traditions, perhaps best demonstrated by the settlers' attempt to maintain their language in the pioneer community. Early on the 1818 immigrants expressed a desire to have a minister who could perform church services in their native tongue. The Gaelic-speaking Reverend Dr. George Buchanan duly arrived in 1822, after Reverend Bell had forwarded a petition, written in English, from the Highland settlers to the Secession Presbyterian Church in Edinburgh. Buchanan's congregation would include the families of Duncan Campbell, Robert Ferguson, and Archibald Dewar. The Dewars, in particular, would be among the strongest supporters of the new minister.[45]

While the Breadalbane settlers went to considerable lengths to retain aspects of their culture in Upper Canada, the 1818 emigrants were part of a much larger migration out of the estate as individuals left to serve in the British Army or look for work in the Lowlands. As a consequence, many residents of the estate could already speak both English and Gaelic; indeed, the Breadalbane estate was situated right along the linguistic border between the Lowlands and the Highlands. It was their ability to function in both societies that had made it possible for the Breadalbane emigrants to obtain government support. Rather than being mere victims of grasping landlords, these families were able to use Britain's imperial claims in North America to their own advantage.

A letter sent in 1858 by a nephew of James McDairmid, one of the 1818 settlers from the Breadalbane lands in Glenlyon, clearly illustrates how those left behind continued to see advantages in becoming colonists. Allan McDiarmid, who was living in Glasgow, wrote to his uncle in Beckwith after visiting his parents on their rented farm in Slatich, near Roro. He believed that it was "foolish" for people to "labour in such a place" where "they merely work for their Landlords," and he asked for his uncle's assistance in convincing his elderly parents to give up their Breadalbane farm and settle in Upper Canada where, from what he had "read and heard … farmers are in a condition quite paradisiacal in comparison to what they are in the Highlands of Scotland."[46]

During the nineteenth century many Breadalbane tenants followed the example of the earlier emigrants and left the estate to farm in the colonies. Despite his best efforts, however, Allan McDiarmid's parents would not leave because "they did not think that they would ever like another place so well." By bringing the Crozier of St. Fillan with them to Upper Canada, the Dewar family had also shown a deep attachment to their homeland and to its traditions. Nevertheless, like the Earl of Breadalbane himself, the Dewars were seeking to improve their standing as well as to preserve their heritage. For the earl, improvement meant wholesale changes in estate practice in order to increase his rents. For the Dewars, improvement was made possible by leaving the estate and settling colonial land. They, like the rest of the 1818 emigrants, were drawn from the class of tenant farmers who had earlier embraced the changes in Highland agriculture, and when the postwar depression undermined the economic basis for those changes tenants like the Dewars were among the first to seek opportunities elsewhere in the empire.

Chapter Four

PAISLEY AND THE EMIGRATION SOCIETIES

Early in May 1820, Daniel Murchie, a forty-five-year-old married weaver with ten children residing at 81 Causeyside Street, Paisley, forwarded a petition from several of the "operative manufacturers" of his Lowland town to the colonial secretary. The document was signed by sixty-three other "heads of families" who collectively represented 361 men, women, and children. Murchie and his neighbours began their address to Lord Bathurst by highlighting the hardships they were enduring, claiming that "[t]o such extremity are the petitioners reduced, that many of them are literally without Bread to satisfy the Call of nature, or Clothing to cover them." In these dire circumstances, these Paisley artisans saw land in other parts of the Empire as the solution to their plight and sought the colonial secretary's assistance in obtaining it. Their petition, however, also demonstrated considerable knowledge of the government's assisted emigration policy:

> The petitioners understand that it is in the Contem-
> plation of His Majestys Government, [to settle] the
> uncultivated Grounds in upper Canada, and to that
> Country the views of the petitioners are particularly
> directed, in preference to the Cape of Good Hope, as
> the Climate of the former is nearly similar to that of
> these Northern parts of Britain, and where ... they
> would have the advantage of being associated with the
> same General Habits, and speaking the same language
> with themselves.[1]

Only a limited number of Scottish settlers had participated in the 1819 government-assisted emigration to the Cape Colony, yet the Paisley petitioners were aware of this initiative and sought to avoid that particular imperial destination. While they cited climate and language as key factors, the petitioners were also likely to have known that the 1819 scheme was designed to protect the eastern frontier from amaXhosa attack, and the reports of the "Caffer Wars" carried in the Glasgow papers undoubtedly encouraged them to seek land elsewhere.[2]

Given that many of the 1815 assisted emigrants and demobilized soldiers who first settled in the Ottawa Valley had come from the Glasgow region, Upper Canada would have provided further appeal. In addition, the month before Daniel Murchie forwarded his petition to the colonial secretary, Lord Archibald Hamilton, the MP for Lanarkshire, had convened the first meeting of the "Glasgow Committee on Emigration," comprised of the leading local politicians, landowners, and industrialists in the region, who had gathered together in order to lobby for the renewal of the assisted scheme. Hamilton's efforts were rewarded on May 8, 1820, when Lord Liverpool's government agreed to support the emigration to Upper Canada of a further 1,100 individuals from the Glasgow vicinity. It is very likely that the Paisley petition was drafted in response to this news.[3]

Only three of the signatories on Murchie's petition would obtain assistance to emigrate, but the document began a campaign that resulted in the formation of the Paisley Townhead Emigration Society, an organization that sent 340 settlers to the Ottawa Valley in 1821.[4] The Paisley petition, and others like it, demonstrate how Scottish Lowland artisans worked together to pressure authorities for support. It also suggests some of the attitudes toward both the homeland and the Empire. The Lowlanders, who took advantage of the renewed government assistance in 1820 and 1821, were drawn from a wide range of industrial towns and villages across the west of Scotland. In these communities, collective petitioning had first been directed toward protecting artisan's livelihoods by demanding a reformed Parliament and, as the postwar depression intensified, many petitioners also began to see the acquisition of colonial land as a means of obtaining greater economic and political independence.[5] Since their petitions often gave details about the signatories, they provide a rare insight into the individual circumstances of Scottish artisans seeking to become imperial immigrants.

The right of all subjects to petition the Crown to obtain redress was well-established in Britain by the turn of the nineteenth century. Petitions were usually sent by individuals and often fell into one of two categories, "petitions of right" that requested royal support with an argument grounded in a legal claim, and "petitions of grace" that requested royal intervention based upon the author's personal circumstances. In the medieval period, petitions were addressed directly to the king, but by the nineteenth century they were far more commonly sent to a king's minister as the preamble to Daniel Murchie's petition suggests: "Unto The Right Honourable Earl Bathurst, principal Secretary of State for the British Colonies." By opening with this formal address the Paisley petitioners were also following the well-established convention for drafting all such documents. They began by recognizing the superior social status of the recipient and ended by begging or praying that the petition be granted. These conventions were indicative of the fact that the majority of personal petitions directed to the Crown asked for clemency for crimes committed or for some form of charitable aid.[6] In other words, petitioners often sought to present themselves as "deserving" objects of charity, as is readily apparent in the Paisley petition to Lord Bathurst:

> In these forlorn and distressing Circumstances, the only opening that presents itself to their View, by which they can prevent themselves from perishing, is that of Emigration to some other Country, where the redundances of Operative trades is not so great as in Britain, and where they can more readily earn Subsistence for themselves, and families; But the means of resorting to this expedient are totally beyond their reach, unless assistance can be procured from those who have the direction of National Finance, and to implore that assistance is the object of the present supplication.[7]

While almost all petitions employed the standard rhetorical form of the charitable appeal, read closely they reveal a great deal more about the attitudes and assumptions of the authors. Daniel Murchie's petition argued that "[t]he trade which they formally earned their Subsistence, and maintained their families in comfort and decency, ha[d] declined, with a rapidity unexampled in the Commercial History of this Kingdom, and left no hope of any amelioration in their Condition, Nor even the smallest prospect that they shall ever again behold the Days of Comfort and Competence, which formerly fell to their lot."[8] The complaint that the postwar decline in trade, especially among handloom weavers like Murchie, was undermining the ability of all Lowland artisans to provide for their families was echoed in petitions sent to the Colonial Office and local elites from across the west of Scotland. These documents also reveal that many artisans believed that they could only be restored to their former "independence" by obtaining farmland in Upper Canada.[9]

The Paisley artisans' belief that little could be expected in Scotland was undoubtedly reinforced by the fact that they had been unable to force local landowners to provide them with regular poor relief. In the summer of 1819, an estimated 825 unemployed cotton operatives in the Abbey Parish had taken their case to the Court of Session but failed to gain any support from that quarter.[10] While the identities of the weavers behind the court session challenge is not known, the petition sent to Lord Bathurst provided the names and addresses of all the applicants. As a consequence, the document provides a rare view of early nineteenth-century Paisley's

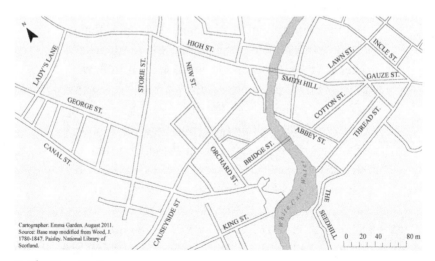

Paisley Town Centre

artisan community. The Abbey Parish encompassed the original medieval town as well as Paisley's southern suburbs along with smaller communities such as Maxwellton and Johnstone to the west and Williamsburgh and Hillington to the east. It was a vast parish that included both large industrial centres as well as numerous small rural villages. Daniel Murchie's petitioners, however, were clearly concentrated in the older town limits of Paisley. Though Murchie's neighbours on Causeyside Street made up the largest single group, they were joined by large numbers of tradesmen in the nearby Gauze, Incle, Lawn, and Thread Streets to the east, and the Canal, Storie, and High Streets to the west. While the majority of the petitioners resided in this area situated within Paisley town limits, a significant number were also located in the suburbs immediately to the south of Paisley, Lylesland, Dovesland, Carrigehill, and Calside. A few others lived in Ferguslie and Maxwellton immediately to west of the town limits. As some of the street names suggest, these locations comprised the industrial districts of Paisley where thousands of handloom weavers worked at their trade in row houses, cottages, and small shops.[11]

Five of Daniel Murchie's petitioners, however, resided in the more distant industrial community of Johnstone, and their presence on his document reflects the wider reach of Paisley's artisan community. The Johnstone petitioners also appeared on the original list for the Paisley Townhead Emigration Society, formed in the autumn of 1820. Unlike Murchie's petition, the emigration society list includes the individual's age, occupation, and place of origin. As with the vast majority of the society members, all five of the Johnstone petitioners were born in Paisley and thus had an intimate connection with the town. Nevertheless, three of the men who appear on both documents were from elsewhere.

Daniel Murchie was himself from Ayr, while Alexander Ferguson and William Robertson were from Glasgow and Govan. The society list further reveals that many other members, or their wives, had originated in other Lowland communities including, among other places, Kilsyth, Hamilton, Rutherglen, and Linlithgow. The list also indicates that all of the society members were married and most had families ranging from four to six children. While some couples were in their twenties and others in their early fifties, the majority were in their mid-to-late thirties and were engaged in a range of occupations. Four of the Johnstone petitioners were listed as miners, while bakers, wrights, gardeners, sawyers, and tailors also appear on Townhead Emigration Society list. Nevertheless, weaving, the occupation of Johnstone petitioner Nathaniel Ferguson, was far and away the most common vocation.[12]

The peripatetic nature of the weaving trade linked widely dispersed groups of artisans across Lowland Scotland, as can been seen in the early career of Alexander Wilson, the Paisley weaver-poet who later gained fame as a founder of American ornithology. Wilson was born in Paisley in 1766 and spent his early years in Seedhill, where his weaver father rented a row house. He attended Paisley Grammar School before starting work as a herd boy on the Renfrew-Ayrshire border. At the age of thirteen he returned to Paisley to be apprenticed as a weaver to his brother-in-law William Duncan, but, after completing his training, Wilson joined his family in rural Renfrewshire at Auchinbathie, where his father ran a small weaving shop and smuggled illegally produced whisky. He subsequently worked as a weaver for Matthew Barr in Lochwinnoch before returning to Paisley to work in James Clarke's two-loom shop in Cotton Street.

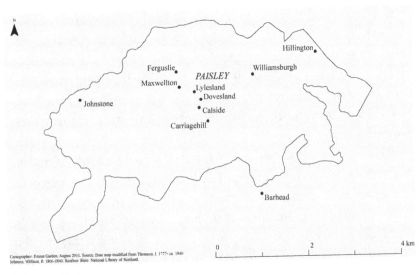

Abbey Parish Map

In each of these moves, Alexander Wilson relied on his family and former workmates to help him obtain employment and these associations extended beyond Lowland Scotland to reach across the Atlantic. When Wilson left Scotland for the United States with his nephew "Billy" Duncan in 1794, the pair first obtained work as weavers in Philadelphia from fellow Scottish artisans like James Robertson, whose brother-in-law had signed Wilson's original apprenticeship certificate.[13]

Although Wilson's career was not typical, it does reflect the highly mobile nature of the weaving trade, and his family's experience of movement between town and countryside would have been shared by many members of Paisley's artisan community, including the signatories of Daniel Murchie's petition. The cloth trade had become increasingly concentrated in Glasgow and Paisley from the middle of the eighteenth century, when Wilson's parents had first arrived in Paisley, contributing to the town's rapid expansion. After the Napoleonic Wars, the number of weavers in Paisley continued to climb, despite the depression in trade, but, like Wilson's father, many still chose to reside in the countryside, often working for the larger Glasgow and Paisley manufacturers.[14]

In addition to reflecting both the urban and rural experience of the Abbey Parish weavers, Wilson's career is also indicative of the high levels of literacy among practitioners of his first trade. Weavers took pride in their ability to educate themselves and their children and this was reflected in Wilson's parents' decision to send him to the Paisley Grammar School. The detailed knowledge of contemporary literary conventions that weavers had obtained from such schooling is demonstrated in a humorous mock petition that Wilson sent to his Paisley friends, asking for financial assistance prior to his emigration:

> The humble petition of A.W. humbly sheweth that your petitioner is, and has for some time past, grievously afflicted with a want of pecunia; the want of which has brought him to such low circumstances that no person ever experienced but himself. He therefore flatters himself that the charitable disposition which always shows

itself in you, on like occasions, will also distinguish itself
in the relief of your poor petitioner.[15]

While Alexander Wilson used the form for comic effect, whereas
Daniel Murchie had compiled his petition for a serious purpose, both
documents illustrate how well Paisley weavers understood the accepted
methods for appealing to those in authority and how they were able to
tailor these conventions to their own ends.

Alexander Wilson belonged to a group of Paisley weaver-poets who
put both their collective pride in their accomplishments and their discontent with the transformations occurring in their trade into vernacular
verse. The first stanza to his poem "The Shark; or Lang Mills Detected,"
a satirical attack aimed at local mill owner William Sharp, encapsulated
these sentiments:

> Ye weaver blades! Ye noble chiels!
> Wha fill our land wi' plenty,
> And mak our vera barest fiels
> To waive wi' ilka dainty;
> Defend yoursels, tak sicker heed,
> I warn you as a brither;
> Or Shark's resolved, wi' hellish greed,
> To gorge us a'thegither,
> At ance this day.[16]

Sharp, who was not amused, made a complaint to the sheriff sub-
stitute, and Wilson was jailed until he provided a "three hundred Merks
Scots, for his good behaviour for two years to come." Upon his release,
Wilson was also required to burn two copies of his offending poem on
the steps of Paisley Tolbooth. A subsequent encounter with authority for
allegedly calling a "Reform" meeting in Stories Street resulted in another
brief imprisonment and contributed to Wilson's decision to emigrate.[17]

The reaction to Wilson's poetry reflected deep fears of social unrest
among Paisley's elite as well as an inclination for mutual support among
the town's weavers. The democratic ideals of the French Revolution that

had circulated among literate weavers like Alexander Wilson raised the spectre of violent insurrection among wealthy industrialists like William Sharp. When the demand for Parliamentary reform, first articulated in the 1790s, remerged among the weavers after the Napoleonic Wars, those seeking to emigrate played on these fears and tried to manipulate them in order to gain assistance from both the local elite and Parliament. Wilson's poem attacking Sharp, however, also revealed a sense of solidarity among Paisley's artisan community. "I warm you as a brither," he wrote, and he did indeed rely on the generosity of his fellow weavers in order to obtain his release from prison.[18]

As Alexander Wilson's experience suggests, banding together in order to provide mutual assistance was already a well-established practice among Paisley's artisans by the time Daniel Murchie wrote to Lord Bathurst. Murchie's document made this explicit with the claim that the petitioners were "known to each other," that they were men of "Principle, & Moral Character" and, as a consequence, they could "mutually depend" upon each other. In return for obtaining assistance to emigrate and settle in Upper Canada, the petitioners promised to "enter into a Bond, Conjunctly and Severally, that the whole to be liable for each individual, or family" in order repay the government. They further promised

This idealized portrait of Alexander Wilson was based on an oil painting by James Craw that is now in the collection of the Paisley Museum and Art Galleries. From Alexander B. Grosart, The Poems and Literary Prose of Alexander Wilson *(Paisley: Alexander Gardner, 1876) Vol. I, frontispiece.*

Public domain.

to remain on their granted land and "... in case it shall so happen, that any family or individual shall fail to pay up their respective proportions, the whole of the others [would be] bound to make good the same."[19] The idea of signing a collective bond would have come easily to Paisley's artisans, since they had been participating in mutual aid societies since the late eighteenth century. These "friendly societies," organized largely by trade, provided support for sick and injured members as well as a burial fund to offset funeral costs for deceased members and provide limited aid to their families.

Entry fees and annual subscriptions were paid by each member creating a common fund, which the ill or distressed might call upon. The system, however, could only operate well when the majority of the members were in full employment, and it was clear even before the end of the Napoleonic Wars that benevolent societies were no longer be able to assist their members. According to William Taylor, a pamphleteer writing in 1814, Paisley had led the way in creating friendly societies but all were now struggling "with pecuniary embarrassment," which had "blotted some of them out of existence."[20]

The postwar depression in trade redirected mutual aid from friendly society organization toward imperial settlement, but the debt owed to the earlier artisan self-help tradition was clearly reflected in the names chosen for several of the newly formed emigration societies. The first petition from a society, sent to Lord Bathurst on July 8, 1819, was from Glasgow's Bridgeton Transatlantic Social Union, and it was quickly followed by others from the city's east end, including the Glasgow Canadian Mutual Cooperation Society and Abercromby Friendly Emigration Society. As with these early examples, the majority of petitions sent to the Colonial Office came from emigration societies located in the industrial districts of Glasgow, but large societies also formed in other important Lanarkshire weaving centres, such as Rutherglen, Hamilton, and Cambuslang, before Daniel Murchie's petition started the process that culminated in the creation of the Townhead Emigration Society in Paisley.

While a complete occupational record does not survive, it is clear that weavers dominated the emigration societies, but their membership also included representatives of most of the trades practised in the west of Scotland's industrial communities. The list for the Glasgow Canadian Society, for example, included a teacher, cooper, nailer, wright, smith, shoemaker, and ploughman, along with three labourers and a sole weaver. More typical was the membership of the Anderston and Rutherglen Emigration Society, which included a sawyer, a mason, two wrights, two calico printers, four labourers, and seven weavers. Paisley's Townhead Emigration Society list, which provides the most complete surviving record of member occupations, reveals that of the 104 heads of families listed, seventy were weavers. It further appears that Daniel Murchie was not unusual in providing leadership, since many emigration society presidents were also weavers.[21]

Since several of the signatories on Murchie's petition had a personal connection to other Lowland weaving communities, it is very likely that they were among the first to learn of the creation of Glasgow's emigration societies.[22] They may also have been aware of the unsuccessful petitions of unemployed weavers in neighbouring Lanarkshire, requesting the creation of small arable holdings from some of the lands held by the Duke of Hamilton, perhaps further encouraging them to seek to be colonists on lands in Upper Canada as a solution to their distress. While most members of emigration societies were located in urban centres like Glasgow and Paisley, where they were seeking to practise their trade, as Alexander Wilson's experience indicates, many of these artisans had recently arrived from the countryside or were among the first generation to be born in town.

One example would be the Paisley weaver-poet and later bookseller, William Anderson, who was born on Storie Street in 1793, but whose father had been a farmer in Ayrshire. Another is John Parkhill, a weaver who published several accounts detailing life in early nineteenth-century Paisley but was born in Bankfoot, a rural area just south of the town, where his father had worked as a farm servant. With their request for one hundred acres for each family, Daniel Murchie's petitioners clearly signalled their intention to return to agriculture in order to support themselves. Several other societies also argued in their petitions that a farm in Upper Canada would not only provide them with a more stable livelihood than weaving, but that it would also benefit the empire by developing the colony.[23]

As their trade expanded during the eighteenth century, weavers in the west of
Scotland often settled in market towns like Lanark, swelling the populations of once
tiny communities. When the handloom-weaving trade collapsed, towns like Lanark
were unable to offer alternative employment. From Black's Picturesque Tourist of
Scotland, *390.*

These arguments appeared to have persuaded the members of Lord
Hamilton's Glasgow Committee on Emigration and Lord Liverpool's
administration, which reluctantly authorized further government assistance to members of the emigration societies. In his published account
of the scheme, Robert Lamond stressed the role of the members of the
Glasgow Committee in obtaining official support for the societies and
the Glasgow Committee's efforts at raising funds in order to support the
scheme. Eager to promote his own role as overseer of the emigrations,
as well as the virtues of the committee members, Lamond stressed that
since many petitioners could not afford the passage money required to
participate in the scheme, efforts were made to obtain contributions
from wealthy Scots in Glasgow, Edinburgh, and London. This allowed

Lamond to portray the assisted emigration as a charitable act, and his version of events is reinforced by the deferential appeals for aid contained in petitions like Daniel Murchie's. All the same, Murchie's document also contained an implied criticism of Paisley's elite, stating that:

> ... although many have been assisted, by the more afflu-
> ent part of the Community, during the Course of last
> winter, yet that assistance being now discontinued, they
> find it impossible any longer to Subsist, as it will be
> entirely out of their power to pay their Yearly rents, due
> at the insuing term, which falls on the 27th and 28th
> of the present month; Consequently their furniture, &
> implements of Trade, will inevitably be seized by their
> landlords, and the petitioners with their families, turned
> out to Starve.[24]

As early as 1817 a public fund had been raised for the relief of Paisley's weavers. In July 1819 the town council had authorized the raising of £100 to aid the distressed, and had hired forty unemployed operatives "to improve a portion of their moss lands" at the rate of one shilling a day. Paisley's councillors rejected the weavers' demand for permanent poor rates, believing that they had already done their utmost, but Murchie's petitioners clearly saw their efforts as inadequate. In a follow-up petition sent to Lord Bathurst, they made this explicit, stating that "... although much assistance has been afforded to operatives by the more wealthy part of the community, yet the transitory nature of all assistance of this kind forbids them to expect permanent relief from contributions from the more opulent classes."[25]

Elsewhere the challenge to those in authority was more direct. In June 1819 an association of weavers met in Carlisle, just across the Scottish border, and appealed for assistance to settle in the colonies, but reinforced their request with a strike demanding a rise in wages before they would return to their looms. The Carlisle weavers appear to have inspired their counterparts in Glasgow to form their own emigration societies, but the first public suggestion to seek assistance to emigrate was made at a "reform" meeting on Glasgow Green, where unemployed weavers had been employed as part of the city's poor-relief measures. Although organizers of that meeting rejected emigration as a solution and argued instead the necessity of Parliamentary reform before weavers' circumstances could improve, the districts where the emigration societies were formed had a history of both labour unrest and radical reform politics.[26]

In Paisley, weavers had been intimately involved in organizing a mass meeting on September 11, 1819, to protest the "Peterloo Massacre," when local yeomanry had notoriously charged into a Manchester reform gathering, killing several unarmed participants. The Paisley meeting was held outside of town but the event ended with rioting all along the High Street. More seriously, several Paisley weavers were also implicated in an abortive rising in April 1820 that came to be known as the "Radical War." In his account, John Parkhill, who had been named commissary general by the Paisley Radical Committee, revealed that the "Smiddy," a weaver's shop on Maxwellton Street, had served as the reformers' regular meeting place and the groups' headquarters during the rising. In addition, five of the seven men charged with high treason in the arrest warrants issued in Paisley following the failed revolt were also weavers, but several of those charged had fled the country before the trials began, as had Parkhill, who fled to Montreal.[27]

In this context, even the relatively mild criticism contained in petitions from weavers like Daniel Murchie could cause alarm among the elite in the west of Scotland. The local estate owners and industrialists, who formed the Glasgow Committee on Emigration, were very concerned that the emigration societies might be used for more revolutionary purposes. By coordinating their activities and lobbying on their behalf, the Glasgow Committee worked to ensure that artisans with more radical goals did not dominate the groups. Kirkman Finlay, the MP and leading Glasgow cotton manufacturer who took over the presidency of the Glasgow Committee in 1821, was particularly worried about the prospect of further unrest, and believed that the government-supported emigrations from the city in the summer of 1820 had done a great deal to undermine support for the revolutionaries.[28] The MP for

Renfrewshire, John Maxwell, argued for the extension of government assistance to Paisley, and reinforced his appeal by highlighting the fact that among the town's unemployed weavers were numerous veterans of the recent war. On June 1, 1820, he reported to Parliament that failure to act would increase discontent among this potentially dangerous group, stating that

> who had fought and exposed their lives by sea and land for the institutions of the country naturally complained, that they could now obtain no assistance from those institutions. They saw, indeed, that they had a House of Commons, but they must lament that it felt no interest for the distressed classes of society.[29]

Furthermore, veterans were trained in the use of arms, and as a consequence they were identified by both radicals and members of the elite as potential insurgents. The possible threat posed by former soldiers undoubtedly contributed to Maxwell's success in having the government-assisted emigration continued for a second season. It was, however, a petition sent to him from Paisley's weavers that had encouraged the MP to raise the issue at all. In this regard, Maxwell was not unusual.[30]

Among the 340 members of the Paisley Townhead Emigration Society, who left Greenock on April 29, 1821, on board the *Earl of Buckingham* for Quebec City, were three of Daniel Murchie's petitioners: Thomas Ferguson, John Hart, and Thomas Briget, accompanied by their wives Mary, Hodgert, and Janet, and their fifteen children. When the group finally arrived at the Lanark depot in July, they were welcomed by Captain William Marshall, a fellow Scot and officer of the Canadian Fencibles who had been given the responsibility of placing the colonists on their lots. Marshall was one of the retired officers who had settled in Perth, but, in August of 1820, he relocated to Lanark and established a government storehouse on the banks of the newly renamed Clyde River. He was joined by fellow officer Captain Alexander Ferguson, who erected a gristmill in anticipation of the arrival of the first settlers from Glasgow.

Marshall's appointment reflected the ongoing leadership role played by former officers in Ottawa Valley settlement. Like their counterparts in Perth, both Marshall and Ferguson would serve in the Second Lanark County Militia when it was formed in 1822. Marshall would play a vital role as the intermediary between the settlers and the colonial government. As early as 1825 he was forwarding a petition requesting additional land from a fellow soldier David Campbell, who had served as a sergeant with the 97th Regiment but had arrived with the one of the emigration societies. Before returning to Scotland in 1830, William Marshall would also become a county magistrate and a trustee of the district grammar school board, but initially he was preoccupied with locating over 2,500 society members in the Lanark, Dalhousie, Ramsay, and North Sherbrooke townships.[31]

The Ferguson, Hart, and Bridget families were located in Dalhousie and Ramsay, but Marshall distributed Townhead Emigration Society members across all four townships. All the same, Marshall did tend to settle individuals belonging to the same society together. This is particularly evident with the Paisley emigrants who settled in North Sherbrooke. In that township, Marshall concentrated the settlers who had arrived on the *Earl of Buckingham*, which included members from the Barrowfield and Anderson, Lanark, Parkhead, and Paisley Townhead societies, between lots 8 to 15 along the first and third concessions. Members of the Camlachie and the Rutherglen Union societies, who had sailed together on the *Commerce*, were located farther south between the third and fifth concessions on lots 2 to 9. Within these emigrant-vessel groupings, members of the same society were placed adjacent to each other. As superintendent of the settlers, Marshall undoubtedly played a significant role in ensuring that individual families were located beside those they already knew before leaving Scotland, but the society members themselves may also have influenced this pattern of settlement.[32]

Mary Stoaks (née Wilson), who arrived in North Sherbrooke with her four children and weaver husband Arthur, was a member of the Townhead Emigration Society whose connections went beyond Paisley. Mary was originally from Kilmarnock, as were several others in the society who settled in North Sherbrooke, and her correspondence with siblings who remained in Scotland reveals that she also knew other

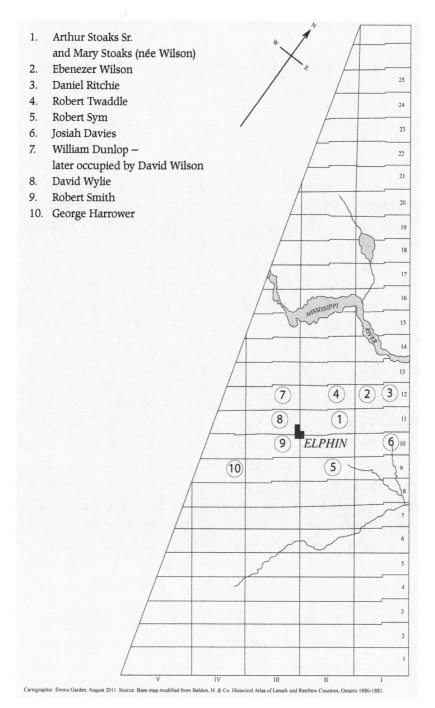

1. Arthur Stoaks Sr.
    and Mary Stoaks (née Wilson)
2. Ebenezer Wilson
3. Daniel Ritchie
4. Robert Twaddle
5. Robert Sym
6. Josiah Davies
7. William Dunlop –
    later occupied by David Wilson
8. David Wylie
9. Robert Smith
10. George Harrower

Cartographer: Emma Garden, August 2011. Source: Base map modified from Beldon, H. & Co. Historical Atlas of Lanark and Renfrew Counties, Ontario 1880-1881.

North Sherbrooke Township

settlers in the township who were from as far afield as Pitlochry, in Perthshire, or Iverary, in Argylshire. Her letters also reveal that before the Stoaks left Scotland, the family were already acquainted with others in the township belonging to the Lanark and the Rutherglen Union Emigration Societies, as well as members of the Hamilton Emigration Society who settled in adjacent lots in nearby Dalhousie Township. It also appears that most of the Townhead Society members who settled in North Sherbrooke were known to the family. Among these were the Paisley weaver Daniel Ritchie, who had played a vital role in organizing the assisted emigration as the president of the Townhead Society, as well as Mary's brother, Ebenezer Wilson, who would emerge as a leader in the new settlement.[33]

Apparently Ebenezer Wilson was "a well educated man — a reader and a thinker" who received newspapers from Montreal and the United States and served as the North Sherbrooke distributor of the Perth paper, the *Bathurst Courier*, which began publishing in 1834. According to Mr. Cromwell, a man who worked for him in the 1830s, Wilson was generous with his own copies and circulated them among his neighbours — as had been the practice among the weavers in Paisley. It appears that early on Wilson developed a reputation for having "some knowledge of medicine" and, according to Cromwell, settlers from "far and near called on him at all hours of the day and night for anything from drawing a tooth to the most serious illness." Wilson was also among the first in the Bathurst District to be awarded a liquor licence, which may have been part of his "medical" consulting, but it is also possible that he briefly ran an inn in his household. His stature in the fledgling community was also reflected in his service as a jury foreman in the Quarter Session trials held in Perth in 1827, and by the fact that he was among the first directors of County of Lanark Agricultural Society when it was formed in 1836.[34]

The correspondence of Mary Stoaks and her brother with family left behind in Paisley also reveals that, in addition to participating in the assisted emigration to Upper Canada, members of the Wilson family had previously settled in Nova Scotia. Ebenezer had come to North Sherbrooke with his second wife, Jean, and their four children, but his son David from his first marriage did not join them until 1823, after stopping first to visit his uncle in Tatamagouche. One account has suggested that Ebenezer had attempted a trading "venture" in Nova Scotia before emigrating with the Townhead Society. While this cannot be established with certainty, his letters home indicate that Wilson family members continued to travel to Nova Scotia to visit his brother well into 1830s. Nevertheless, Ebenezer Wilson could not persuade other family members to join him in North Sherbrooke, although his son David remained as a settler in the township. A decade after the Paisley Townhead Emigration Society had taken place both the Wilson and Stoaks families had established themselves on their land, but found that they did not have the means to finance further emigrations from Scotland.[35]

Early on there were several reports of struggling colonists and many turned once again to petitioning in an effort to obtain some assistance. In 1828 when John MacIntyre, an emigration-society settler in Dalhousie Township, successfully petitioned for tools from the government stores with the claim that he was too poor to buy them, it encouraged at least thirty other Lanark-area emigrants to do the same.[36] Among them was Robert Craig, a former weaver and member of the Townhead Society, who had also settled in North Sherbrooke. By 1831 Craig had abandoned his lot in the township and was living with his wife and two young children in Lanark village, where he joined eleven other society members in petitioning the lieutenant governor requesting the cancellation of the £10 debt each settler owed the imperial government under the terms of the assisted-emigration scheme.

In addition to two other members of the Townhead Society, the signatories of the petition included members from the Bridgeton Transatlantic Society, the Abercrombie Street Friendly Emigration Society, and the Lesmahagow Emigration Society. The petition provided a detailed economic argument for the settlers' difficulties, including the high price of provisions and inadequate markets for agricultural produce, and stated their grants were on "the worst tract of land on which any extensive settlement was ever attempted in Upper Canada."[37]

A subsequent survey of Sherbrooke, while finding that the Wilson and Stoaks families possessed better-quality land, agreed that Robert Craig's

lot, like most of the township, was "good for nothing." As a result of similar survey reports and further coordinated petitioning and lobbying by
the emigrants, the British Treasury finally agreed to cancel all outstanding
debt owed by the society members in 1836.[38] While the successful petitioning campaign launched by settlers like Robert Craig indicates that the
weavers' collective approach to self-help evident in Paisley had crossed

*While little remains of Ebenezer Wilson's farm in North Sherbrooke, the stone pile in
the centre of this surviving field is an indication of the difficult labour that was needed
to cultivate the township's land.*

Photo by M. Vance.

the Atlantic with settlers, the 1831 petition also revealed that the emigrant artisans, as with their more radical brethren in Scotland, remained convinced of the need for obtaining greater political rights in order to protect their livelihoods.

A proposal, which they attributed to William Marshall, for transforming the assisted emigrants' outstanding debt into an annual rent was especially troubling, no doubt because it recalled the evictions for nonpayment that many had experienced in Scotland. While insisting on their "loyal attachment to the institutions of the country that gave them birth," the petitioners complained that their debt to the imperial government had denied them title to their land and thus to political rights in the colony since "they have been and still are accounted as Aliens ... in their father's house." Furthermore, the petitioners argued that "whilst they are obliged to perform all the duties of freeholders they cannot make a requisition for a Road, to the Quarter Sessions, and whilst they pay for a member of Assembly, they must be passive in his election." By forgiving their debt, the imperial government ensured that all such barriers to emigration society members' full participation in the political life of the colony were removed. By 1840 Ebenezer Wilson was holding township meetings in North Sherbrooke, in order to obtain support for his "Reform" candidacy in that years' Legislative Assembly elections.[39]

Paisley's weaving community had been intensely involved in contemporary politics, and Ebenezer Wilson would undoubtedly have been well aware of the petitions that had been sent from the town's artisans, promoting various legislative initiatives. Among these were documents demanding an end to the African slave trade and the adoption of a minimum wage for weavers, as well as the reform of Parliament itself. In the 1830s, artisans in Paisley sent further petitions to Parliament in support of the Reform Bill and the Peoples' Charter. While the former, which extended the right to vote to Britain's middle class, was passed in 1832, the Chartist's demand for universal suffrage, first promoted by Paisley's supporters of the French Revolution, was not fully realized until after the First World War.[40]

Given this high degree of political mobilization, both prior to the departure of the society members and following their emigration, it is not

surprising that Ebenezer Wilson and his fellow Townhead Society emigrants would emulate this practice in the colonies. In the imperial capital,
however, the assisted schemes themselves became the focus of a political
debate that resulted in a parliamentary committee being struck in 1826 to
examine the entire question of government-supported emigration.

The Select Committee on Emigration from the United Kingdom
reviewed the costs and accomplishments of the assisted-emigration
schemes and concluded that the expenditure was not warranted, especially
since the land was now firmly under imperial control. The committee
heard evidence suggesting that emigrants continued to proceed to Upper
Canada without government support and that the schemes had done little
to alleviate distress in the west of Scotland. It was suggested by several committee members that migrants from Ireland had quickly taken the place
of the departing weavers, and, as a consequence, wages continued to be
depressed. While its conclusions were deeply disappointing to many of
Paisley's weavers, the parliamentary committee had met largely in response
to the overwhelming numbers of petitions that the Colonial Office had
received calling for further assistance to emigrate.

In Renfrewshire nearly eight hundred heads of families from thirteen
emigration societies had sent petitions asking for a renewal of the scheme.
John Tait and John Wilson, two weavers representing the five groups
from Paisley, went to London to speak on behalf of all the members. In
his testimony, John Tait emphasized the positive accounts received from
friends already in the Ottawa Valley, but when pressed about the suitability of weavers to the hard work of pioneering, Tait pointed out that
many society members "have been accustomed to out-door labour" and
that in the summer of 1826 many of the towns' unemployed weavers had
been "breaking stones," which was "a species of labour harder than that
of felling trees." He further reinforced the point made in the society petitions that the weavers were prevented from proceeding to Upper Canada
on their own because of the continuing decline in their trade. According
to Tait, a loom that "would have cost 5 *l*. about three or four years ago ...
cannot get above 10 *s*.," and "not one among fifty" of the society members owned their household furniture. As a consequence, the weavers
had nothing to sell to pay for their passage.[41]

As early as the autumn of 1821, Daniel Murchie had made a similar argument in one more petition to Lord Bathurst. He wrote to the colonial secretary, on behalf of ninety heads of families enrolled in the Paisley Townhead Society who had been unable to obtain passage money in time to participate in the scheme. In that petition, Murchie stated that the weavers' hopes of a revival in their trade had been "blasted" and that they were more anxious than ever to join those who had already departed. He reiterated the claim that, unless they emigrated, the weavers would become a burden on the "wealthy part of the community," but he also solicited the aid of William Mure, the vice-lieutenant of Renfrewshire and a Glasgow Emigration Committee member, who wrote his own letter to Bathurst supporting the petitioners.[42]

While Murchie's strategy was unsuccessful in obtaining further government assistance, other groups in Paisley would continue to organize themselves into emigration societies and solicit support from the local elite throughout the remainder of the nineteenth century. Upper Canada remained a favoured destination, although Paisley societies were also formed in order to facilitate emigration to other parts of the Empire, including New Zealand in 1840 and British Columbia in 1858.[43] As with the friendly societies, members of these later groups were required to contribute weekly deposits in order to build a communal fund to pay for members' passages. Impoverished weavers like Daniel Murchie would have been unable to participate in these later societies, but, according to William Mure, by the autumn of 1821 Murchie, being "past middle age," had given up on the idea of emigrating and was arguing instead on behalf of younger members of his group. All the same, although he chose not to leave Paisley in the end, Murchie's original petition to Lord Bathurst had begun the process of establishing the artisan led "Townhead" Society that had successfully lobbied for assisted emigration to Upper Canada for at least some of its members, and firmly established imperial land as a desirable commodity among the town's artisans.

Chapter Five

IMMIGRANT POLITICS AND RELIGION

O pening a copy of the October 23, 1829, edition of the *Bathurst Independent Examiner* published in Perth, immigrant readers found four large pages of densely packed type, crammed with information. Under a masthead that incorporated the Royal Coat of Arms, and thus proclaimed loyalty to the British Empire, the locally produced newspaper provided the latest details concerning the conflict between Russia and the Ottoman Turks, and an account of the current state of the wool trade in Britain, as well as a notice of the famous actor Edmund Kean's latest performance in Manchester. A mention of a steamboat explosion in Antwerp harbour shared space with a traveller's account of voyaging on the Red Sea and news that the city of Baltimore was planning to erect a "colossal" statute to George Washington.

While the tastes of Scottish readers were appealed to with an excerpt from Walter Scott's *Tales of a Grandfather*, the editor's own background was echoed by a poem reprinted from the *Irish Shield*. John Stewart had come to Perth in 1823 to teach in the newly opened Bathurst District Grammar School, and had branched out into newspaper publishing in 1828 when he brought the first printing press to the community. By 1829 he claimed to have over five hundred subscribers, and had

As the signature indicates, this copy of the Independent Examiner *once belonged to Dr. John A. Gemmill, the Lanark depot physician and Secessionist Presbyterian clergyman.*

Courtesy of Library and Archives Canada, Amicus 7678033.

established a network of agents to distribute the paper throughout the surrounding townships.[1]

Stewart's newspaper was not at all unusual in being dominated by stories gleaned from foreign papers and extracts of published literary work as well as unpublished works of local authors. Like other Upper Canadian papers, the *Independent Examiner* also specifically catered to its local audience with notices of land sales, advertisements from local merchants, and personal notices. After the Napoleonic Wars, however, Upper Canadian editors like John Stewart began to publish a great deal more political news — giving accounts of proceedings of both the imperial and provincial parliaments. Indeed, it has been suggested that the dramatic increase in the number of newspapers after the war in both Upper Canada and the British Isles resulted in the extension of political debate from the exclusive preserve of those sitting in Parliament to the wider reading public.[2] Although addressed to Upper Canada's Provincial Parliament, it was to this wider public that the petition from the "Inhabitants of the District of Bathurst," published on the third page of the *Independent Examiner*, appears to have been directed, especially since a follow-up article in the October 30th edition makes it clear that signatures were still being gathered for the document.

At first glance, the petition appears to be a straightforward request for government support toward the district's road-building expenses and the reduction of the court costs involved in the recovery of outstanding debts. The tone of the document, however, implied criticism of the legislature's performance, stating that the petitioners "have borne the fatigue, danger, and inconvenience of such a state of communication with their neighbours in the hope that the Legislature would grant them relief, by the appropriation of a sum of money, for the improvement of the original roads in this section of the Province ... It was therefore, with extreme mortification and surprise that they learned of the failure of the measure of the last session." When discussing the law regarding debtors, the petitioners further lamented that "by it His Majesty's subjects are often deprived of their liberty without sufficient cause, and costs are accumulated to gratify, in many instances, malicious dispositions" and requested that the legislature make "amendments in this Law."[3]

While these claims imply that the authors of the document were sympathetic to those in the colony who were calling for legislative reform, the composition of the committee charged with obtaining signatures for the petition suggests a complex set of motivations. Ebenezer Wilson, undoubtedly a supporter of the Upper Canadian reform movement, was named, but the list was headed by William Morris, the Paisley-born local MPP, who was unabashedly conservative in his politics representing, as he did, the merchant interests in the community. Morris had served with distinction in the 1st Leeds Militia during the War of 1812, and when he arrived in Perth in 1816 he joined the clique of Scottish former officers who dominated the commercial life of the town.[4] Although he had little time for radical reformers, Morris nevertheless had his own longstanding disagreement with the colonial administration over the lack of support for the Church of Scotland in the colony. Throughout his political career, Morris advocated tirelessly for the granting of equal status between the Anglican and Presbyterian churches. Other signatories to the petition were also known for religious convictions that differed from those of the officially supported Church of England.

John Toschach (Toshack), a member of the Rutherglen Union Society settled in Ramsay Township, was a lay preacher who had held the earliest services in the community, but as a Congregationalist belonged to neither the Anglican or Presbyterian church.[5] What early settler newspapers, like the *Independent Examiner*, reveal is that the political antagonisms of the imperial homeland were transferred to the Ottawa Valley, and church records indicate that denominational splits and sectarian animosities also accompanied the immigrant Scots to the settler community. Nevertheless, the petition published in the October 23rd edition illustrates how these divisions could occasionally be overcome in order to promote the practical work of colonization.

At least seven of the sixteen men charged with collecting signatures for the petition from the "Inhabitants of the District of Bathurst" were Scottish immigrants, and this reflected the disproportionate influence of immigrant Scots in early history of political petitioning in the colony.[6] Indeed, Robert Gourlay, an "improving" farmer from Fife, who came to Upper Canada to claim his wife's inheritance in 1817, was among the first to use the tactic initially employed by British reformers of public petitioning to affect change. Influenced by the reformers' criticism of the homeland government, Gourlay had come to believe that the overriding authority exercised by the appointed Legislative Council, reinforced by an excessive use of patronage in the awarding of land grants and office appointments, was damaging the economy of the colony.

For Gourlay, the solution lay in restructuring the colonial constitution in order to give the elected House of Assembly greater control, and he sought to persuade the imperial government of the popularity of such reform by initiating a colony-wide petitioning campaign. Emulating similar efforts in the homeland, Gourlay organized public township and district meetings to obtain signatures for his petition to the Crown and then published the proceedings and announcements of future meetings in pamphlets and local newspapers.

Although he was unsuccessful and forced to leave the colony, Gourlay's model for mobilizing public support was followed by others — especially William Lyon Mackenzie, the former Dundee tradesman and eventual leader of the 1837 Rebellion in Upper Canada. In 1827, Mackenzie joined with others in organizing and publicizing petitions protesting, among other colonial policies, the setting aside of "Clergy Reserves" for the support of the Anglican church, and followed this with a successful campaign to represent York in the 1828 election. His platform recalled Gourlay's call for reform, and when he was unable to achieve change through the Provincial Parliament, Mackenzie emulated Gourlay, again, through a colony-wide petitioning campaign in 1831. Starting with an announcement in his paper, the *Colonial Advocate*, Mackenzie called for public meetings to petition the king to address, among other matters, the executive council's exercise of patronage as well as the colony's high legal costs, which it was claimed limited access to justice, and to consider the abolition of all land reserves except for those required for education, roads, and bridges.[7]

By identifying court costs and road construction as pressing issues, the Bathurst petitioners anticipated Mackenzie's subsequent list of grievances, but they also emulated the earlier petitioning efforts by first holding a public meeting to draw up their petition and then having the local newspaper report on their activities. Indeed, there was considerable overlap between the names on the Bathurst petition committee and John Stewart's list of local agents who distributed the *Independent Examiner*. Three men, Morris, Bell, and Gemmill, were merchants, and at least two

The caricaturist John Kay's representation of a melee during the 1790 general election between gentleman supporters of the government and reform-minded colliers (dressed in long trousers). The battle took place in an inn run by Johanna Baxter in Kinghorn, Fife. From John Kay, A Series of Original Portraits, *Vol. III (Edinburgh: H. Paton, Carver and Gilder, 1838), 400.*

Courtesy of Mount Saint Vincent University Library.

others, Craig and Nowlan, were innkeepers, which made them ideal candidates for both purposes because their businesses were regularly frequented by local settlers. Publishers were particularly keen to ensure that copies of their papers were available in local taverns and inns, since these were places where news was often debated. Some contemporaries went as far as to suggest that the combination of radical reform papers, like Mackenzie's *Colonial Advocate*, with strong drink had turned many taverns into "dens of sedition" prior to the 1837 Rebellion.

Despite such claims, recent research has shown that groups with varying political orientations all used the public meeting space that early taverns provided, and there does not appear to have been any evidence of support for armed rebellion in the Upper Ottawa Valley. All the same, during the 1840s and the 1850s several meetings of the Reform Association were held in Ramsay Township at the Rosebank Inn, run by Alexander Snedden, who had left Cambuslang for Beckwith Township in 1819. Malcolm Cameron, whose mother, Euphemia, had hosted the 1829 petitioners at her inn, would go on to become a leading member of the Upper Canadian reform movement.[8]

Although born in Canada, Malcolm Cameron remained connected to his parents' homeland, and, during a visit to Scotland in 1833, married his cousin Christina McGregor. As a boy, he had met many of the Lowland weavers who stopped at his father Angus's tavern on the road to Lanark, and he had his own labouring experience as a stable boy in Montreal before taking a clerk's position in a Perth brewery and distillery. By 1829 he had embarked on a career in business that began with a general store in Perth and would branch out into land speculation, first in the Perth region and then in Sarnia, and culminate in railway development. Nevertheless, he remained popular with the Scottish artisan colonists in Lanark County and was able to translate this support into four election victories in 1836, 1841, 1844, and 1845.

In his first campaign, Cameron relied on his local reputation, and, in a statement to the electors published in the *Bathurst Courier*, refused to make any pledges other than to act in "the best interests of the country."[9] The extent of Cameron's local reforming reputation can be seen with the history of the *Courier* itself. Conceived as successor to the *Independent*

Examiner, the paper was founded in 1834 by Malcolm and his brother John, who served as its editor, but they were forced to sell a year later when it became clear that the majority of Perth's merchant community refused to advertise. Despite, or perhaps because of, the opposition from the town's elite, Cameron easily won the Bathurst District for the reform movement two years later.[10]

Among those who refused to advertise in the Cameron-run *Bathurst Courier* was William Morris, who had himself represented the Bathurst District until he was appointed to the Legislative Council in 1836. While Cameron had appealed to a rising desire for change among the Lowland settlers who had become recently enfranchised with the cancellation of the debt they owed to the imperial government, Morris's support had come from the former officers and merchants of the community who had been among the first to hold the right to vote. Prior to appending his name to the 1829 Bathurst District petition published in the *Independent Examiner*, Morris had supported a public petition welcoming the Duke of Richmond to the district, as well as a petition to the governor requesting that an annual fair be established in Perth. These acts reflected his support of the imperial establishment as well as the economic interests of the merchant community. This type of advocacy would continue with the championing of the Tay Navigation Company, which sought to connect Perth to the Rideau Canal system. Morris undoubtedly supported the anti-reform petitions that circulated in response to the activities of William Lyon Mackenzie. As a consequence, Morris came to be identified with the privileged elite of the colony and would become the target of attacks from Cameron, one of which resulted in a prosecution for libel.[11]

It is tempting to view the two politicians as emblematic of the changes occurring within the settler community by the 1830s. The older military elite, represented by Morris, were beginning to lose their dominant position in the community, and the artisan colonists, represented by Cameron, were asserting their political rights as they gained free title to their land grants. Yet despite their public differences, both men shared an interest in land speculation and the commercial development of the colony, if only to increase their own personal wealth. More importantly, both men were opposed to the nature of government support for religion in the province. Like earlier reformers, Cameron was a "voluntarist" and sought to abolish the Clergy Reserves. Morris was unwilling to go that far, but was determined to get equal recognition for the Presbyterian Church in Upper Canada. Like the Anglican Church in England, the Presbyterian Church was the "established" church in Scotland, a reality that had been recognized in the Act of Union in 1707. According to Morris, if the imperial homeland could accommodate two established churches, the same should hold true for the colonies.[12] While their solutions differed, both men, and a great many of their constituents, believed that the existing religious establishment was unacceptable.

The Ottawa Valley Scottish community was divided along religious lines from the start, with a few Scottish settlers, particularly Glengarry Fencible soldiers, sharing the Roman Catholicism of the demobilized deWatteville, de Meuron, and Irish regiments. Some Scots also adhered to Anglicanism, but the vast majority were Presbyterians, although not all

While the kilted boy standing in a canoe clearly replaces the indigenous paddler with a Scot, the image on this 1872 election poster may also have been an allusion to Malcolm Cameron's first occupation, ferrying travellers across the Mississippi River from his parents' inn.

Courtesy of Library and Archives Canada, C-120987.

were affiliated with the Church of Scotland. The community's first minister, Reverend William Bell, was himself a Secessionist and ordained by the Associate Synod in Edinburgh.[13] He had followed the first group of assisted settlers to the colony in 1817, under an arrangement with Lord Bathurst, who agreed to provide him with a land grant and £100 annual salary. Although Bell worked tirelessly, travelling and preaching in all the townships settled by the Scots, and, by 1819, had erected the First Presbyterian church in Perth, he was not the choice of either the 1815 emigrants along the Scotch Line or the Scottish officers who dominated the town. As a consequence, he found himself embroiled in controversy early on.

John Halliday, who had been selected by the emigrants to serve as their schoolteacher, had several disagreements with Bell, culminating in 1827 with a public attack on the minister's choice of hymns for the Sunday school, which, according to Halliday, had no basis in scripture. Halliday, who had originated from Moffat in Annandale, was deeply influenced by the Cameronian idea that only hymns based upon the Psalms were legitimate. He suggested that those used by Bell included "Arminian doctrines."[14] The schoolteacher's challenge was a reflection of the divisions within Scottish Presbyterianism that extended to dissenting groups, and demonstrates that these disagreements clearly travelled with the emigrants to Upper Canada. For some, like Halliday, conflicts arose out of theological differences, but others were more concerned about the exercise of church discipline.

Reverend Bell appears to have had an intense dislike of the aristocratic lifestyle. Early on he attacked the "decadent" past-times of Perth's retired officers — coming into open conflict with Roderick Matheson and Alexander McMillan over their fathering of illegitimate children.[15] His strict Sabbatarianism and public denunciations of the desecration of the Lord's Day increased the dissatisfaction with Bell among Perth's elite, who successfully petitioned the General Assembly in Edinburgh to send out a Church of Scotland minister. When Reverend Thomas Clarke Wilson, who was ordained in Lanark before departing Scotland, founded Perth's St. Andrews Church in 1830, several former officers, including Roderick Matheson, Alexander McMillan, and

William Morris, joined the new congregation, as did the disgruntled John Halliday.[16]

Differences with ministers also extended to neighbouring Beckwith Township, where Reverend Bell had been instrumental in obtaining the services of Reverend Dr. George Buchanan. Apparently many settlers had not known that Buchanan, like Bell, was a Secessionist, and, by 1831, they were petitioning for their own Church of Scotland minister. When Reverend John Smith arrived in 1833 to preach in the newly built St. Andrews Church, he found a deeply split congregation. The rifts only began to heal when Reverend Buchanan died in 1835.[17]

Reverend Smith had been sent to Upper Canada by the Glasgow Colonial Society, which had been established in 1825 to provide Church of Scotland clergymen for Britain's North American colonies. The society's president was Kirkman Finlay, who had served in the same capacity for the Glasgow Committee on Emigration, but the group was largely run by the Paisley minister Reverend Robert Burns. Several members of the Glasgow committee had already heard from the society settlers asking for assistance, and, as early as 1823, the Duke of Hamilton had raised funds to erect a church at Lanark depot — receiving glowing thanks in return from settler James Hall.[18]

When the assisted emigrants learned about the formation of the Glasgow Colonial Society from Scottish newspapers sent to the colony, a Presbyterian committee was formed in the village and a letter was sent to Reverend Burns requesting that a minister be sent to them. According to Captain William Leech, who headed the committee, religious services were being performed in Lanark by Reverend Dr. John Gemmill, another Secessionist, who had served over thirty years as a minister in Ayrshire before emigrating with the Glasgow Trongate Society. However, the "old man" could only provide a sermon once a month and settlers elsewhere in the township were not being attended to at all. William Morris also wrote to Burns on behalf of the emigration-society settlers in Lanark and Dalhousie. As a consequence, William McAlister, a Church of Scotland minister from Skye, arrived to serve both townships in 1830. According to Morris, the arrival of the minister was particularly welcome since a "Cameronian body" in New

York had sent a missionary to Upper Canada "who has lately visited Lanark, Ramsay & some other townships."[19]

Given Morris' disagreements with the Secessionist minister William Bell, it is not surprising that he would be concerned about the Cameronians, who were particularly hostile to the notion of an established Presbyterian church, but his correspondence with Burns also highlighted the threat posed by missionary work of other non-conformists denominations — especially the Methodists. Captain Leech echoed this concern, writing to Burns in 1828:

> If we do not get a Presbyterian Clergyman among us soon[,] and one too of Piety and ability[,] there will not in all likelihood be many Presbyterians among us in a few years as the Methodists have two very zealous Missionaries itinerating in this and the neighbouring townships. The People not having an opportunity of hearing a Preacher of their own persuasion are likely to fall in with them.[20]

Reverend John Fairbairn, who served as the first minister of the St. Andrews "Auld Kirk" Church in Ramsay Township, believed that Church of Scotland missionaries should be sent to counter the influence of the Methodists who had "penetrated into the most dreary solitudes in search of perishing sinners." According to Fairbairn, the Methodists were setting an example to be emulated but many of their preachers were "too controversial, & too fond of politics for their high office."[21]

The evangelical fervour found among the Methodists was distrusted by the social and clerical establishment in both Scotland and Upper Canada, but what Morris, Leech, and Fairbairn failed to communicate to Reverend Burns was that a number of the assisted emigrants already belonged to dissenting Protestant groups. A small group of Congregationalists and Baptists from Breadalbane had participated in the 1815 scheme, and a number of the emigration society members also belonged to these denominations. These groups did not attract large numbers of followers in Scotland, but their greatest appeal was among artisans and weavers, and this was reflected in the Scottish settler community. John Toshack, the lay Congregationalist preacher who settled in Ramsay, was a millwright, while Duncan McNabb, who hosted a small Baptist congregation in his Beckwith home, was a weaver. In North Sherbrooke, a Baptist community was established by artisan members of the Barrowfield and Anderston, Rutherglen Union, and Paisley Townhead emigration societies that included the head of the later group, Daniel Ritchie.[22]

Reverend Bell believed that Ebenezer Wilson was also a member of the group, and, while there is no direct evidence that this was the case, there is no doubt that members of his family were important members of the congregation since the Baptist church and burying ground were located on the lot belonging to his sister, Mary Wilson, and her weaver husband, Arthur Stoaks. Josiah Davies, a stonemason from Paisley, was another key member of the church and one of the first in the community to move to Perth, where he worked on Reverend Wilson's St. Andrews Church. In 1842 his daughter Mary became one of the original members of Perth's First Baptist Church, despite the fact that she had been baptized and received into the First Presbyterian Church by Reverend Bell. In the 1830s, Robert Sym, who had emigrated with the Rutherglen Union Society, would become a leading figure in the community established by North Sherbrooke Baptists in Sarnia Township on land purchased by his friend and fellow political reformer, Malcolm Cameron.[23]

The unsettling influence of these early Baptists was commented upon by Reverend Dr. Gemmill, in Lanark, and Reverend Bell, in Perth, who both highlighted the controversy provoked by the denomination's prohibition of infant baptism. Reverend Fairbairn had James Wilkie, the son of a Cambuslang Emigration Society member, struck off the list of Auld Kirk members for "being immersed by a Baptist preacher."[24]

Mary Davies was the focus of considerable comment when she married her employer, Captain Alexander McMillan. The concern, however, was not over her Baptist background, but the fact that as a domestic servant she had married outside of her social rank. The subsequent shunning from his fellow officers provoked McMillan to fight a duel with Dr. Alexander Thom — for which he later had to seek public absolution from the St. Andrews' kirk session. According to

William Bell, shortly after the marriage had taken place there had also been an attempt to "get up a chivari," but that the organizers had been unable to get enough participants to go to his house because it was rumoured that McMillan had threatened to shoot "the first that came." The attempt may have been a further popular reflection of the perceived mismatch between master and servant, or a commentary on the former officer's previous sexual relationships with his female servants, but Baptists in Perth did not suffer as a consequence, and both Mary's father and her brother appear to have obtained building contracts as a result of the marriage.[25]

Social exclusion, however, also appears to have occurred in the townships. According to oral tradition, the women of North Sherbrooke would not have anything to do with Deborah "Donohow," the wife of the Glasgow weaver Robert Love, who had emigrated with the Camlachie Society. During the Napoleonic Wars, Robert Love had served as a private soldier with the 42nd Regiment of Foot and the 5th Garrison Battalion in Ireland, where he met and married his wife. Deborah Donohow was not the only Irish woman in the community, but her Catholicism marked her out.[26] At first glance, anti-Catholic attitudes also appear to have given rise to clashes between Scottish emigration society members and Irish Catholic settlers in the spring of 1824. In April of that year, the fourth regiment of the local militia was mustered at Morphy Falls in Beckwith, and rioting broke out between two of the companies at Alexander Morris' tavern after the drilling.

The dispute may have been encouraged by Captain Glendinning, one of the company officers, but appears to have originated with the resentment that the emigration society members held toward recently arrived Irish Catholic government-assisted settlers from Cork. It was believed that their leader, Peter Robinson, had arranged for the Irishmen to receive better land and more generous provisions than the Scots, who had experienced a devastating crop failure, run out of aid from the military stores, and found themselves unable to repay their government debts.

When reports were received in Perth of continuing "Irish" disturbances in Ramsay Township, an armed party of one hundred militiamen

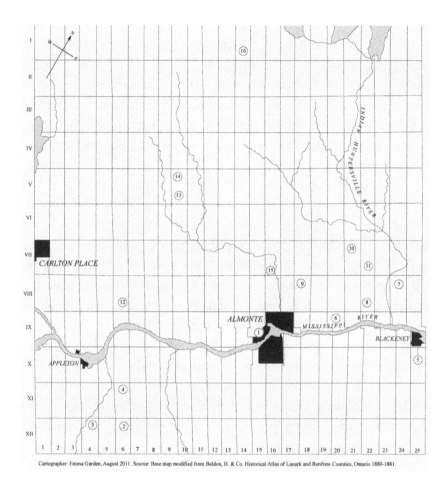

Cartographer: Emma Garden, August 2011. Source: Base map modified from Beldon, H. & Co. Historical Atlas of Lanark and Renfrew Counties, Ontario 1880-1881.

Ramsay Township

1. John Gemmill
2. John Neilson
3. John Lochart
4. Alexander Duncan
5. William McQueen
6. James Sneddon
7. John Toshack
8. Robert Carswell
9. James Craig
10. Walter Black
11. Alexander Steel
12. William Davie
13. Andrew Smith
14. Alexander Galbraith
15. Auld Kirk Church
16. Arthur Lang

were sent to Shipman's Mills (later Almonte) to arrest those involved in "rioting and assault." There, a party under the command of the deputy sheriff, Alexander Matheson, fired on the house of William Roche, wounding several people and killing one. While there was considerable blame to go around for the incident, the only men sentenced for their part in the violence were Robinson's settlers. Many prominent Scots, including Reverend Bell, believed that the Irish Catholics were, by nature, predisposed to violence and necessarily responsible for the disorder.[27] While some of Beckwith's Irish Protestants tried to calm the situation — particularly the tavern keeper and 1829 petition committee member Patrick Nowlan — it appears that Perth's Irish Protestant Orangemen, led by Matheson, rather than the Scottish society settlers, were responsible for escalating the conflict. Nevertheless, it is likely that the Scottish artisans were sympathetic with the anti-Catholicism of the Orange Order, since many had found themselves in direct competition with Irish weavers who had moved to the west of Scotland in large numbers after the end of the war.[28] In this regard, the riots of 1824 can be seen as an extension of the sectarian conflict that was on the rise in the imperial homeland.

It has been suggested that shared Protestantism was one of the unifying elements in the emerging "British" imperial identity that emerged after the Parliamentary union of 1707 and certainly the 1824 disturbances, attributed to both Protestant and Catholic Irish settlers, had shocked many colonial officials who had expected emigrants from the British Isles to stabilize the colony. It was at the parish level, however, where the Presbyterian churches founded by Scottish immigrants were most evidently working to maintain order among the colonists.[29] Records of the kirk sessions reveal how important these institutions were in the settlers' daily experience, since almost every aspect of early community life was monitored by these bodies.

An indication of this intrusiveness can be gleaned from the session minutes of the "Auld Kirk" in Ramsay moderated by Reverend Fairbairn. Even before their church was erected, the congregation appointed five elders to the kirk session, which held its first meeting on June 9, 1834, and immediately began to administer discipline. Each elder was given the task of investigating complaints in his own district, thus ensuring that the entire township was covered. After the Reformation the Scottish kirk sessions had assumed responsibility for dealing with matters pertaining to parishioners' conduct and morality, and offences as wide ranging as drunkenness, Sabbath breaking, riotous behaviour, and slander were all worthy of their attention.[30] As the minutes of the Ramsay kirk session reveal, this role was self-consciously replicated in the colonial settlement.

One of the first incidents investigated by the Ramsay session was a report that William Drynan, a settler who had arrived with the Milton Dunbartonshire Emigration Society, "had been guilty of drunkenness." Drynan would be called twice more before the session and admonished for the same offence, while John Bennie, the son of Rutherglen Union Society member James Bennie, was called to answer the same charge with the added claim that while inebriated he had "been engaged in a quarrel, whereby reproach was brought on his own character as a professing Christian."[31] The linking of drunkenness with unchristian behaviour was also evident in the case of another emigrant's son, John Galbraith. In addition to public intoxication, Galbraith was charged with failing to attend church, and when the elders learned that this was due to a lack of "decent clothes," they hoped that he would obtain them soon.[32] While the entry is perhaps a reflection of the poverty that many settlers were experiencing in the pioneer community, the elders were more concerned that Galbraith resume regular attendance, and in this regard they were not alone. In the 1830s, Reverend Wilson's kirk session in Perth investigated several cases of both the failure to attend church and respect the Sabbath.[33]

In Scotland, charges of Sabbath breaking had declined dramatically during the second half of the eighteenth century, largely due to the fact that strict Sunday observance had become the norm by that time. Nevertheless, in the homeland the Church of Scotland was dominant, but in the colony it was merely one of several denominations, and the policing of Sunday observance by the Ottawa Valley kirk sessions can be seen as an attempt to reassert lost control.[34] The session minutes, however, demonstrate that the immigrants, too, looked to the kirk session to enforce "Christian" standards in their new settlement by reporting objectionable behaviour, particularly among the younger members of the community.

In 1838 the Ramsay kirk session admonished the sons of two emigration society families, Allan Gilmour and William Bowes, when the men acknowledged the truth of a report that they had been "guilty of profane swearing and giving way to anger on two separate occasions." While this clearly fell under the mandate to correct personal conduct, at times even criminal matters could be brought to the session's attention. In 1841 Janet Hart, possibly the daughter of Paisley Townhead Emigration Society member John Hart, was accused of theft and lists of missing items and testimony for various parishioners were submitted to the elders for their consideration. The session found her guilty of the theft, as well as falsehood for previously denying the charges against her, and suspended her church privileges.[35]

Janet Hart had allegedly stolen items while she was residing in the house of Robert Yule, where she was likely working as a domestic servant for the family. The minutes indicate, however, that she had been called on previous occasions to appear before the kirk session, at which time she admitted that she had been guilty of fornication. As Captain McMillan's reputation suggests, household servant girls were often the focus of sexual attention. At the same time that Janet Hart appeared before the Ramsay session, Margaret Dickson confessed to Reverend Smith's kirk session in Beckwith that she was guilty of the sin of fornication "a short time previous to her departure from Scotland ... and again more recently while employed as a servant in the neighbouring village of Richmond." She was required to submit to rebuke from Smith in front of the congregation on two Sabbaths, before being absolved and readmitted to "the privileges of the church." When William Mitchell and Jean Bryson admitted to the same sin, both were similarly rebuked before the Ramsay congregation. The Beckwith session, while recognizing that "the laws obliging those guilty of scandalous offences" to offer public penance had "become obsolete in Scotland," believed that the practice should be maintained, suggesting, once again, that in colonial circumstances it was believed necessary to firmly assert church authority.[36]

By the middle of the eighteenth century cases involving sexual behaviour dominated the kirk session minutes in Scotland, where women who gave birth to illegitimate children were of particular concern, but the preoccupation with parishioners' conduct also extended to the premarital relations of married couples. This was also true of the kirk sessions in Beckwith, Perth, and Ramsay, where cases of illegitimate births were often heard and where cases of antenuptial fornication came to dominate the minutes. When John Paterson acknowledged this sin to the Ramsay session, he and his wife were absolved and an "intimation" of this was read out to the congregation, but session minutes also suggest that the concern was with both premarital sexual relations and the "irregular" marriages of some parishioners.[37]

In some cases the lack of a sanctified and documented marriage was a consequence of the unsettled conditions in the pioneer community; in others, it was the continuation of older popular custom. John MacTaggart, in his *Three Years in Canada*, reported encountering Peter Armstrong from Hawick who had cleared seven acres in the "wild woods." His wife, Tibby Patterson, had worked as a "byre women" on the Branksome (Brankholm) estate, where Armstrong had worked as a "herd lad" before leaving for Upper Canada in 1813. After several years they met again in Perth, had

This log house in Appleton, Ramsay Township, is one of several that still stand in Lanark County. While many of these early settler structures have disappeared, those that remain deserve to be properly recorded and studied.

Photo by M. Vance.

three children together, and "read their bible on Sunday" but did not have an officially recognized marriage.[38] In addition to ensuring that all marriages of this kind were properly formalized, the kirk sessions tried to ensure that they were harmonious. Incidents of domestic violence appear in several entries of the Ramsay session minutes, including the distressing case of the Duncan family of the Paisley Townhead Emigration Society. John Lochart, the local elder, informed the session that the public reports of fighting among the family were accurate, and, when they appeared before the session, Alexander Duncan admitted to striking his wife, Sara Ann Robinson, but only in self defence. While Mrs. Duncan's own admission of suicidal intentions strongly suggest that she was suffering from mental distress, the sessions' response was to suspend her church privileges. In order to restore some domestic tranquillity, Alexander Duncan later requested that he be suspended as well.[39]

Sara Ann Robinson had briefly left her home as a consequence of the family discord. Advertisements placed in local papers by men refusing to honour debts contracted by their absent wives reveal that others had done the same. The newspaper notices do not reveal why the women left, but the kirk session records offer a possible explanation. James Dunlop admitted beating his wife "on one occasion," but was absolved by the Ramsay session after acknowledging his sin.[40] The embarrassment of such public admissions was the only deterrent that the kirk elders could offer abused wives.

In some cases even this was not possible. In 1837 Robert Carswell, a member of Cambuslang Emigration Society who had been cited as a successful settler in testimony given to the Select Committee on Emigration, was confronted by two kirk elders with reports that he had been guilty of "striking his wife," Helen Russell. Carswell's response was to both deny the charge and declare that these were matters in which "the session had no business." He refused repeated requests to appear before the kirk session, and in the end all that could be done was to suspend him from the church privileges that he did not appear to have been exercising in the first place.[41] Robert Carswell's defiance demonstrates the limitations of church discipline in the colony, which could have contributed to women fleeing violent situations, but the case also demonstrates the extent to which church elders were prepared to go to impose order on the immigrant community.

Late in 1825, the *Paisley Advertizer* reported that William Jamieson and Jean Walker had failed to appear before the Glasgow Presbytery to answer the charge that they had "connected together in forbidden degrees." According to the paper, the couple had already left Scotland for "America."[42] In attempting to escape the discipline of the church by becoming colonists, Jamieson and Walker were following the example of many radical reformers who had crossed the Atlantic to avoid persecution.

Early politics in the Ottawa Valley, as in the rest of Upper Canada, indicates that Scottish artisan immigrants continued to hold reform ideals first formed in the homeland, and this was particularly evident in the electoral successes of Malcolm Cameron. William Morris's early domination of local settler politics, however, demonstrates that other Scots, particularly among the merchant community, were keen to maintain the conservative social order that imperial planners envisioned for the colony. The intensity of these opposing views, first developed in Britain, was reflected in the reports of the raucous polling days that accompanied the earliest elections in Lanark County, but when examined from the perspective of daily religious practice, the social conservatism of all members of the immigrant community is striking. Prior attempts had been made to assert church discipline in the west of Scotland, where many of the settlers had originated, but the need to control a widely dispersed settlement, which contained rival and competing denominations, gave the kirk sessions a particularly vital role in creating a stable pioneer community.[43] In the colony, as in the imperial homeland, female misconduct was viewed as the most serious threat to that stability.

One case in the kirk session minutes of the St. Andrews Church in Perth illustrates the extent of the immigrant church's reach into individual settler women's lives. In the summer of 1839, the kirk session investigated a report of "light behaviour" brought against Margaret Paton, the wife of the schoolteacher Adam Paton, by Alexander Ferguson, a successful Scottish settler in Drummond Township. The Patons occupied a house on Ferguson's land, and he and his family charged that Mrs. Paton had behaved inappropriately with James Hicks, his farm servant.

Examination of the case proceeded over several months and accusations of Mrs. Paton's "adulterous" behaviour were countered with charges of Alexander Ferguson's unfair dealing. In the end, the kirk session found no evidence of adultery, but did find that Mrs. Paton was guilty of behaviour unbecoming a married woman, and suspended her from church privileges when she refused to acknowledge any "misconduct." The Patons relocated to Ramsay Township and became parishioners of Reverend Fairbairn, but were denied church privileges there when the case became known. Three years after the initial complaint had been lodged, Margaret Paton finally relented and travelled to Perth to admit her misconduct, which had merely entailed the "attempt to take a handkerchief," rubbing Hicks's face with flour, and the use of language "unbecoming the profession of a Christian."[44]

The contrast of the successful pursuit of Margaret Paton by the St. Andrews kirk session with the inability of the Ramsay elders to compel Robert Carswell to answer charges of spousal abuse, underlines the inequality at the heart of both the religious and political life of the

The "Auld Kirk" stone church in Ramsay Township was built between 1835 and 1836. Before the building was erected, the kirk session met at John Gemmill's store in Shipman's Mills (later Almonte).

Photo by M. Vance.

immigrant community. As the wife of a schoolteacher, whose livelihood depended upon an upright reputation in the settler community, Mrs. Paton found it difficult to resist the authority of the kirk elders — even for comparatively trivial matters. But Robert Carswell was, like the church elders and the district's voters, an independent landholder and there was no economic or social lever that the kirk session could use to compel him to recognize their authority. Since only men could vote or serve as elders, both the religious and political life of settler society was governed by this inequality between the sexes.[45] What may have been accepted as natural by the community was reinforced by notions of patriarchal authority that, like their politics and their religious practices, were first developed in the imperial homeland.

Chapter Six

PIONEER PATRIARCHS

In May 1821 Ann Adams left Scotland with her husband, John Gemmill, and two children, John and Mary, along with the other members of the Glasgow Trongate Emigration Society. Ann's family settled in Ramsay Township, where her husband established himself as the first merchant in what would eventually become the town of Almonte. Ann, however, did not live to see the remarkable success of her husband's business. Although the Gemmills were members of a Glasgow society, like many others, the couple were originally from the rural Lowlands. John Gemmill had been born in Dunlop, a small community in Ayrshire, and he continued to correspond with members of his family still in the county. When James Gemmill, who resided in Irvine, received the news of Ann's death, he responded with the following lines:

Dear Brother,

I received your letter of 29th Septr 1828 about the beginning of Decbr following — I was very sorry to here [sic] of the loss you have met with in the death of your wife it is no doubt a heavy tryal [sic] but the will of the Lord must be done. — You mention altho with reluctance you must have another wife[.] [T]here are some going from this place to get Husbands[.] My old Landlord Mr. Gardners Daughter is just fitting out to go to Jamaica to get married to an old sweethart [sic], and there is another from this place going to Montreal to get a husband, by this you see the ladys on this side are none affraid [sic] to venture over the water where a sweethart comes in the way — So if you still be in want of a wife if you recollect any of your old friends you have no more

to do but commission me and I will do all in my pow[e]r
to forward the business in this country.[1]

For James, his brother's situation in his Upper Canadian pioneer
settlement was no different than other Scotsmen within the British
Empire, whether an unmarried factor on a Jamaican estate or a mason
in Montreal. His emphasis on overseas alliances, however, reveals how
marriage provided some single Ayrshire women with the opportunity to
settle within this wider British imperial world without the aid any official
emigration schemes. It is not known if James Gemmill played a role, but
shortly after his brother's letter was sent, John Gemmill did enter into a
second marriage with Margaret Muirhead, another native of Scotland.[2]

In recent years emigrant correspondence like John Gemmill's has
been subjected to considerable scholarly scrutiny. Some have suggested
that these documents are so heavily influenced by conventional formulas
and a desire to influence their readers that they are of limited value in
understanding what actually occurred in the past. Immigrant writers,
in particular, were keen to justify their departures from the homeland,

*As the postmarks and address labels indicate, James Gemmill sent his letter to his
brother via the emigrant vessel* Favourite *of Montreal. The ship left Greenock with
the letter in August and arrived in Quebec at the end of September, a year after John
Gemmill had written with the news of Ann Adam's death.*

Courtesy of Archives of Ontario, MU 7424 Series 1–2.

and as a consequence would often minimize their difficulties and portray their circumstances in the best possible light — often with the goal of encouraging others to join them.

It has been suggested that the main purpose of such letters was not to convey information but to maintain a physical connection with relatives in the homeland, hence the conventional request to write soon. As James Gemmill's letter reveals, the exchange of letters took place over many months or indeed years, and each document was eagerly anticipated and often carefully preserved by the recipient. Over the course of time, as the immigrant family became more established in their new communities, the correspondence often diminished or ceased altogether.

While studies of what has been termed the "ethics of the personal immigrant letter" have revealed a great deal about the conventions and psychological significance of letter writing, others have emphasized how these documents are critical for understanding actual immigrant experience. Rather than focusing on the conventions that the letters share, these studies have sought to identify the particular incidental information they contain and then place those details in context by reading the letters alongside other available documentation. When letters are treated in this critical fashion they reveal aspects of the immigrant experience largely unavailable in other types of document.

This is particularly true for women, who seldom appear in official sources like the earliest censuses, which recorded only male heads of households. In addition, since letters are personal, they provide details about household life that are largely absent from sources like local newspapers or government land records.[3] In early nineteenth-century popular literature the household was increasingly viewed as the natural sphere for women's activity, and letters are therefore critical for uncovering how this popular perception affected women's actual experience, as well as the role they played in fulfilling settlement plans for the Ottawa Valley.

One aspect of female experience highlighted in James Gemmill's response to Ann Adam's death was the indispensable value of marriage — not only for settlers like his brother John but also for labouring people in general. In offering his brother further details of the marriages in his own community, James mentioned that Jean Nisbett had married a Mr. Henderson and that together they had established a grocer shop in Paisley. Such joint working relationships were far from uncommon, and indeed characterized handloom weavers' families in which men commonly worked the loom while the women did the spinning in addition to caring for the household and the children. Marriage was therefore an economic necessity, and this, in part, accounts for John Gemmill's reluctant decision to remarry. The letters he received from relatives in Scotland, however, also demonstrate the deeply ingrained assumption that all women would marry. An earlier letter from Ann's nephew Alexander Adams, a weaver in Saltcoats, Ayrshire, indicated that his aunt and uncle had suggested that if "Aunt Jean was not married to send her out to America [where] she would soon get a husband." Alexander was able to report that there was no need since she had already married John Kingan, a widowed school-master with eight children, and that she just had her first child and was living in Shettleston in Glasgow, where Kingan ran a school.

The exchange reveals how emigration was seen as a part of the choices available to women seeking a marriage that would remove them from the distressed conditions of the weaving communities of Lowland Scotland, but it also demonstrates that marriage, whether at home or abroad, was expected. Indeed, Alexander Adam further reported that his sisters, Janet and Marion, were "working at the needle" and not yet married, declaring that "we will have to send them out to you to look for husbands for them" as there were "no good chances here." After Ann Adam's death, John Gemmill offered Janet Adams his wife's clothes. But instead of coming to Canada to receive them, as he hoped, Janet requested that Ann's garments be sent to Scotland "not so much upon account of the value of them but for the sake of whom they belonged."[4]

The concern with the matrimonial state of the single women belonging to the extended family members still in Scotland, so apparent in John Gemmill's correspondence, was also reflected in the letters of numerous other immigrants. Ebenezer Wilson, the community leader in North Sherbrooke, opened his letter to his sister and brother-in-law, John Colquhoun, in Paisley by stating that a letter sent by his daughter Marion had told him of his niece Nancy's marriage and that he was eager to know more: "I should have learned what kind of match Nancy had made but nothing except the bare name of the man was given which not happening to know we could not judge." Wilson was deeply concerned about deteriorating conditions in his hometown, but was unable help his daughter Marion and her husband to rejoin the family in Upper Canada.[5] Since marriage offered the possibility of escaping hardship, it is little wonder that Wilson wanted more details about his niece's husband.

Marriage also linked Scottish immigrants together after their arrival in Upper Canada. There are examples of Scots entering into marriages with members of other immigrant groups, but the careful work done by genealogists suggests that this was relatively rare among the first generation of immigrant families. More typical was the marriage, in 1829, of another of Ebenezer Wilson's nieces, Betty Stoaks. His sister Mary in a letter to family still in Paisley reported:

> Our Betty was married last Wednesday with Andrew Harroer [Harrower] a young man of 21 years age they live about 2 miles Distant from us he was brought up in Fort Augustus in the North of Scotland. They had about eight miles to go meet the minister and he had about seven miles to come meet them and they come home here in the afternoon and sat down to dinner a company of upwards 40 people of Friends and Neighbours and had all plenty to eat and drink.[6]

The Harrower family patriarch, James, was a native of Crieff, Perthshire, and a career soldier who had served the British Empire in both the American Revolutionary War and the Napoleonic Wars. He and his wife, Ann Tulloch, had ten children together — four of whom emigrated to Upper Canada. The first to do so was Margaret Harrower, who settled in Lochiel Township in Glengarry County, in 1818, with her husband John McDonnell. They later moved to North Sherbrooke, where they joined Margaret's brother George Harrower, and Walter Sym, the husband of Ann Harrower. Robert Sym, also a native of Perthshire, had arrived in North Sherbrooke as a member of the Rutherglen Union Emigration Society in 1821, and his brother and brother-in-law joined him in the township as independent settlers the following year. Walter Sym quickly returned to Scotland to rejoin Ann, who had stayed to care for her ailing father. The couple only returned to the township after the death of James Harrower in 1832, and, given the date of the wedding, Andrew Harrower was probably residing with his brother George during the couple's courtship.[7] Nevertheless, the chain of migration that led to the union of these two Scottish families in Upper Canada was initiated by Margaret Harrower.

While marriages like James Harrower and Betty Stoak's are empha-sized in the immigrant correspondence, the letters also reveal that women's work was also of great importance in consolidating the settle-ment. In an earlier letter to her sister in Scotland, Mary Stoaks reported that "most of the young girls ... gowed [sic] away to service and gets from it 2: to 4: dollars a month," and that before her marriage her daughter had done the same "about 60 miles down the country." Nor was this unusual, as several other North Sherbrooke settlers, including the Twaddle, Gilmour, and Wylie families, all had daughters working as domestic ser-vants away from home.[8] In this regard the unmarried women were no different than the men of the settlement, who had travelled as far afield as New York State in search of wages to supplement their family income while simultaneously trying to establish their farms.

Indeed, a letter written by William Davie of the Parkhead Emigration Society to his adult children who chose to remain in Scotland suggests that families often initially relied on their daughters to supplement their earnings while the men began clearing the land. A severe illness, contracted upon his arrival in Upper Canada during the summer of 1821, had prevented William from occupying his hundred-acre grant in Ramsay Township until September, but, by November of that year, both of his daughters were already "at service." Jess was working for a family in Prescott and "Betsay" was doing the same across the river in Ogdensburgh, New York.[9]

Alexander Adam's letter to John Gemmill illustrates that this reli-ance on women's earnings was not merely a product of pioneering circumstances, but was already a feature of labouring family life in Scotland before families chose to emigrate. In addition to indicating to his uncle that his sisters were employed in sewing, Alexander stated that his Aunt Janet was living near Edinburgh "working at the needle and doing very well," and that his mother was "working away as usual altho[ugh] there is little doing as money is so scarce [sic]."[10]

Women's labour was so vital to immigrant prospects that Robert Forrest, a Lanark County settler with the Lesmahagow Emigration Society, advised his weaver brother John in Lanark, Scotland, that he should try to raise his passage money, but that he should bring his family with him. In an earlier letter to his parents, Robert stressed, in particular, the psychological consequences of family separation:

The genteel women shown in the foreground of this engraving depicting Irvine in the early nineteenth century give little indication of the intensive labour that occupied the majority of the community's female inhabitants. Only a few figures faintly visible in the fields in the background reflect most women's actual experience. From John Wilson, The Works of Robert Burns *(Glasgow: Blackie & Son, 1857) Vol. I, cxlii supplemental plate.*

As for sending John to me — I do not think it proper nor
do I advise a family to separate so far their mind is never
easy and altho Johns help would be of great service to
me it is a great chance if he could raise as much money
serving any other as would bring his fathers family all
out — if John cannot give up the thought of coming here
— The next thing I would advise — for him to come out
with his son John himself — and if they both kept their
health they could send for the rest of their family in two
years at farthest but if it can be helped a family should
never be separated.[11]

John Forrest did finally emigrate with his family from Scotland to
Upper Canada, settling in Renfrew County, where his brother had settled
in 1827 after having exchanged his unproductive lot in Lanark Township
for better land in Horton Township.

Robert's advice was likely informed by knowledge of the fact that
some women, like Sarah Neilson of Glasgow, found themselves stranded
in Scotland after their husbands had left for Upper Canada, or of the
difficulties that many families, such as the Gardners of the Hamilton
Emigration Society, experienced in trying to maintain contact across the
Atlantic after separation. Indeed, Margaret Gardner had left Scotland in
1822 with her two young boys not knowing what had happened to her
husband Robert, daughter Mary, and son William, who had sailed the
previous year. Although she was reunited with the rest of her family in
Dalhousie Township, her son Archibald, who was nine years old when
he travelled to Upper Canada with his mother, later recounted how the
whole episode had been an emotional ordeal.[12]

While Robert Forrest was opposed to the practice of separating families during emigration, he had no such qualms once they were settled in
Upper Canada. He reported to his parents that his wife, Nelly, had been
staying with her brother Bob for four months in Kingston: "Their meeting was very agreeable and no wonder having not seen one another 11
years."[13] Family ties were clearly important to Robert. He even advocated
the emigration of elderly female family members to his brother John,

but the reminiscences of other Scottish settlers reveal how separation in Upper Canada was vital for establishing families on the land and meeting the settlement duties laid out by the colonial government.

After the first clearings had taken place and the support from the government stores for assisted immigrants ran out, many family heads had to leave the settlement in order to find wage work, leaving the women to look after the farm and the children. One Paisley weaver, who had settled in Ramsay Township, later recalled how construction work on the Oswego Canal in New York State had provided employment for many of the men. In an anonymous article in the *Perth Courier*, he wrote that in 1823 "most of we menfolk went to work at it, leaving our women and children in the wilds of Canada, without one penny of money, they to plant potatoes in the spring and sow any little clear spot."[14] He went on to describe how the construction firms in Oswego exploited the men and sought to ensure that they would not leave the diggings by withholding their wages. Early nineteenth-century canal building was hazardous work, and many men lost their lives at Oswego. Indeed, John Hamilton, a Lanark Township settler who had emigrated with his wife and young son as members of the Kirkman Finlay Emigration Society, was one of the men who did not return from canal building in the United States. Rather than risk a similar fate, the anonymous author of the *Courier* article had decided not to wait for his full wages and to return to his family:

> When I reached home at Ramsay, the wife and weans had eaten up the last mouthful of meal the day before and knew not where to look for more. The potatoes were in the ground only half grown. They had looked to Heaven for help and the Lord directed me home, even with a third of my lawfully earned wages.[15]

Although faced with similar circumstances when her husband went to work in Oswego, Mrs. McLellan looked back in later years with some pride in what she was able to accomplish in her husband's absence. The Cambuslang couple had arrived in Dalhousie Township with the

Anderston and Rutherglen Transatlantic Society in 1820, and John McLellan, a former weaver, left to work in the United States three years later, leaving his wife with their four children all under nine years old. But according to her account, published years later in the *Bathurst Courier*:

> soon as the gude man went away I took heart and with the [eldest] boy began to dig between the stumps and plant potatoes. When the fall of the year came and we had gathered them in, how many do you think we had? No less than 350 bushels of potatoes, and 30 bushels of corn raised by myself and my little boy.[16]

But while Mrs. McLellan remembered her pioneer trials with fondness, other women were clearly placed in distressed circumstances by their husband's absence and their isolation. The experience of Ellen Gunnan, the wife of the Dumfriesshire-born wheelwright, Walter Black, was perhaps more typical. The Blacks had arrived in the township in 1821 with other members of the Glasgow Canadian Society. By 1825 Walter was working in the United States, and Ellen was left with their children on the family's backwoods clearing in Ramsay Township. Her son James later recalled how the crops had failed and his mother had been spurred on by the hungry "cries of her little ones" to leave her home early one winter's morning and thread her way through the woods to Snedden's Mills, four miles away, in order to obtain some cornmeal.[17]

In comparison to Ellen Gunnan, Mary Stoaks was frequently away from home as a consequence of her popularity as a midwife. She began assisting women in childbirth on board the *Earl of Buckingham*, and, in her first letter to Scotland, described her activities in the new settlement:

> ... about 6 weeks ago a man came 16: miles for me on foot: and got the loan of a Boat and we sailed about 9 miles to his place and all was well: and I got home again the same way next day — I was with Mrs. Eliot about 3 weeks ago. She wanted a few days of 16 when she was delivered of a Daughter. The mother is quite well but the

child is weakly. [I]t was born in the 7th month and is not likely to live long.[18]

While such visits ensured that Mary Stoaks kept in contact with her fellow settlers, she remained concerned about her children during her travels and wrote that she felt "the want of Betty in the family when I am from home."[19] The absence of her eldest daughter, first through service and later through marriage, was clearly a source of anxiety for Mary and her difficulties were compounded when illness occurred.

The Stoaks were among several Scottish settlers who continued to weave as well as farm in Upper Canada, and, in her letter of January 6, 1829, Mary reported that she and her son David had journeyed to Perth with some wool for carding. They both became ill ten days later, and at the time of writing her son was "stil[l] taking the ague and fever every

Entitled The Beginning, *this mid-nineteenth century engraving shows the pioneer family engaged in the work of clearing the forest. It glorifies the muscular activity of the husband while relegating his wife to the supervision of the cook pot.*

Courtesy of Killam Library, Dalhousie University.

day or two" while Mary herself was "very ill and very weak" and had "no freedom in going to the door or tasting or handling anything that is cold." Mary's experience with the "fever and ague" was all too common among the settler families, and her letter revealed that her brother Ebenezer's family had also been stricken but were "better long ago."[20]

While illness could isolate even relatively well-travelled women like Mary Stoaks in their homesteads, the roads themselves presented hardships. In the first few decades the settlements were connected in the most part by rough trails or crude corduroyed roads, and Reverend Bell's early circuit took him over most of them. In his *Hints to Emigrants*, Bell reported seeing female settlers struggling along such roads in the rain, knee-deep in mud with their children on their backs, "grumbling out ... reproaches to themselves for their folly in leaving comfortable homes for a howling wilderness." He claimed to have often seen women "sitting at the side of the road, resting their weary limbs, or crying till they were sick, and expressing unavailing wishes that they were back in their native land."[21] For Bell, such scenes represented the foolishness of emigrants who travelled to Canada with unreasonable expectations and thus suggested that the women were responsible for their own circumstances.

While many women undoubtedly encouraged husbands and family members to consider emigration, many others, such as Reverend Bell's own wife, Mary Black, were left with little choice but to follow their husbands overseas. At the time of their emigration, five of the six Bell children were under the age of nine, and Mary had lost her youngest son James at age four to the measles less than three years earlier. Her preference to remain in Scotland appears natural in such circumstances, but while Bell claimed that she was free to do as she pleased, he did not offer to support her if she did stay, and entreated her to join him with the following lines:

> The sacrifice you are required to make is, after all, but
> trifling, in comparison of what every female mission-
> ary has to make. Mrs. Glen, in the prospect of going to
> Astra[k]han, displays a firmness and a resolution that
> do honour to both herself and her husband ... If you

really think you are making a great sacrifice, when you accompany me to Canada, it will be much to your credit, as well as mine, that you do it cheerfully; for everyone admits that the cause is the noblest and best that can engage the attention of mankind.[22]

This letter not only reveals Bell's unwavering faith in his imperial mission, but also the pressure that could be exerted on women to emigrate by appeals to prevailing ideas about marital obligation and female duty.

Reverend Bell's letter to his wife also demonstrates that notions of proper female conduct were formed in the homeland and travelled with the immigrants to Upper Canada. Indeed, John Gemmill appears to have literally carried them with him from Glasgow, since he contributed his two-volume translation of Jeanne-Marie Le Prince de Beaumont's female conduct manual, *The Young Misses Magazine*, to the Ramsay Library when it was established in 1829.

Many emigration society members greatly valued learning and some had brought their prized books with them to the colony. The list of original donations provides insight into what individual settlers considered to greatest benefit to their new community. Thomas Shepard's seventeenth-century sermons on the *Parable of the Ten Virgins*, donated by John Toshack, reflected the immigrants' widespread concern with maintaining religious observance in the colony, while their interest in radical politics was echoed by Findlay Sinclair's donation of Thomas Paine's *The Rights of Man*. Arthur Lang, a weaver with the Paisley Townhead Emigration Society, may have developed some of his ideas about his destination from his three-volume edition of the Scottish historian William Robertson's *History of America*, which he contributed to the Ramsay collection. Once enough revenue had been generated through entrance fees, the Ramsay Library also acquired Sir Walter Scott's Waverley novels, and these joined other volumes of Scottish literature in the original collection such as an edition of *Ossian's Poems* donated by the Cambuslang settler David Snedden and *The Poetic Works of Robert Burns* contributed by Malcolm Cameron.[23]

The *Young Misses Magazine*, donated by John Gemmill, was also fiction since it records imagined conversations between a governess, one Mrs. Affable, and her young charges, which include, among others, a Lady Witty, a Lady Sensible, and a Lady Tempest. For her lessons, however, which included geography and European history, Mrs. Affable drew heavily on classical and biblical texts as illustrations for her instructions on proper female behaviour. As a consequence, Gemmill's donation was also similar to the religious tracts contributed by other settlers, like Reverend John Wilson's *The Afflicted Man's Companion*, donated by the Paisley Townhead Emigration Society member, John Shaw, as well as the texts containing practical knowledge, such as Daniel Fenning's *New System of Geography*, donated by William Morris.[24]

While the *Young Misses Magazine's* specific emphasis on female instruction made it unique to the early collection of the Ramsay Library, its lessons correspond to ideas of appropriate female conduct found in a number of sources in both Upper Canada and the imperial homeland. Mrs. Affable warned her pupils of the sin of pride, and, through a dialogue with Lady Tempest, the importance of controlling one's temper, but she also stressed the importance of sacrificing personal pleasure to social duty. According to the governess, idle diversions, in particular, were to be shunned. Reverend Bell's Upper Canadian journal indicates that he agreed with such sentiments. While he was disturbed by the lack of respect for the Sabbath demonstrated by many former officers in Perth, it was his daughter's encounter with one of her peers that provoked the following entry for Monday, August 29, 1825:

> [Isabella] met Miss Lane who told her that she had been at Captain LeLievre's the evening before where they had such fun! Fiddling & dancing, singing &c. What profanation of the Sabbath. Thomson was there. What would his father think, who is an elder in Greenock, did he know how is son was employed?[25]

The attention that was later paid to Margaret Paton's behaviour by kirk sessions in both Perth and Ramsay illustrates how the male church elders, as with the real life Reverend Bell and the fictional Lady Affable, were particularly keen to discourage what they viewed as inappropriate female public conduct, since it could lead to sinful behaviour and undermine the settlement. This concern, however, also reflected the spread of what has been termed the "separate spheres ideology" both in the homeland and in the colony.[26]

It is possible to trace the development of this ideology in the popular literature being produced in Scotland at the time of the assisted emigrations to Upper Canada. While many of these cheap broadsides and pamphlets were, unlike the *Young Misses Magazine*, designed to entertain rather than instruct, they do clearly reflect the idea that men should act in the public world as family breadwinners and that women needed to focus on running their households as private refuges from that world.

The London illustrator, Thomas Hosmer Shepherd, specialized in books on "modern" cities for middle-class readers like the woman he depicts here in her Edinburgh garden. From T.H. Shepherd, Modern Athens! or Edinburgh in the Nineteenth Century *(London: Jones & Co., 1829).*

The topic of emigration featured in several broadsides that were sold by peddlers and chapmen on the streets of Scotland's town and cities in the early nineteenth century and one, printed by John Muir of Glasgow, focused on emigrant women in Upper Canada.

The document, dated the February 12, 1827, purported to be a "Copy of a very Curious Letter from a Cotton Spinner in Canada, to his friends in this Country, containing a particular invitation to all men going out to America to take a Cotton Mill Lass along with him, as they make the far best Wives there; with many other curious particulars." Rather than reproducing a genuine letter, this broadside was intended as a parody of letters that had been published — notably in Robert Lamond's account of the 1820–21 assisted emigration. The letter's "author" reports that while he and his cousin Rab were drinking rum in a Perth tavern with an English neighbour named Holden, the conversation turned to the subject of their wives. Since they were settled only three miles apart from each other, the men agreed to visit each of their homesteads and "bet a gallon of rum, agreeing that the person who had the laziest, the dirtiest; and most uncivil wife, and the clartiest house, was to pay the rum":

> … so away we went to our cousin Rab's … when we came to Rab's door we could hardly get in for muck — but save us, such a house and such a wife wi' dirt, you never did see the like with your eyes. No wonder though they call the Scotch dirty, for her and her house were a disgrace to our country; and I must say most of the braw country lasses when they become wives are little better. You know she has black hair; it was all loose, hanging down the back and side of her head; her mutch and face were like as if they had been smoked up the lum for half a year; her blue plaiding petticoat, once of true blue, was shamed into black wi' greim; the cogs, luggies, plates and spoons, were all barkened wi' kail and porridge, for I suppose she never washed them. She had two bairns half-dressed, trailing through thee ashes.[27]

The three men then proceeded to the Englishman's house where they were treated civilly, yet coldly, but when they arrived

> ... everything was in good order — just like a little pal-
> ace. Jean was frank, clean, and decent, as usual. Here's
> my Cotton Mill Lass, said I to the Englishman; do you
> think more of her or of Rab's country girl. Faith, said plain
> spoken John Bull, there is a mighty difference; the one is
> like an angel of light, the other like an angle of darkness.
> Before we could look about us Jean set down plenty of tea
> and bread and butter — and when that was done, plenty
> o'gude tody to mak' a' comfortable and pleasant. We were
> all very hearty but Rab; but he soon overcame his dulness,
> for we boused away till morning. Then off we would all
> go to drink the gallon of rum at New Perth, as we were
> resolved to mak' Rab pay for it, as he was so positive about
> his braw country Jenny.[28]

While Scots words do appear in genuine emigrant letters, this broad-side's use of contrived dialect and conventional stereotypes is similar to those that appear in many works of contemporary popular literature. Indeed, the supposed unclean, or "clarty," nature of "country lasses" was a stereotype that had been popularized in Scotland with Elizabeth Hamilton's 1808 novel *The Cottagers of Glenburnie* — a copy of which had been donated to the Ramsay Library by John Nielson, a weaver with the Paisley Townhead Society.[29]

Scholars who have studied Scottish broadsides have noted that com-mercial printers attempted to increase sales by publishing material that reflected the domestic and marital lives of labouring people, but rather than present realistic portrayals these usually took the form of satires, melodramas, or, as in the case of the "Curious Letter," comedies.[30] But despite its apparently fabricated nature, the "letter" does provide some clues as to the attitudes toward marriage among Scottish artisans. The narrator clearly wishes to praise the domestic skills of his "cotton mill lass," and yet behaves like a drunken lout. This tension is also apparent in broadsides relating artisan marriage from the 1790s onward, which frequently portrayed conflicts, often violent, between husband and wife over the husband's drinking. For example, in "Watty and Meg; or the Wife Reformed" by Alexander Wilson, the Paisley poet-weaver and American ornithologist, Watty, stops Meg's nagging over his drinking by threatening to leave her and join the army. The strategy was suggested by Mungo, his drinking companion, who offered the course of action in order to prevent Watty from assaulting his wife. The Glasgow Police Court records reveal that such attacks were far from uncommon and indeed reflect an increased incidence of assaults as the city expanded in the early nineteenth century.[31]

Labouring women are clearly evident in this early nineteenth-century representation of Bridgegate Street in Glasgow. A domestic servant is airing out sheets in an upper-storey window while other women carry various baskets and bundles in the street below. From Joseph Swan, Selected views of Glasgow and its Environs *(Glasgow: Joseph Swan, 1828), 66–67.*

It has been suggested that as the Lowlands industrialized men's social life came to focus increasingly on the all-male workshops and on the ale houses built beside them. The men employed in these workplaces only reluctantly left this social world to enter into marriage and resented any limitations it imposed. As a consequence, there was, in addition to higher levels of assault, an increase in casual relationships, abandonment, and illegitimate births among the labouring population of the city.[32] These industrial developments were in marked contrast to the domestic life experienced by the handloom weavers who worked at home and relied on the labour of their wives and children. For weavers, a family was crucial for success, and, as a consequence, they often sought marriage partners who were skilled and hard-working. The young women who entered the newly established cotton spinning factories, such as the Deanston Mill mentioned in the "Curious Letter," often came from textile-producing families. Their employment was essentially an extension of the family approach to work, reflected in John Gemmill's correspondence.[33] In this respect, the letter's cotton-mill lass, Jean, represents the ideal hard-working partner of the weaving family, but her accommodation of her visitors presents her as an understanding supporter of the emerging all-male social world focused on work and drink — thus she avoids the conflict of "Watty and Meg" and gains the high esteem of her husband's associates.

All three of the wives in the "Curious Letter" are presented as working in their homes, and the author suggested that a suitable wife was needed "for washing, sewing, knitting, carding and spinning, keeping a house in order, and … to bring up a family of bairns clean and decent." In this sense it echoed the idea that a women's proper place was in the family home. While it is possible to trace this notion in popular literature, by the 1820s very few labouring families in Scotland were able to have wives working solely in the household. A few textile workers do appear to have maintained the practice, but evidence drawn from the British census suggests that only families with several teenage or adult wage earners could afford the luxury of having a mother employed solely in housework.[34]

In the British Isles this "domestic ideal" was only readily attained by the middle class, but, as the "Curious Letter" indicated, a farm in the empire appeared to offer Scottish immigrant families the chance to achieve this goal — a further attraction for many weaving families in their distressed postwar circumstances. The vision represented in the "Curious Letter" of an Ottawa Valley settlement comprised of independent family households was apparently shared by the Colonial Office, since unaccompanied females were discouraged from departing to the colony at the outset. John Campbell had been sent explicit instructions on the subject in 1815. Single women were not to depart with the assisted emigrants unless they were the daughter or sister of a male settler. The Colonial Office excluded single women on the grounds that they were supposedly unsuited to the hard physical labour involved in establishing a pioneer settlement, but the policy also reflected deeply ingrained patriarchal attitudes. Campbell hinted at these when he suggested that it would not be "proper" for women to proceed to Upper Canada without the "protection" of a male relative. Nevertheless, the regulations recognized that women and their labour were needed in order for the settlement to succeed.[35]

Some of the letters to the Colonial Office from women left behind in Scotland during the assisted emigrations tended to reinforce the patriarchal idea that women required male accompaniment. Margaret Tait wrote to Earl Bathurst from Blackcraig, a farm near Newtown Stewart, in the summer of 1820, explaining that her husband Nathaniel had left for Upper Canada the year before and now had two hundred acres near Perth, but that she and her six children did not have the means to join him.

> I have been advised to apply to your lordship to request that you will have the goodness to direct me to be informed how I can proceed with and to applying for the allowance by Government that may enable me & my children to get to my husband — I humbly beg that your Lordship will pardon this presumption & comply with my request.[36]

Two years later, Sarah Nielson's letter to Earl Bathurst also presented herself and her young daughters, Janet and Margaret, as vulnerable in her husband's absence: "My husband, Robert Neilson, sailed last year with part of the family on the ship Commerce and as I now remain behind with two children, having sold what furniture I had with the view of sailing to Canada to him, and am in consequence doing nothing for my support." In order to ensure that her account would be accepted, Sarah Nielson had her letter endorsed by male authority figures, two elders from the Gorbals church she attended — Andrew Rankin and Thomas Murdoch.[37]

The importance placed on male "protectors" by the Colonial Office also appeared to be justified by cases that came to the attention of officials in Upper Canada. Jane Brown, a member of the Hopetown Bathgate Society who arrived in Upper Canada with her husband James Dick, found herself alone with her eleven children — six under the age of twelve — when her husband drowned in the Saint Lawrence River. It fell to her eighteen-year-old son, John, to inform his uncle, also John, a merchant who had remained in Scotland, of the tragic news. James Dick had two brothers, but since his brother William had died in Jamaica in 1803, John was the only one who remained alive in 1822. He would be the only one of five children not to predecease their parents when his sister Agnes died in 1826.

The family history illustrates the draw of Empire for Lowland artisans, but it also demonstrates the hazards of emigration for parents with young families. Jane Brown died a month after her husband, possibly from fever, and the family became objects of charity and the special project of Reverend Dr. Gemmill in Lanark and Reverend Bell in Perth. The two clergymen arranged for some of the youngest children to be placed in temporary foster homes until John Dick and his older siblings could clear their lot. The law stated that one had to be nineteen to hold land, but local pressure resulted in the regulation being waived. While her brother and several other members of the family were ill with fever, twenty-one-year-old Janet Dick arranged for neighbours to put up the first "house" on their father's Lanark Township lot.[38] Similar desperate circumstances faced Grizel "Grace" Wallace, who had emigrated with her husband James Craig as a member of the Barrowfield and Anderson Society, when James, a former collier, was killed by a falling tree in the spring of 1823. Her situation came to the attention of the governor general, Earl Dalhousie, when she wrote to him asking that she be granted the deed to Craig's lot in Dalhousie Township. The earl sent her five pounds on his own account, but was unable to transfer ownership since, in contrast to the accommodation shown to John Dick, Grace was informed that Upper Canadian law did not allow a widow to inherit the land directly but only to enjoy the use of it until an heir came of age. She was therefore unable to sell the lot and use the money to return to Scotland as she had hoped — leaving her and her two daughters in "a most deplorable predicament."[39]

Other letters sent back to Scotland also implied that women who were widowed in the colony found themselves unable to cope. A letter written by John Toshack, and reproduced in Robert Lamond's account of the assisted emigrations from Glasgow, was delivered by a Mrs. Graham who had lost her husband in the colony and returned to Scotland.[40] All the same, the ability of many women to run their pioneer homesteads while husbands were absent earning wages indicates that many were clearly able to manage without a husband's "protection." Andrew Boag, the author of another letter in Lamond's *Narrative*, died in 1830, and, according to the survey undertaken in 1834, his widow Mary was still on the Lanark Township lot raising her young children.[41]

Indeed, as Robert Forrest's letters reveal, some emigrant women travelled on their own back to Scotland for reasons other than personal tragedy. An exchange of letters between Forrest and his parents in Lanark was facilitated by his neighbour Marion "Minnie" Barrowman of the Bridgeton Transatlantic Society, who made a return visit to Scotland in 1824. Mrs. Barrowman undertook her solo journey in order to visit her eldest daughter, Margaret, who had remained behind when the family departed in 1820.[42] In addition, there is evidence in both Scotland and Upper Canada suggesting that many immigrant women were quite able to manage their own property. In a letter to Lord Dalhousie, Robert Lamond reported that Janet Bulloch, a member of the Bridgeton Canadian Emigration Society, had remained in Scotland in 1820 in order to dispose of a farm that she held "in her own right along with a sister." In Upper Canada, Malcolm Cameron's mother was also able to re-establish herself as an innkeeper in Perth after her husband died in 1822 at the tavern they ran together on the road to Lanark.[43]

As the widow of a respected elder in Reverend Bell's congregation, Euphemia Cameron (née McGregor) appears to have had little difficulty in conducting business, but women who combined boarding house and tavern-keeping were under far greater scrutiny than the women who remained on the settlement's farmsteads, fulfilling what was considered to be their natural domestic role. Although both men and women frequented Upper Canadian taverns, elaborate steps, such as the provision of separate rooms for accompanied females, were taken in order to ensure the "respectability" of both the patron and the proprietors.

Despite being frequented by conservative patrons, Montgomery's Tavern north of Toronto became associated with disorder when the 1837 rebels adopted it as their headquarters. As Mrs. Kippen's experience indicates, the rapid transformation of the reputation of a tavern could occur as a consequence of far more trivial incidents. From Charles Lindsay, The Life and Times of William Lyon Mackenzie *(Toronto: P.R. Randall, 1862), Vol. II, 62.*

In contrast to the positive reputation enjoyed by Mrs. Cameron, Catherine Kippen drew the ire of the St. Andrews kirk session for apparently failing to keep a proper house. She first attracted the attention of the church elders for holding a ball on New Year's Day in 1838, and again on the same day the following year. The men of the session were concerned about the drunkenness witnessed at these occasions, but when Mrs. Kippen was questioned she stated that she saw "no evil in such things" and claimed that she had arranged the balls "to help make a living." In order to have her conform to their wishes and stop holding such events, the elders suspended her from the church and arranged for a private meeting with the minister. Under this intense pressure, Mrs. Kippen reneged and was restored to church privileges, only to have them withdrawn again after it was reported that she had "falling people drunk in her house on Sabbath day." To the male elders, Catherine Kippen's behaviour was unacceptable, but her defence to the session reveals the awkward position in which independent immigrant women could be placed if they lost their "respectable" status. The record of her testimony stated:

> ... these men came into her house in a state of intoxication and insisted on getting liquor and that for peace she had given them a glass each in order to get rid of them. The Session considering that repeated complaints have been made against Mrs. Kippen as to various irregularities in her house at different times resolved to withhold a token from her at present till this matter is farther investigated.[44]

Since they were unable to "substantiate the truth" of the claims against her, Catherine Kippen was restored again on December 7, 1839, but her repeated conflicts with the St. Andrews elders undoubtedly undermined any claims that she had to "respectability" in the community.

The need for "respectability" was shared by both men and women and was behind one of the most celebrated episodes in the early history of the Ottawa Valley settlement. On June 3, 1833, Ebenezer Wilson's son, John, shot and killed fellow law student Robert Lyon in an "affair of honour" that has become part of Ontario folklore — memorialized in Perth with the "Last Duel Park" on the site of the contest. John Wilson had left Paisley with his parents in 1821, but, unlike his elder half-brother David, did not remain in North Sherbrooke to farm. He was instead sent to the District Grammar School in Perth to complete his education. There he joined Reverend Bell's congregation, and, after a brief stint as a schoolteacher, articled with James Boulton. Robert Lyon, who was born in Inverurie, Aberdeenshire, left Scotland to join his elder brother George sometime after the former officer with the 99th Regiment of Foot settled at the Richmond depot in Carleton County. George Lyon then used his wife's family connections to have his younger brother articled with one of Boulton's rivals, Thomas Radenhurst. The duel between the two young men — Wilson was twenty-three and Lyon was nineteen at the time of the contest — has frequently been attributed to the baneful influence of Perth's retired officers by both contemporaries and later chroniclers.

While duelling, despite its illegality, was frequently used to settle disputes between high-ranking military men throughout the Empire, in Upper Canada such contests primarily arose out of a perceived need to defend a professional reputation, and lawyers far outnumbered soldiers in the documented cases. Indeed, Wilson claimed that his reputation had been damaged when Lyon "knocked him down" in public, and that the only way he could recover his standing was to issue a challenge. In his subsequent trial, witnesses suggested that Wilson's relatively humble origins made him more sensitive to such "insults," and it is clear that in order to advance his subsequent legal and political career he deliberately aligned himself with the colonial elite. He eventually returned to the reforming politics of his father, but as a young man Wilson believed that his prospects depended upon an unblemished reputation among Perth's elite, which included Alexander McMillan and Alexander Thom, who had fought their own duel the previous winter.[45] Although a sensitivity to status undoubtedly played a role in both the Wilson-Lyon and the McMillan-Thom contests, notions of proper female behaviour were ultimately behind both exchanges.

While McMillan had reacted to the respectability of his wife being questioned because of her previous position as a servant in his household, Wilson had become embroiled in a complicated contest for the attention of Elizabeth Hughes, a recently arrived schoolteacher from England, that resulted in questions being raised about her "character." As part of that intrigue, Wilson had repeated claims made by Robert Lyon that Miss Hughes had allowed him physical contact "which no woman of spirit would permit" in a letter to her employer and protector Gideon Ackland. It was this communication that provoked Lyon's assault and ultimately led to the fatal duel, but the consequences were not limited to that exchange of pistol shots. The trial, which resulted in the acquittal of Wilson, was widely reported, and it appears that the reputation of Ackland's school suffered and had to close. In 1835 Ackland relocated to St. Thomas to practise law, with Elizabeth accompanying him. Wilson also had to relocate, settling in nearby London, and, in 1835, he married Elizabeth Hughes in an obvious

Almost from the day it occurred, the scene of the Wilson-Lyon duel became a pilgrimage site for visitors to Perth. The Perth Museum currently houses the pistol set that was purportedly used in the contest.

Photo by M. Vance.

bid to reclaim "respectability" for them both.[46] The concern with "respectability," however, went well beyond the social circles of John Wilson and can clearly be detected in the townships where the emigration society members settled.

The Ramsay kirk session minutes record a complaint made by John and Daniel Galbraith against David Smith, whom they claimed had falsely stated that he "had a criminal connection" with their sister Margaret and that "in giving an account of his conduct with her, he had used a great deal of licentious language." Both the Galbraith and Smith families had been members of the Glasgow Canadian Society, had travelled together onboard the *George Canning*, and had settled on neighbouring lots in the township. It would appear that David Smith may have been trying to tease his boyhood companions, but the Galbraith brothers took the jest seriously, as did the Ramsay elders. Smith was admonished on three separate occasions for his "slander" and "language unbecoming a Christian."[47]

What all of these disputes shared was an underlying patriarchal assumption that women required male protection. One wonders what the women themselves thought of their would-be champions' behaviour, but both duelling and the exercise of church discipline were undertaken exclusively by men, to whom women's opinions were not considered relevant in determining a course of action. While churchmen were deeply opposed to duelling, the kirk session of Ramsay and the Perth combatants shared a view of society that placed women in a subservient and submissive role. Indeed, the emigrant correspondence examined in this chapter reveals that Scottish immigrants, regardless of social status, had already formed these attitudes prior to their departure from the homeland. It has been argued that in the British Isles it was the middle class that firmly embraced the "separate spheres" vision of society, but the letters sent from the Ottawa Valley, both real and imaginary, strongly suggest that this patriarchal ideal was also embraced by Scottish artisans.[48] Land in the empire provided the opportunity to realize the ideal, however the letters home also make it clear that women's work was vital in making the colony a success — just as it had been vital for labouring families in Scotland. Yet despite their importance, women were expected to defer to men and those who left the settler homestead to work in service, or those who ran their own businesses, faced tremendous scrutiny from a society that had become increasingly preoccupied with female "respectability" regardless of social status. In this regard, the experience of the women whose labour enabled the colonization of land claimed by the British Empire anticipated that of the Scotswomen who remained in the imperial homeland.

Chapter Seven

RECALLING AND RETELLING

Reverend William Bell was a dedicated diarist. Over the course of his lifetime he compiled seventeen volumes that range from his earliest memories to his daily activities in both Scotland and Upper Canada. These "journals" provide a detailed picture of daily life in the immigrant community, and are frequently cited by those who have written about the pioneer settlement. Diaries and journals are, however, deeply personal documents and by their very nature give a very particular slant on past events.[1] Because he left such a valuable archive, Reverend Bell's interpretation of events has tended to dominate the histories of Lanark County, which the clergyman likely would have been gratified by. The journals appear to have been written with posterity in mind, and show the signs of having been rewritten and reworked later in life. Short initial entries were often later embellished in order to make a moral judgment about the event in question.

On Sunday February 1, 1824, Bell made a short entry indicating that a sick indigenous woman, along with her infant, two other children, and elderly female companion, had been taken by John Robson to Mrs. Cameron's inn to allow the woman to recover her health. The story was later rewritten in order both to give Bell a much greater role in the events and to illustrate several lessons. A lack of Christian charity was apparent in the inaction of the town wardens, but the uncivilized nature of the original inhabitants was also criticized on several fronts. The woman's refusal to allow herself to be bled was a reflection of "the Indians ... great aversion to surgical operations," presumably a consequence of superstition, but more troubling still was the fact that when she recovered other "Indians" came to visit them with "spirits with which they got drunk." Bell was a stern critic of alcohol abuse by settlers as well, but the trouble, in this case, had originated with the First Nation's "usual employment of hunting in the woods." According to Bell, it was this activity that had resulted in the sick woman being left in a "wigwam" near the town, where she would "probably perish if not brought to some shelter." Shelter that only the colonists possessed.[2]

Reverend Bell's retelling of this encounter reflects several features of the narrative recalling the Scottish settlement in the Ottawa Valley that emerges during the course of the nineteenth century. The first is the focus on male figures, in this case Bell himself, and the under-estimation

A detail from William Henry Bartlett's Wigwam in the Forest *showing a seated First Nations woman with her infant cradled behind her.*

Courtesy of Killam Library, Dalhousie University.

of female efforts. Indeed, in the rewritten version Bell uses the tale to chastise his imaginary female readers, "soft and delicate dames who sit on carpets in comfortable apartments," while underplaying the charity of Euphemina Cameron who actually took care of the Native woman and children.[3] The second is an emphasis of the pioneers' heroic struggle to carve a settlement out of the wild and unfamiliar forest. In contrast to the First Nations, who merely "wander the woods," the colonists settle and tame the land, despite initial fear and trepidation. In the same volume, Bell provides a detailed description of the fear that the forest generated for a lost anonymous Glasgow family, stating that "[b]its of rotten wood around them had assumed the appearance of fire but their terror made them believe that they were the glaring eyes of wild animals."[4]

Robert Forrest suggested a possible origin for such fears, stating in a letter to his parents in Scotland that the idea they had "of this country" was "perfectly wrong" and that while settlers had hardships "those you speak of are none of them — Indian, bears, wolfs, snakes and ugly reptiles does well enough to frighten the Credulous at home who are willing to believe everything put in print about Canada." He added that "[t]hese accounts answers another purpose[,] it swells the pages of those Vagabonds who must write something wonderful to astonish the people and make their Books sell."[5]

While Reverend Bell might have objected to Robert Forrest's claim, his own *Hints for Emigrants*, written as a series of letters, had appealed to the same audience that would read travellers' accounts, like John MacTaggart's *Three Years in Canada*, or see William Henry Bartlett's illustrations in Nathaniel Willis's *Canadian Scenery*. Tales of encounters with exotic, wild environments, like those found in the backwoods of Upper Canada, were what British publishers were seeking, and Bell's rewritten journals could have also been intended for that market.

It also appears that John McDonald's often cited pamphlet *Narrative of a Voyage to Quebec, And Journey From Thence to New Lanark in Upper Canada* was designed for this audience at the outset — as indicated by its subtitle: *Detailing the Hardships and Difficulties which an Emigrant has to Encounter before and after His Settlement: With An Account of the Country, As it Regards Its Climate, Soil and Actual Condition of the*

Inhabitants.[6] This was reinforced by the introduction, that claimed readers would find "a faithful and impartial account of the hardships through which our unhappy and deluded countrymen are doomed to pass, the privations they must undergo, the sufferings they must endure, with the deplorable consequences resulting from these, before they can be settled in their cold, comfortless, and solitary log-house." While the *Narrative*, purportedly based upon a "diary or journal" kept by McDonald, did indeed provide factual information, its style was in keeping with the contemporary romantic literary conventions, which tended to emphasize the dramatic and unusual. This is seen clearly in McDonald's description of the bird life of Upper Canada:

> Black birds are to be seen in the woods, but they have no song like those of Scotland. Indeed there are no feathered songsters of the groves, as at home, nor is the lark ever heard warbling delightful melody as it ascends to the sky. — Your ears are never saluted whilst traversing the Canadian woods, with the delightful and varied notes of the winged choristers. No sound of music is ever heard there, but a melancholy death-like stillness reigns through the forests, except when they are agitated by the tempest or the storm.[7]

McDonald's prose emulated that found in contemporary novels, which were also often written as a series of letters or journals, but his *Narrative* and Bell's *Hints* did more that echo the prevailing romantic style — they also helped to establish the ocean voyage, the impassable colonial roads, and the forest as severe trials with which individual pioneer settlers had to battle. This was reinforced by the personal recollections of Scottish emigrants that began to appear in local newspapers by the 1860s. By the turn of the century, these accounts were supplemented by the boyhood recollections of those who had arrived in the colony as children. In 1892, one anonymous author, who incorrectly identified his emigrant vessel as the *Govan Cannon* rather than the *George Canning*, provided the following account of the departure:

On the second day out, all hands took the last linger-
ing look at the blue mountains of Auld Scotland, and
on the third day, a little gale sprang up, the ship rolled
badly, and sea sickness set in when vomiting was the
order of the day. There was much grumbling amongst
the women, but after a few days the sickness began to
wear off, although there were some who got sick every
little gale that blew.[8]

The romanticized "last look" found in many accounts had also been
captured in several famous Victorian paintings like John Watson Nicol's
Lochaber No More. The author's depiction of the emigrant women as
weak, complaining dependents was also reflected in earlier accounts, like
Reverend Bell's. In contrast, the men were represented as embracing the
challenges presented. An account, written in 1901, of the life of William
Lang, the son of the Paisley Townhead Society member Arthur Lang,
was typical:

... the women and children of the party were left while
the heads of the families went out into the almost path-
less forest in search of land upon which to locate....
People of today can form very little idea of what that
journey was like — through woods and swamps, over
fallen trees and rocky ridges, beset by myriads of good
healthy mosquitoes, and loaded with provisions and
accoutrements necessary for the trip ... [Arthur Lang
selected lot 14 on the tenth line in Ramsay] ... A little clearing was made and a log shanty with a roof of
scooped out logs was built and made ready by Mr.
Lang for the coming of his family. It was a rude shelter to bring them to, but it was to be home to them,
and "home" to those people under such circumstances
meant a great deal more than it does to many today who
live in affluence and dwell in palatial residences.[9]

Since most of the published personal recollections were from Scotsmen, the newspapers, often themselves published by Scots and their descendents, reinforced the notion that their countrymen had played a disproportionate, and, indeed, critical role in the colonization of the district. As early as 1877, a history of Lanark County, published in Ottawa, made this explicit:

> ... the fame of the fertile tract of land on which the "fair town of Perth" now stands, had travelled abroad, and reached the ears of some canny Scots, and with the fore-thought of their race, Joshua-like, they sent out scouts into the promised land, and these returned with such favorable reports, that in 1815 a large number of families left Scotland and settled in 1816 on what is now called the "Scotch Line" ... forming as it were, a little trans-Atlantic Scotland, a peaceful, thrifty, and industrious community, who, in after years, by their own handiwork, and almost unassisted, built up for themselves and their posterity independencies.[10]

A short history of the village of Balderson, five miles north of Perth, went further and linked the origin of the settlers with the "conquest" of the land. After noting the contribution of the English soldier Sergeant John Balderson, along with a few other early arrivals, the history claimed that

> ... [t]he great bulk of the rest of the first settlers ... were from the Highlands of Scotland, chiefly from Perthshire ... they fought a stern but successful battle with the wild forest and the forces of nature and though the battle was long and stubborn in the end they won a splendid victory and their sons and their son's sons are to-day reaping the fruits of that victory.[11]

The Balderson history appeared in a special issue of the *Perth Courier* published in 1905 to commemorate the town's first "Old Boys

Reunion." While the contribution of "some English and Scottish gentle-men" to the establishment of the settlement was noted in a "History of Old Perth and the Perth District" in the same issue, that article, along with others in the paper, did not dwell on the collective contribution of Scots, but instead focused on individual accomplishments. These served to reinforce the success of the town itself. According to one writer, Perth's modern development had begun when the town had secured a branch line of the railway, which would bring the "Old Boys" home from across North America. The exact site of the Wilson-Lyon duel was mentioned as a point of interest for the visitors, anticipating more recent tourist promotions, but it held equal status with Otty Lake, a scene of natural beauty, and "the phosphate, plumbago and mica mines," a reflection of the region's industrial development.

This new story of modernization and industrial progress was repeated at "Old Boys" reunions held throughout the Upper Ottawa Valley in the opening decades of the twentieth century, and probably appeared natu-ral to the "Old Boys" themselves, who had used the railway to leave the region to help colonize the North American west or to pursue profes-sional careers.[12] The reunions sought to reflect their experience, rather than that of their parents and grandparents. Nevertheless, echoes of the earlier settlement story were still apparent. As late as 1936, the Winnipeg solicitor J.G. Harvey, in an address to the to the city's Lanark Old Timers Association, would claim that the first pioneers had "made the uninhab-ited wilderness a place of habitation, and where only wild animals had roamed, the laughter of children was heard. These settlers came, men and women, from a civilized well-settled country, with all its conveniences, and took possession of the wilderness and conquered it."[13]

J.G. Harvey's complete dismissal of the original inhabitants was not reflected in all accounts of the Ottawa Valley's history, but when mem-bers of First Nations were discussed they were marginalized. A 1916 article marking Perth's centenary, published in the *Courier*, acknowl-edged that "the Cree Indians" had used and frequented "the prolific wilds in the vast expanse of this part of Ontario," and that they had "left their marks of occupation on the shores of Otty, Rideau, Christy, Dalhousie and Mississippi ... in the way of pottery, flint arrow heads, stone implements of war, hunting and domestic use ... now in the collections of antiquarian fanciers, in the museums, or in a hundred private houses in the community." But the article firmly placed these individuals in the past, and suggested that their main contribution to the settler community was to teach the newcomers how to make maple syrup.[14] At times the "Old Boy" reunions made reference to the original Indian "camps" and "wigwams," but only in order to contrast the wild nature of life before the colonists brought "civilization" and "progress." This was made explicit in the historical pageant performed at the Pembroke reunion in 1928. During that program, the audience was treated to a scene in which the children of a pioneer family camped in the woods are terrorized when the father goes off to hunt for dinner and the mother goes to a nearby creek to wash clothes:

> A girl of six and a boy of five, are happy in their play around the campfire, little realising the danger of a nearby tribe of savage Indians who are sneaking and crawling, upon the camp. With one blood curdling yell, the Indians kidnap the girl and scalp the boy, leaving his limp body as mute evidence of their visit.[15]

There is no evidence that any such event ever occurred in Ontario. Instead, at the time the Pembroke pageant was being performed First Nations' communities were marginalized on reserves, denied the opportunity to pursue their hunting and fishing rights guaranteed in earlier treaties, and actually having their children taken from them and placed in residential schools. The widespread popularity of the "savage Indian" stereotype, along with the associated "captivity" story, overrode the actual experience of aboriginal-settler relations in the region. Nevertheless, stories of "Indians" taking women and girls as captives first became popular during the Seven Years War and continued to be widely circulated during the nineteenth century. These tales appear to have been behind the Pembroke pageant scene, and may have been responsible for the fear of indigenous peoples exhibited by some of Scottish emigrants.[16]

The view from the Mississippi River looking east toward Green Landing on the left-hand shore. This wide tranquil portion of the river made it an ideal stopping point for camping and trade.

Photo by M. Vance.

William Lang's boyhood recollections of an early encounter reflected the apprehension. According to the 1901 newspaper account of Lang's life, as the family journeyed down Mississippi Lake on the way to their land grant "they stopped at an island, and while preparing a meal a big Indian hove in sight coming towards the camp in majestic strides."

> Instantly stories of blood-thirsty doings of these wily savages flashed across the minds of the company and fear filled every heart. Equal to the occasion, however, was the late John Steele, who was one of the party, and he seized a huge loaf of bread and presented it to the Indian as an evidence of their friendly intentions. The peace offering was not accepted, and the Indian passed by on his way to his camp on another part of the island and paid no attention to them, but they breathed easier when he was out of sight.[17]

Once again a male settler, John Steele, is presented as the hero of the narrative facing down another pioneering "danger," but as the article recognized this was not reality but fiction. Captivity stories circulating in Scotland also appear to have influenced the reaction of the wife of Paisley weaver Hugh Adam to the presence of indigenous people in the settlement. According to a local oral tradition in North Sherbrooke, the couple arrived from Scotland in the 1850s and took up a land grant in neighbouring Palmerston Township known as the "Indian lot." The land bordered the Mississippi River and a camping site known as "Green Landing" that was used by the First Nations on a seasonal basis. Occasionally, travellers would come to the Adam's house to trade "beadwork, venison, furs and fish" for "meat and potatoes." According to one account, "Mrs Adam was scared of these Indians, not only for her own sake, but because of her children. When she would see the Indians coming, she would have one of the older children take the young ones into a back bedroom out of sight, as it was heard that the Indians were not averse to stealing babies." As a consequence of this "fear," the Adams traded lots with James and Elizabeth Miller, who had been among the original Scottish settlers of North Sherbrooke.[18]

The North Sherbrooke oral tradition provides a glimpse of another story that has been neglected as a consequence of the heroic pioneer narrative that dominated the early accounts of the region; that is, the story of the indigenous response to these imperial immigrants from Scotland. According to the Adam's daughter, Ethel Adam Linton, indigenous peoples continued to make use of their traditional waterway and landing place right up to the end of the nineteenth century.[19] As Reverend Bell noted much earlier, Native peoples kept on hunting and trading in the region, despite being displaced by the arrival of the newcomers who not only occupied the land but deforested large portions of it. But even when it was no longer possible to use the land in traditional ways, First Nations people did not "disappear" as many accounts implied.

The family history of Annie McInnis, who in 1890 settled with her husband Solomon Benedict on a farm in Pembroke Township near North Sherbrooke, illustrates both the continuing Native influence in the region and the intimate relationships that could develop between people of indigenous and settler origins. Annie was of "Scottish descent" while Solomon was connected to the Abenaki Odanak Reserve east of Montreal. While her husband was listed as a farmer in their marriage record, he had lost an arm in a hunting accident and made his living stripping ash for basket makers on the Odanak Reserve. In addition to supporting this growing Native economy based upon the demand for "traditional" handicrafts, the family were all skilled in traditional healing. Solomon's grandmother had been a medicine woman and Annie's daughter Lila used this inherited knowledge to help treat community members in North Sherbrooke. She also aided Dr. Kerr, the physician in McDonald's Corners, as a midwife, and her sister Adele would become a professionally trained nurse. Annie McInnis' family thus bridged the Native and non-Native societies by maintaining traditional practices and regional connections while also participating in "modern" health care.[20]

The heroic pioneer story that emerged in the nineteenth century largely ignored experiences of people like Solomon and Annie Benedict. It downplayed the role of the imperial state, and its institutions, in making colonial settlement possible in the first place, and drew attention away from the daily interaction between peoples in the settlement. Scotsmen were given a privileged place in the pioneer pantheon, and the patriarchal assumptions brought from the imperial homeland resulted in the experiences of women being discounted. But genealogical research is continuing to uncover the history of families and individuals like Annie McInnis, and we are beginning to revise the older story and understand in much greater detail the consequences of this particular episode of imperial immigration for one corner of the former British Empire.

The figures in William Henry Bartlett's engraving Canoe Building at Papper's Island, on the Ottawa River *appear to be dressed in both First Nations and European influenced clothing. This melding of cultures was also reflected in the birchbark canoes, an indigenous craft that was readily adopted by the settlers. From* Canadian Scenery, *Vol. I, 10.*

Appendix I

RIDEAU PURCHASE SUPPLEMENT

"Return showing the present scale of Annual Presents made to Chiefs of the Mississauga tribes of Bay of Quinty and Kingston and additional proposed to be made in account of the surrender of land agreed for in 1819 — and commonly called the Rideau purchase."

Present Scale		**Proposed Addition**	
298 lbs	Ball & Shot	31 pairs	Arm Bands (silver)
34	Blankets of 1 point	300 pairs	Ear bobs (silver)
36	Blankets of 1 ½ point	500	Brooches (silver)
40	Blankets of 2 point	9	Blankets 1 point
112	Blankets of 2 ½ point	9	Blankets 1 ½ point
98	Blankets of 3 point	10	Blankets 2 point
49 yards	Broad cloth	20	Blankets 2 ½ point
76 yards	Caddis	20	Blankets 3 point
324 yards	Calicoe	6 cwt	Ball & Shot
50 yards	Irish linen	180 yards	Bath Coating
98 yards	Stroud	196 yards	Calicoe
76 yards	Striped Cotton	37 yards	Broad cloth
34 yards	Embossed Serge	82 yards	Striped Cotton
62 yards	Flannel	20 dozen	Horn Combs
34 yards	Ratteen	21 dozen	Ivory Combs
131 yards	Molton	140 yards	Flannel
22	Fish lines	228 lbs	Gun Powder
200	Fish hooks	10	Chief guns
250	Sewing needles	14	Common guns
5 lbs	Sewing thread	7	Plain Hats
62	Butcher knives	180 lbs	Brass Kettles
800	Gun flints	50 yards	Irish Linen
100 lbs	Gun Powder	144	Looking glasses

Present Scale *(cont...)*		**Proposed Addition** *(cont...)*	
3	laced hats	84 yards	Molton
71	plain hats	84 yards	Ratteen
230 lbs	Tobacco	8 groce	Hunters Pipes
180 lbs	Brass Kettles	6 pieces	Ribbon
30 lbs	Copper Kettles	175 yards	Stroud
1 ½ ?	Tin Kettles	3 lbs	Sewing Thread
-	-	1 piece	Russia [shirting?]
-	-	181 yards	Osnaburgs
-	-	4 dozen	Clasp knives
-	-	3 dozen	Scissors
-	-	6 dozen	Silk handkerchiefs
-	-	112 lbs	Tobacco
-	-	3 groce	Silk renneting
-	-	1000	Sewing needles
-	-	150 yards	Embossed Serge
-	-	5lbs	Beads
-	-	10 groce	Hawk Bells

Total value 642/10 /0

£ / s /p

Archibald Kennedy Johnson, Indian Department, Fort George, 1st May, 1820, Secretary for Indian Affairs

[Also signed by:]
William Claus, Deputy Superintendent General for Upper Canada.
Joseph Brant Clench, Indian Department.
John Johnson, Superintendent General & Inspector General of Indian Affairs.

Source: LAC, RG8, Vol. 263, p. 194 (micro-film C-2854).

List of Mississauga leaders appended to the final Rideau Purchase Treaty
— November 28, 1822.

Nawacamigo

Antenewayway

Kabratsiwaybiyebe [Kabiatsiwaybegebe]

Wabakeek [Wobukeek]

Shewitagan [Shiwitagon]

Nawaquarkecom [Nawakeshecom]

Shawandais [Shawondaise]

Pejehejeck [Kakekijick]

Papewan [Papiwom]

Wabeckeneme [Wobekenense]

Nagansaway [Nongonseway]

Shebeshe[e]

Naiquakan [Nakawagan]

Wabanzick [Wabosek]

[ ] = *spelling given on May 31, 1819 treaty.*

Source: *Indian Treaties and Surrenders from 1680 to 1890*, Vol. I (Ottawa: 1891), 63, 65.

Appendix II

SERGEANT SIMON GRAY'S DISCHARGE PAPERS

HIS MAJESTY's 4th Royal Veteran Battalion, whereof General LOWTHER LORD MUNCASTER is Colonel.

THESE are to certify, that *Simon Gray Sergeant* in *Captain John Jenkins* Company in the Regiment aforesaid: born in the Parish of *Inverness* in, or near the Town of *Inverness* in the Country of *Inverness hath* served in the said Regiment for the Space of *four* Years and *one hundred twenty three* Days, as likewise in other Corps, according to the following Statement, but in consequence of *the Battalion being ordered to be disbounded~Being wounded in action is Right hand & Leg in the island of Grenada W.I. 8th April 1795~and is desirous of residing in Canada until the decision of the Commissioners of Chelsea is known.*

is considered unfit for further Service Abroad, and is proposed to be discharged; and has been ordered to remain in *Quebec* ~~Canada~~ until his case may be finally determined on, having first received all just Demands of Pay, Clothing, &c. from his entry into the said Regiment, to the Date if this Discharge, as appears by the Receipt on the Back hereof, [except*] *and that he has no Claims, whatever one the 4th Royal Veteran Battalion*

And to prevent any improper Use being made of this Discharge, by its failing into other Hands, the following is a Description of the said *Simon Gray* He is about *Sixty One* Years of Age, is *five* Feet *9* Inches in height, *Brown* Hair, *Grey* Eyes, *Swarthy* Complexion, and by Trade a *Labourer.*

*Any Claims reserved for Investigation at Home, are to be here specified; if none. Care must be taken that the Blank is filled up with the following Words, viz. "and that he has no Claim whatever upon the Regiment."

STATEMENT OF SERVICE

In what Corps	Period		Serjeant Major.		Qr. Mnst. Serjeant		Serjeant.		Corporal.		Trump or Drummer		Private.		Total Service.		In East or West Indies included in the aforegoing total.	
	From	To	Yrs	Dys	Yrs	Dys	Yrs	Dys	Yrs	Dys	Yrs	Dys	Yrs	Dys	Yrs	Dys	Yrs	Dys
68th Foot	1775 1st May	1803 24th Sept					12		3		Dolleys 2		11	208	32	25	W 7	
R. Nfdland	1803 25th Sept	1812 26th May					8	242							8	242		
4th RVB	1812 25th May	1816 24th Sept					4	123							4	123		
Total							25		3		2		11	208	45	25	7	

Given under my Hand and Seal of the Regiment at *Quebec* the *Seventh* Day of *January* 1817

Wllm Macpherson Commanding *Officer*
Lt. Col (late 4th R. V. Bn)

I certify that the above mentioned _____ is unfit for further Service. ___ Day of _____ 18___

In Consquence of the above, _____ is hereby Discharged. ___ Day of _____ 18___ Commandant.

I *Simon Gray* do acknowledge I have received all my Clothing, Pay, Arrears of Pay, and all just Demands whatsoever, from the Time of my enlisting in the Regiment mentioned on the other side, to this Day of my Discharge, / vide / *24ᵗʰ September 1816,*

his
Simon X Gray
mark

As witness my Hand this *Seventh* Day of *January* 1817
Witness   Saml Brazier
             Segt Major 4 R.V.Bn.

I do hereby certify that the Cause of which has rendered it necessary to discharge the within-mentioned *Sergeant Simon Gray* as stated on the opposite side, has not arisen from Vice of Misconduct, and that he is not, to my Knowledge, incapacitated by the sentence of a General Court Martial from receiving his Pension. *His General Character is* very good & is highly Recommended

Surgeon   *Wllm Macpherson* Commanding *Officer*
             Lt. Col (late 4th R. V. Bn)

N.B. *When a Soldier has lost an Eye of Limb, or has been wounded or disabled in the Service; the Discharge must particularly express the*

Cause from whence proceeding, as when, where, and how it took place. Should any mark remain in consequence, it is to be noticed in the Man's description; the Surgeon, or Assistant Surgeon in his absence, will sign his Name in the Margin, opposite the Cause assigned for the Discharge being granted, which will be considered the Commanding Officer's Certificate above. The Period of Service in the Body of Discharge, *is to filled up in* Words at length, *and in Figures. Service* prior to the Age of Eighteen, *is not to be included in the within Statement.*

Appendix III

LIST OF 1815 ASSISTED SCOTTISH EMIGRANTS SETTLED IN LANARK COUNTY

The following list has been compiled by comparing the Ship Lists [National Archives (UK) CO385/2 ff.3-26] with Upper Canadian Land Records (Library and Archives Canada R11465-0-3-E). Township names have been abbreviated as follows: **B**=Bathurst; **BR**=Burgees; **D**=Drummond; **E**=Elmsley. This list can be compared to the full ship list published in Campey, *Scottish Pioneers of Upper Canada*, Appendix I, 191–96.

Name	Former Trade or occupation	Residence in Scotland	Original Concession & Lot #
John Flood [Ire. 34] *wife* Janet McKechnie [30] & 2 ch. [15,2]	Farmer & Weaver	Anderston [Glasgow]	B C1 W23
Samuel Purdie [45] *wife* Isobel McKechnie [32]	Wright	West Calder [Midlothian]	B C1 E12
Hugh McKay [33] *wife* Betty Ross [35] & 5 ch. [11,8,6,5,9m]	Farmer & Weaver	Gorbals [Glasgow]	E C10 W29
Alexander McFarlane [33] *wife* Ann McCulloch [36] & 7 ch. [10,8,7,5,3,18m,6m]	Labourer [farmer]	Kilbirnie [Ayrshire]	BR C10 E1
John Brash [34] *wife* Catherine McLean [27] & 3 ch. [7,4,6m]	Plowman [labourer]	Port Dundas [Glasgow]	BR C10 E3
Archibald Morrison [28]	Farmer [servant]	Glasgow	E C10 W4
John Christie [24] *wife* Isobel Wright [20]	Farmer	Primrose [Kincardine]	B C2 W4

William Old [33] *wife* Agnes Brakenridge[37] & 5 ch. [10,9,4,2,9m]	Labourer [farmer]	Canongate [Edinburgh]	**B** C1 E20
John Miller [21]	Labourer	Restonbell [Berwickshire]	**BR** C10 W4
George Wilson [56] *wife* Isobel Wilson [43] & 7 ch. [15,14,12,10,5,2,6m]	Farmer [labourer]	Glencapelquay [Dumfries]	**B** C1 E16
Thomas Barber [35] *wife* Janet Hannah [35] & 4 ch. [8,6,3, 8m]	Tailor [labourer]	Torthorwold [Dumfriesshire]	**BR** C10 W8
James McLaren [39] *wife* Euphemia Jamieson [33] & 6 ch. [15,12,10,8,5,2]	Weaver [labourer]	Callander [Perthshire]	**E** C10 E28
James MacDonald [37] *wife* Margaret McDonald [37] & 4 ch. [11,9,6,2]	Blacksmith [private soldier]	Edinburgh	**BR** C10 W1
John Allan [24]	Labourer	Cockburnspath [Berwick]	**B** C1 W25
Francis Allan [22] *wife* Janet Cowie [17] & 1 ch. [9m]	Teacher [labourer]	Edinburgh	**B** C1 W20
Thomas. Cuddie [22] *wife* Marion Fiffe [20]	Gardener [labourer]	Corstophine [Edinburgh]	**B** C1 W26
John Ferguson [50] *wife* Catherine McIntyre [42] & 7 ch. [17,15,13,11,9,7,4]	Farmer [labourer]	Callander [Perthshire]	**B** C1 E23
James Taylor [46] *wife* Margaret Cowie [44] & 5 ch. [19,17,11,9,7]	Labourer & Dyer	Carnwath [Lanarkshire]	**E** C10 W1
Thomas Borrie [38] *wife* Agnes [Whale ?] [Eng. 36] & 9 ch. [17,15,14,12,10,8.6,3,18m]	Shoemaker [labourer]	Dundee [Angus]	**B** C1 E8
John Campbell Kerr [22]	Saddler [labourer]	Edinburgh	**B** C1 E21
John Simpson [45] *wife* Margaret Petrie [38] & 5ch. [13,11,9,6,2]	Shoemaker [labourer]	Rothes [Morayshire]	**B** C1 E26

John Halliday [37] *wife* Margaret Johnston [33] & 7 ch. [12,11,9,8,4,3,1]	Schoolmaster [farmer]	Hatton [Dumfriesshire]	**BR** C10 A
Robert Wood [33] *wife* Helen Scott [30] & 3 ch. [9,7,5]	Farmer	Inverkeithing [Fife]	**D** C3 E7
David Oliphant [45] *wife* Clementina McKenzie[39] & 3 ch. [17,15,12]	Printer & Labourer	Leith	**B** C1 E25
Robert Gardner [32]	Farmer [labourer]	Paisley	**BR** C10 E4
John Ritchie [47] *wife* Janet Luke [42] & 9 ch. [21,19,17,13,12,10,7,5, 1m]	Blacksmith [labourer]	Fintry [Stirlingshire]	**B** C1 E10
John Hay [32]	Labourer	St. Vigeans [Angus]	**B** C1 E19
John McLeod [42] *wife* Janet Campbell [33]	Labourer [soldier]	Glasgow	**B** C1 E13
John Ferrier [31] *wife* Charlotte McGlasham [36] & 4 ch. [9,5,2,3m]	Labourer & Weaver	Dumbartonshire	**BR** C10 W7
Abraham Ferrier [33] *wife* Christian [Rowat ?] [38] & 4 ch. [10,8,5,18m]	Labourer & Weaver	Glasgow	**BR** C10 E8
James Miller [48] *wife* Mary [Friend ?] [38] 3 ch. [12,7, 21m]	Farmer [sailor]	West Kilbride [Ayrshire]	**BR** C9 lot A
Thomas McLean [23]	Mason [labourer]	Dunscore [Dumfriesshire]	**E** C6 W23
John McDonald [28] *wife* Christian Campbell [27] & 2 ch. [2, 6m]	Mason [labourer]	Killin [Perthshire]	**E** C3 S14
Alexander McDonald [brother of John- 24] *wife* Marjory Campbell [22]	Mason [labourer]	Killin [Perthshire]	**B** C3 W18
John Oliver [40] *wife* Mary Munn [36] & 6 ch. [17,15,12,11,8,2]	Farmer [labourer]	Kilmarnock [Ayrshire]	**E** CR5 F21

William Rutherford [25]	Wright [labourer]	Liff [Angus]	**B** C1 W11
William Spalding [26] *brother* Alexander Spalding [15]	Mason [labourer]	Liff [Angus]	**BR** C10 W3
Wlliam McGillivray [38] *wife* Isobel McLean [32] & 6 ch. [11,10,8,6,4, 4m]	Labourer [farmer]	Barrowfield [Glasgow]	**BR** C10 E2
Donald McDonald [31] *wife* Ann Campbell [33] & 2 ch. [3, 1.5]	House Carpenter [labourer]	Killin [Perthshire]	**E** C4 E16
William Johnston [31] *wife* Janet Nicol [25] & 1 ch. [6]	Farmer	Stobotule [Peeblesshire]	**B** C1 W16
Thomas Scott [37] *wife* Janet Gardiner[26] & 2 ch. [5,2]	Labourer & Tailor	Tundergarth [Dumfriesshire]	**B** C1 W12
George Gray [60] *wife* Isobel Lessly [43] & 8 ch. [18,14,13,11,9,5,3, 1.5]	Farmer	Banff [Banffshire]	**B** C3 W21
Alexander Kidd [34] *wife* Christian White[34] & 7 ch.[10,9,8,6,5,3,1]	Cartwright	Blackburn [Edinburgh]	**B** C1 E18
Robert Gibson [54] *wife* Jean Greed [44] & 5 ch. [14, 9,7,5,3]	Stocking Weaver	Edinburgh	**B** C1 E15
Thomas Donaldson & *sister* Isobella Donaldson & 2 ch	Farmer	Kinglassie [Fife]	**E** C5 lot 22
David Donaldson {brother-in-law:} *wife* Jean Donaldson did not arrive in Perth.	Farmer	Kinglassie [Fife]	**E** C5 lot 23
Andrew Donaldson [brother of Thomas]	Farmer	Kinglassie [Fife]	**E** C4 lot 23
John Donaldson [brother of Thomas]	Farmer	Kinglassie [Fife]	**E** C3 SE22
James Donaldson [brother of Thomas]	Farmer	Kinglassie [Fife]	**E** C3 NE22

Appendix IV

NAMES, FAMILY DETAILS, AND ADDRESSES OF THE SIGNATORIES ON THE "PETITION OF THE OPERATIVE MANUFACTURERS OF PAISLEY, MAY 1820."

Name	Males	Females	Trade	Address
Andrew McLachland*	2	1	[weaver]	73 Causeyside St.
John Sproule	1	1	-	Abbey Parish
Daniel Murchie*	7	5	[weaver]	81 Causeyside St.
Mathew Jaap*	1	1	[weaver]	Smithhills
Nathaniel Ferguson*	2	6	[weaver]	Johnstone
John Greenlees	2	2	-	Lawn St.
David Robertson	2	2	-	6 Incle St.
Alexander Greenlees	2	2	-	6 Gauze St.
John Sommervile	2	-	-	George St.
Archibald Thorton	5	3	-	Dovesland
John Graham*	2	2	-	Lylesland
James Thomson	5	4	[weaver]	Carriagehill
John Whyte	3	1	-	38 Wells St.
David Smith	3	3	-	Maxwellton St.
Thomas Bridget*+	2	4	[weaver]	Williamsburgh
James Cowden[?]	3	2	-	Dovesland
James Keir	2	2	-	Dovesland
Malcolm McCallum*	2	4	[weaver]	13 Storie St.
William Leas*	3	3	[weaver]	Storie St.
Archibald McLain	2	5	-	Dovesland
Peter Stewart	4	1	-	52 High St.
James Pollock*	1	1	[baker]	34 High St.
David Carswell	8	2	-	Carriagehill
James Hill	4	2	-	26 Orchard St.
Grenelan[?] Fox	2	1	-	11 Incle St.

John McAll	1	2	-	14 Gauze St.
James Rowan*	3	2	[weaver]	Hill Foot
Neil Dunlop	2	1	-	Hill Foot
William Grant	2	2	-	71 Causeyside St.
James Robertson	3	5	-	15 Lawn St.
James Muir	3	1	-	Lylesland
Mathew Sprowl*	4	1	[weaver]	Lylesland
John Adam	1	1	-	Carriagehill
Michael Richmond*	1	3	[weaver]	Carriagehill
James Fleming	4	5	-	8 Thread St.
James Stephens	5	2	-	Williamsburgh
Thomas McMillan	2	1	-	8 Thread St.
Andrew Stewart	3	5	-	8 Thread St.
David Polson*	2	4	[weaver]	9 King St.
William Robertson*	5	5	[weaver]	15 Incle St.
Thomas Crookshanks	1	3	-	Incle St.
Alexander Ferguson*	3	6	[weaver]	Calside
Alexander Sloan	7	5	-	Dovesland
William Alison	3	3	-	Dovesland
John Miller*	5	5	[weaver]	Dovesland
Robert Lang*	4	2	[weaver]	13 Storie St.
Thomas Barr	2	2	-	1 Canal St.
Thomas McKutchen	2	3	-	Calside
John Allieson	1	1	-	79 Causeyside St.
Andrew Boyd	2	4	-	74 Causeyside St.
John Allison	5	2	-	101 Causeyside St.
Daniel Connel*	4	5	[Baker]	18 High St.
Thomas Ferguson*+	4	4	[miner]	Johnstone, Rankine St.
Robert McLeod	1	1	-	Lylesland
Patrick Aitcheson	3	3	-	Johnstone
John Leishman*	3	4	[miner]	Johnstone
John Hart*+	2	6	[miner]	Carton[?] [Johnstone]
William Arthur*	2	4	-	Johnstone
William Campbell	2	-	-	2 Fergnslie
John McNair	4	3	-	Abbey Parish

Alexander Borland	1	2	-	Dovesland
Andrew Campbell	3	2	-	2 Fergnslie
William Tait	3	5	-	81 Causeyside St.
Peter Davidson	3	5	-	83 Causeyside St.

Males over 15: 100

Males under 15: 84

Females over 15: 96

Females under 15: 81

Total: 361

[* subsequently a member of the Paisley Townhead Emigration Society]

[+ emigrated to the Ottawa Valley]

[Sources: *NA(UK)* CO 384/6 ff. 796, 541 & CO 42/189 f.538]

SELECTED ENTRIES FROM "AULD KIRK" KIRK
SESSION MINUTES, RAMSAY TOWNSHIP

November 20, 1836

The Moderator stated that a public foma [*sic*] existed against Alexander Duncan, Mr. Duncan + their daughter Helen, alleging that they had been quarrelling + fighting amongst themselves + that Mrs Duncan had in consequence left the house. Mr Lockhart confirmed the truth of the foma, stating that he had been called to act as arbitrator in the matter for the purpose of bringing about a reconciliation.

December 1, 1836

[*Duncan family called to appear before the Session*]

Mrs Duncan acknowledged that she was often so excited + angry that she left the house + remained out all night — that when Mr Wilson was present, the statements made by her husband + the rest of the family had put her into a terrible rage + that she was once in such a state of mind that she went upstairs + attempted to hang herself — Alexander Duncan acknowledged that he had once struck his wife, but was convinced that if he had not done so, she would have taken his life, or that of some other member of the family — Helen Duncan acknowledged that she sometimes when much provoked said things to her mother that she should not have said + and for which she was afterwards vexed.

[*The session attributed the conflict to Mrs. Duncan's conduct and suspended her from church privileges until she showed* "signs of repentance + reformation of character."]

April 7, 1839

John Patterson + his wife appeared, and acknowledged their guilt of the sin of antenuptial fornication + expressed sorrow for the same. Whereupon they were admonished by the Moderator + absolved + it was agreed that an intimation to this effect should be read from the pulpit on Sabbath next.

James Dunlop appeared before the meeting + acknowledged that he had been guilty on one occasion of beating his wife. After admonitions, he was absolved.

September 27, 1839

[John Galbraith] acknowledged that on ... occasions he had been worse for ardent spirits, though not incapable of transacting business, and expressed his regret for the same. He also stated that he had resolved to abstain entirely for the future for the use of intoxicating liquor as an ordinary drinker ... He stated as the reason for his absence from church, his want of decent clothes, but that he hoped soon to have such as would enable him to make his appearance again in public. The Session, sympathizing with him in his difficulties, resolves to leave this matter for the present to his own consideration, hoping that he would use his utmost endeavours to provide himself with suitable clothes soon.

September 26, 1840

James Wilkie Junr has within the last year been engaged in several disorderly and irregular practices ... but having since been immersed by a Baptist preacher, it was agreed to strike his name off the roll.

November 28, 1840

Daniel McPherson laid before the Session an accusation against David Campbell for having slandered him in a public meeting, calling him a man of no principle. He admitted that he had first called David Campbell a liar.

[*both admonished and absolved*]

February 18, 1841

Janet Hart appeared to answer the charge of theft. A list of articles was produced by Robert Yule which it was alleged she had taken while residing in his house last year. These she acknowledged that she had

taken … it was proved that several other articles belonging to other persons had been found in her possession.
[*suspended from church privileges*]

Extract from Kirk Session minutes of St. Andrews Presbyterian Church, Perth.

12 March 1842
[Testimony of Margaret Paton, wife of Adam Paton, school teacher]
I participated in the foolish joke of the attempt to take a handkerchief from a man: and also, that being at the back of my own house picking up a few chips or sticks to bake a loaf, I happened to come near the stable attached to the barn situated there at the time Mr. Ferguson's man was attending to his oxen feeding in it, I just stood in the door + looked in (so it may either be called in the stable or out of it, it was just at the door) + my hands being over with flour at the time I rubbed them on his face: and also that I used language unbecoming the profession of a Christian; and for these things I express my regret.
[*The Ramsay Session admonished and absolved her*]

[Source: *UCA* "Ramsay Kirk Session Minutes"]

NOTES

Preface

1. See R.E. Graves, revised by Anne Pimlott Baker, "Bartlett, William Henry (1809–1854)," *DNB*, and Alexander M. Ross, "Bartlett, William Henry," *DCB*, VIII (1851–1860).

Chapter One: Land and Empire

1. Rideau Purchase Supplement, see Appendix I.

2. The Mississauga leaders present in 1822 are listed in Appendix I. Six of the leaders who negotiated the 1819 agreement, Itawobenon, Ketchegom, Komonjeveweny, Katouche, Kiwiashe, and Nitinowinin, did not endorse the later agreement. Since the Native names were written phonetically, spelling varies greatly in each document. R.W. Shaw translated the leaders' names into English and while some, such as *White Hawk, Muskrat,* or *Grey Feathers,* appear to reflect the totems recorded on the original document, this author has not been able to confirm the accuracy of Shaw's work. See R.W. Shaw, "The Treaty Made with the Indians at Kingston, May 31, 1819, for the Surrender of Lands," *Ontario Historical Society Papers and Records,* Vol. 27 (1931), 540–42; and *Indian Treaties and Surrenders from 1680 to 1890,* Vol. I (Ottawa: Queen's Printer, 1891–1971). Facsimile edition, Coles Pub. Co., 1971, 63, 65. For the careers of Sir John Johnson (1741–1830) and William Claus (1765–1826), see their respective entries in the *DCB,* VI (1821–1835). See also Robert J. Surtees, *Indian Land Surrenders in Ontario, 1763–1867* (Ottawa: Department of Indian Affairs and Northern Development, 1984), esp. 73–74.

3. Point Blankets are discussed in Harold Tichenor, *The Blanket: An Illustrated History of the Hudson's Bay Point Blanket* (Toronto: Quantum/HBC, 2002), and the significance of Scottish silver-heart brooches is examined in George R. Dalgleish, "Aspects of Scottish-Canadian Material Culture: Heart Brooches and Scottish Pottery," in P.E. Rider and H. McNabb, eds., *A Kingdom of the Mind: How the Scots Helped Make Canada* (Montreal: McGill-Queen's University Press, 2006), 122–29. For Osnaburg fabric, see Alastair Durie, "Imitation in Scottish Eighteenth-Century Textiles: The Drive to Establish the Manufacture of Osnaburg Linen," *Journal of Design History,* Vol. 6, No. 2 (1993), 71–76.

4. It has been claimed that there is no evidence of "Mississauga occupancy" in the Ottawa Valley, but many First Nations did make use of its waterways. See Peter Hessel, *The Algonkin Nation, The Algonkins of the Ottawa Valley: An Historical Outline* (Arnprior, ON: Kichesippi Books, 1993), 69–70, revised edition.

5. See Peter S. Schmalz, *The Objibwa of Southern Ontario* (Toronto: University of Toronto Press, 1991); Olive Patricia Dickason, *Canada's First Nations: A History of Founding Peoples from the Earliest Times*, second edition (Oxford: Oxford University Press, 1997); Donald Smith, *et al.*, *Aboriginal Ontario: Historical Perspectives on the First Nations* (Toronto: Dundurn Press, 1994); Howard M. Brown, *Lanark Legacy: Nineteenth-Century Glimpses of an Ontario County* (Perth, ON: County of Lanark, 1984), 2–8; and the following web sites: *www.aafna.ca; www.algonquinsofpikwakanagan.com; www.aincinac.gc.ca/al/ldc/ccl/agr/ont/algn/fna-eng.asp*.

6. The Ohio Valley First Nations, who fought beside the British during the Seven Years War, were outraged that their successful struggle against the French had merely resulted in a flood of American colonists pouring into their territory. For many American colonists, the Royal Proclamation was yet another example of British misrule and contributed to the revolutionary sentiment developing in the Thirteen Colonies. See Dickason, *Canada's First Nations*, 154–58; Robert J. Surtees, "Land Cessions, 1763–1830," in Smith, *et al.*, *Aboriginal Ontario*, 92–94.

7. Surtees, *Indian Land Surrenders in Ontario*, 22.

8. *Ibid.*, 19–34. The Crawford agreements were apparently confirmed with the exchange of wampum belts — a practice that had also been used to seal alliances and peace agreements.

9. Glenn J. Lockwood, "The Pattern of Settlement in Eastern Ontario, 1784–1875," *Families*, Vol. 30, No. 4 (1991), 238–39. Jean S. McGill, *A Pioneer History of the County of Lanark* (Toronto: T.H. Best Printing Co. Ltd., 1968. Reprint edition, Clay Publishing, 1979), 12–13. Since no new treaty emerged until 1819, it appears that the Indian Department may have considered the land already surrendered under the terms of the Crawford agreements. Francis Gore's departure for Britain may have also contributed to a lack of urgency on the matter.

10. Lieutenant-Colonel Pilkington may have provided the incorrect location for Richmond as a consequence of an earlier proposal to locate a military depot in Oxford Township, Eastern District. NA(UK) CO 700/CANADA 77 "Plan of the Principal Settlements of Upper Canada, 1817." It appears that Bathurst, Drummond, and Beckwith Townships lay above land purchased from Mynass, but Goulburn Township would have been above the land ceded by the Oswegatchie Iroquois.

11. Surtees indicates that survey crews were interfered with in the interior lands ceded by Mynass and the Oswetegatchie. *Indian Land Surrenders in Ontario*, 25, 34.

12. QUA, Bell Journals, Vol. I, August 6, 10, 1817; Vol. III, September 26, 1819. Some of William Bell's journal entries have been reprinted in Brown, *Lanark Legacy*, and Isabel Skelton, *A Man Austere: William Bell, Parson and Pioneer* (Toronto: Ryerson Press, 1947). See also Reverend William Bell, *Hints to Emigrants; in a Series of Letters from Upper Canada* (Edinburgh: Waugh and Innes, 1824), 180. For Ojibwa treaty objectives, see J. Michael Thoms, "Ojibwa Fishing Grounds: A History of Ontario Fisheries Law, Science, and Sportsmen's Challenge to Ojibwa

Treaty Rights, 1650–1900" (University of British Columbia: unpublished Ph.D. thesis, 2004).

13. In the early eighteenth century, members of Algonquin First Nation settled at Oka, the site of a Sulpician mission, and hunted and trapped in the upper Ottawa Valley. In 1857, Algonquin families at Oka successfully petitioned for the creation of their own reserve at Golden Lake in South Algona Township. Hessel, *The Algonkin Nation*, 68–72, 85.

14. Cole Harris estimates the entire aboriginal population of southern Ontario in the 1760s to be a few thousand, but, by the 1860s, there were close to 1.5 million people in the same territory. Olive Dickason quotes an 1824 estimate of 18,000 indigenous people, excluding those living "wild" in the forests, for both Upper and Lower Canada. See Harris, *The Reluctant Land: Society, Space, and Environment in Canada before Confederation* (Vancouver: University of British Columbia Press, 2008), 306; and Dickason, *Canada's First Nations*, 205–06.

15. Lord Bathurst was colonial secretary from 1812 to 1827. For his background and career, see Neville Thompson, "Bathurst, Henry, third Earl Bathurst (1762–1834)," *DNB*, and *Earl Bathurst and the British Empire, 1762–1834* (Barnsley: Leo Cooper, 1999). For the early development of the Colonial Office, which was not fully functioning until 1801, see D.M. Young, *The Colonial Office in the Early Nineteenth Century* (London: Longmans, 1961); and Zoë Laidlaw, *Colonial Connections, 1815–45: Patronage, the Information Revolution and Colonial Government* (Manchester, UK: Manchester University Press, 2005), who notes on pages 21–27 that many of the officers who served with Wellington in Spain obtained colonial appointments after the war.

16. Lord Bathurst to Sir George Prevost, October 29, 1813, quoted in Haydon, *Pioneer Sketches*, 10–11.

17. Haydon, *Pioneer Sketches*, 11.

18. *Ibid.*, 10–14. Sir Gordon Drummond (1772–1854) was born in Quebec, where his father was the agent for a leading London firm, but Drummond returned to Britain for his education before joining the army. See Kenneth Stickney, "Drummond, Sir Gordon," *DCB*, Vol. VIII (1851–1860).

19. For Highland military service and conduct in Upper Canada, see Andrew Mackillop, 'More Fruitful than the Soil': Army, Empire and the Scottish Highlands, 1715–1815 (East Linton: Tuckwell Press, 2000), and Marianne McLean, *The People of Glengarry: Highlanders in Transition, 1745–1820* (Montreal: McGill-Queen's University Press, 1991).

20. John Graham, after whom Grahamstown is named, was born in Dundee, and was the second son of the landed family the Grahams of Fintry in Forfarshire. While with the Sutherland Highlanders, he had fought at the Battle of Blaauwberg during the conflict that reasserted British control over the Cape. Graham made his proposal to

settle Highlanders in South Africa in May 1813, after visiting the Sutherland estate. Lord Bathurst sent his proposal to settle emigrants from Caithness or Sutherland in Upper Canada in October 1813. See K.S. Hunt, "Graham, John (1778–1821)," *DNB*; Ben Maclennan, *A Proper Degree of Terror: John Graham and the Cape's Eastern Frontier* (Johannesburg: Ravan Press, 1986), esp. 161–62; and H.J.M. Johnson, *British Emigration Policy, 1815–1830: 'Shovelling Out Paupers'* (Oxford: Clarendon Press, 1972), 16.

21. Rideau Purchase Supplement, see Appendix I.

22. For the support provided by First Nations to the British forces during the War of 1812, see Dickason, *Canada's First Nations*, 190–98. See also Bathurst to Prevost, September 9, 1814, quoted in Richard Reid, ed., *The Upper Ottawa Valley to 1855: A Collection of Documents* (Toronto: The Champlain Society, 1990), 8–10; Eric Jarvis, "Military Land Granting in Upper Canada following the War of 1812," *Ontario History*, Vol. LXVII, No. 3 (September 1975), 126; and Lillian F. Gates, *Land Policies of Upper Canada* (Toronto: University of Toronto Press, 1968), 86.

23. In 1817 the desire to direct Britons away from the United States had also led Lord Bathurst to support free passages and land grants in the Cape Colony for emigrants with sufficient capital to employ and settle ten families. Johnson, *British Emigration Policy*, 28.

24. Johnson, *British Emigration Policy*, 17–21.

25. *Ibid.*, 21–31, 37–40, 50–55, 77–85; and Michael E. Vance, "The Politics of Emigration: Scotland and Assisted Emigration, 1815–1826," in T.M. Devine, ed., *Scottish Emigration and Scottish Society: Proceedings of the University of Strathclyde Scottish Historical Studies Seminar 1990–91* (Edinburgh: John Donald, 1992), 37–60.

26. Robert Legget, *Ottawa River Canals and the Defence of British North America* (Toronto: University of Toronto Press, 1988), 35.

27. *Ibid.*, 16–17, 34–36; Jarvis, "Military Land Granting," 121–22.

28. Jarvis, "Military Land Granting," 123–25; Reid, *The Upper Ottawa Valley*, 11–13; and Gates, *Land Policies*, 86–88.

29. For Sir Francis Gore (1769–1852), see S.R. Mealing, "Gore, Francis," *DCB*, Vol. VIII (1851–1860). See also Jarvis, "Military Land Granting," 124–25; Gates, *Land Policies*, 88; and McGill, *Pioneer History*, 12.

30. The Clyde River is a tributary of the Mississippi, while the Jock feeds into the Rideau. The latter appears to have derived its name from the French Rivière Jacques. Colonel Cockburn sent his report to the governor-in-chief, the Duke of Richmond, on November 29, 1818. See Haydon, *Pioneer Sketches*, 41–42, 65–66; McGill, *Pioneer History*, 15–16; Glenn J. Lockwood, *Beckwith: Irish and Scottish Identities in a Canadian Community* (Carleton Place, ON: Township of Beckwith, 1991), 16–18; and Jarvis, "Military Land Granting," 126.

31. See A. Godlewska and N. Smith, eds., *Geography and Empire* (Oxford: Blackwell Pub., 1994); and J.B. Harley, *The New Nature of Maps: Essays in the History of Cartography* (Baltimore: Johns Hopkins University Press, 2001) for the relationship between map making and imperialism. Jeffers Lennox provides a detailed discussion of this relationship in the founding of Halifax, Nova Scotia, in his "An Empire on Paper: The Founding of Halifax and Conceptions of Imperial Space," *Canadian Historical Review*, Vol. 88, No. 3 (September 2007), 373–412. Gore's map [LAC NMC 19505] is reproduced in Lockwood, *Beckwith*, 11.

32. For a summary of Beckwith's career, see Glenn A. Steppler, "Beckwith, Sir Thomas Sydney," *DCB*, Vol. VI (1821–1835). Henry Goulburn (1784–1856), who was ambivalent about slavery and agreed with its abolition, would later serve as chief secretary for Ireland and chancellor of the exchequer. The township that bears his name was settled primarily by demobilized Irish soldiers from the 99th Regiment of Foot and assisted emigrants from Tipperary and Cork. See Brian Jenkins, *Henry Goulburn, 1784–1856: A Political Biography* (Montreal: McGill-Queen's University Press, 1996) as well as Bruce S. Elliott, *Irish Migrants in the Canadas: A New Approach* (Montreal: McGill-Queens University Press, 1988); "Emigration from South Leinster to Eastern Upper Canada," in K. Whelan and W. Nolan, eds., *Wexford History and Society: Interdisciplinary Essays on the History of an Irish County* (Dublin: Geography Publications, 1988); and "The North Tipperary Protestants in the Canadas: A Study of Migration, 1815–1880" (Carleton University: unpublished Ph.D. thesis, 1984).

33. A synopsis of Montague's naval exploits can be found in "Montagu, George, 1750–1829," *DNB*. While the careers of Russell (1733–1808), who had served in the imperial army in the Mediterranean and North America before settling in Upper Canada, and Elmsley (1762–1805), who, although London-born, was from an Aberdeenshire farming family, are outlined in Edith G. Firth "Russell, Peter," and "Elmsley, John," *DCB*, V (1810–1820). Ironically, both men were embroiled in Upper Canadian land-granting controversies. It has been claimed that Burgess Township was named for Thomas Burgess (1756–1837), the bishop of Salisbury. This is unlikely as Burgess was a relatively minor figure in the church in 1794, when the township was first surveyed, and his first major appointment as bishop of St. David's did not come until 1803 — although he was active in the Sunday school movement and had published an anti-slavery tract in 1789. See D.T.W. Price, "Burgess, Thomas (1756–1837)," *DNB*; and Brown, *Lanark Legacy*, 10. Both Burgess and Elmsley Townships were later divided, with the north and south designations being separated by Rideau Lake.

34. The Earl of Dalhousie (1770–1838) is perhaps best remembered in Canada for his educational initiatives as reflected in his founding of Dalhousie University in Halifax. He also took a keen interest in the Scottish settlers in the upper Ottawa Valley and provided books for a pioneer library they established at Watson's Corners in Dalhousie Township. Haydon, *Pioneer Sketches*, 173–96. See also Peter Burroughs, "Ramsay, George, 9th Earl of Dalhousie," *DCB*, VII (1836–1850), and "Sherbrooke, Sir John Coape," *DCB*, VI (1821–1835).

35. For the careers of the Duke of Richmond and Colonel Cockburn (1780–1868), who would later serve as governor of British Honduras and the Bahamas, see George F.G. Stanley, "Lennox, Charles, 4th Duke of Richmond," *DCB*, V (1801–1820); and Ed McKenna, "Cockburn, Sir Francis," *DCB*, IX (1861–1870). See also Brown, *Lanark Legacy*, 9–18; Lockwood, *Beckwith*, 18; and Haydon, *Pioneer Sketches*, 40–44. The fact that Perth, U.C., was printed on the location tickets suggests that the name for the depot had been selected sometime before. For more on the superintendent of the Perth settlement, Alexander McDonell, see Chapter Two.

36. It is possible that the tavern keeper, Alexander Morris, a native of Paisley, was responsible for the name change from Morphy Falls to Carleton Place. An alternative explanation suggests that a desire to indicate the town's central location in Lanark and Carleton County was responsible for the change, but when the name was adopted the original spelling apparently followed the Scottish model. See Lockwood, *Beckwith*, 96–97.

37. Harris, *Reluctant Land*, 316–18; Lockwood, *Montague: A Social History of an Irish Township, 1783–1980* (Smith Falls, ON: Township of Montague, 1980), 25; NA(UK) MR 1/137.

38. In 1817 the British Government agreed to fund the surveys from the Military Chest. Gates, *Land Policy*, 90. See also Lockwood, *Beckwith*, 14–15; Haydon, *Pioneer Sketches*, 45–48; AO RG 1-59, "Crown Land Survey Diaries, Field Notes and Reports."

39. Even though Reuben Sherwood (1775–1851) had been demobilized after the war, Drummond arranged for him to be put back on military pay while he was surveying the settlement. Haydon, *Pioneer Sketches*, 27, 45–47. See also Legget, *Ottawa River Canals*, 34–35; Reid, *Upper Ottawa Valley*, 11–12; and McGill, *Pioneer History*, 13–14, 19.

40. Lockwood, *Montague*, 26–27; AO RG 1-59, "Crown Land Survey Diaries, Field Notes and Reports."

41. Most non-Native commentators agree that "Mississippi" derives from an indigenous name, but there is no agreement on the precise origin. R.W. Shaw suggested that it derived from *Mishi-sippi*, which he claimed was Algonquin for great or large river, while Howard Brown proposed the Massanoga rock on Bon Echo Lake as a possible origin. See Shaw, "Treaty Made With the Indians," 542; and Brown, *Lanark Legacy*, 6.

Chapter Two: Early Settlement and the Imperial State

1. The extent of military mobilization in the British Isles during the French Wars is examined fully in J.E. Cookson, *The British Armed Nation, 1793–1815* (Oxford: Clarendon Press, 1997). For the influence of postwar conditions on policy-making, see Johnson, *British Emigration Policy*, 10–31; and J.E. Cookson, "Early Nineteenth-Century Scottish Military Pensioners as Homecoming Soldiers," *The Historical Journal*, Vol. 52, No. 2 (2009), 319–41.

2. On June 30, 1817, Simon Gray was awarded Con. 9, lot 6SW, in Burgess Township and Con. 10, lot 2 SW, in Yonge Township. The Burgess lot had been awarded previously to Jacob Mayer of the de Watteville Regiment, but he had left the area. Gray's land settlement is recorded in LAC Perth Military Settlement R11465-0-3-E, Microfilm Reel C-4651, "Upper Canada Located Settlers (Monthly Returns)," 31. For more on the difficulties of recovering women's experience in the settlement see Chapter Six.

3. Sergeant Simon Gray's Discharge Papers, NA(UK) WO 97/1125/295. See Appendix II.

4. The suppression of the slave rising in Grenada and general conditions of military service are examined in Roger Norman Buckley, *The British Army in the West Indies: Society and the Military in the Revolutionary Age* (Gainesville: University Press of Florida, 1998), 186–87, 256–57.

5. The Veteran Battalions were units composed of experienced soldiers. The 10th Royal Veteran Battalion (later renamed the 4th) saw action early in the War of 1812, but performed garrison duty in Lower Canada for much of the conflict. See Philip J. Haythornwaite, *The Armies of Wellington* (London: Brockhampton Press, 1998 edition), 177; and "The War of 1812 Website," *www.warof1812.ca/10thrvb.htm.*

6. Buckley, *British Army in the West Indies*, 277.

7. In 1814 a number of army units that had fought in the Peninsular War and the West Indies arrived in Canada — including the 90th Perthshire Light Infantry, which had fought in Martinique and Guadeloupe. See Donald E. Graves, "The Redcoats are Coming!: British Troop Movements to North America in 1814," *Journal of the War of 1812*, VI. No. 3 (Summer 2001), 12–18; and Arthur Swinson, ed., *A Register of the Regiments and Corps of the British Army* (London: The Archive Press, 1972).

8. Simon Gray's pension record can be found in NA(UK) WO 23/147 f.5. In order to qualify for free title, the land had to be occupied and at least four acres had to be under cultivation for each year of occupation. See Haydon, *Pioneer Sketches*, 44–45.

9. The specific impact of soldier settlers on Lanark County is discussed in Virginia Howard Lindsay, "The Perth Military Settlement: Characteristics of its Permanent and Transitory Settlers, 1815–1822" (Carleton University: unpublished M.A. Thesis, 1972). Larry Turner in *Perth: Tradition & Style in Eastern Ontario* (Toronto: Natural Heritage Books, 1992) notes the impact of half-pay officers on Perth's architecture.

10. Cookson, "Early Nineteenth-Century Scottish Military Pensioners," 323–26.

11. McLean, *People of Glengarry*, 82–87.

12. Alexander McDonell's selection as superintendent of the Department of Settlers was probably facilitated by personal connections, since his wife, Ann Smith, was the sister of Colonel Samuel Smith, a prominent Long Island Loyalist who had served in the Queen's Rangers and had been a member of Upper Canada's Executive Council since 1813. Several historians have been highly critical of McDonell's efforts at Baldoon, and in examining his correspondence with Lord Selkirk have argued that he was more interested in his political career in York than attending to the settlers' needs. If

Gore was aware of these complaints, he chose to ignore them. Gore had also served in the army in Europe, early in the French Wars, and this was probably another factor contributing to his endorsement of a fellow soldier. See J.M. Bumsted, "McDonell, Alexander [Collachie] (1762–1842)," *DCB*, VII (1836–1850); S.R. Mealing, "Gore, Francis (1769–1852)," *DCB*, VIII (1851–1860). For the difficulties at Baldoon, see L. Campey, *The Silver Chief: Lord Selkirk and the Scottish Pioneers of Belfast, Baldoon and Red River* (Toronto: Natural Heritage Books, 2003), 51–76.

13. McLean, *People of Glengarry*, 198; "McDonell, Alexander (1762–1840)," *DCB*, VII (1836–1850).

14. QUA, William Bell Fonds, Vol. 8, March 1832, 90–91.

15. It is possible that Farquhar Matheson had joined the Canadian Fencibles, which had been recruiting in the Highlands in 1803. Intriguingly, rumours that the regiment was to be sent to India instead of North America had undermined those efforts and the regiment and its Scottish officers left for Quebec the following year. Farquhar was killed at Fort Wellington (Prescott) on November 7, 1813. See Donald F. Sherwin, "Roberick Matheson: Pillar of 19th Century Perth," *Perth Upon Tay Papers* (Perth Museum), No.1, 2006; and George Mainer, "Matheson, Roderick (1793–1873)," *DCB*, X (1871–1880).

16. H. Winston Johnston, *The Glengarry Light Infantry, 1812–1816: Who Were They and What Did They Do in the War?* (Charlottetown: Benson Publishing, 1998), 219–20, 235–36, 248–49.

17. William Marshall was unmarried when he was awarded land in Elmsley and Beckwith Townships in 1816. He would receive further grants in Drummond and Elmsley Townships in 1817 and 1818, LAC, "Upper Canada Located Settlers (Monthly Returns)," 23. Thom, who settled with his two young daughters in Perth in 1816, received land in Bathurst, Elmsley, Drummond, and Sherbrooke Townships between March 1816 and May 1821. LAC, "Upper Canada Located Settlers (Monthly Returns)," 27. Thom's daughters were children from his first marriage in 1811 to Harriet E. Smythe, who had died in 1815. Thom would marry twice more, first to Eliza Montague (d. 1820), and then to Bestsy Smythe, with whom he had a son and two daughters. Charles G. Roland, "Thom, Alexander (1775–1845)," *DCB*, VII (1836–50).

18. For John Watson, see Johnston, *Glengarry Light Infantry*, 256; McGill, *Pioneer History*, 20, 54, 56, 135; and Brown, *Lanark Legacy*, 273. In recording his land grants, Watson was credited with also serving in the 76th Regiment. He was initially awarded Con. 3, lot 27, in Bathurst; Con. 3, lot 16, in Beckwith; and Con. 3, lot 16, in Kitley. George Ferguson was single at the time he was awarded Con. 12, lot 17SW; Con. 2, lot 7; and Con. 8, lot 18, in Drummond. He was also awarded Con. 3, lot 14SW, in Beckwith, and Con. 5, lot 2, in Wolford. James Gray was given Con. 10, lots 37 and 41, and Con. 2, lot 16, Burgess, in addition to lots in Elizabeth and Bastard Townships. [LAC "Upper Canada located Settlers (monthly returns)," 18, 22, 31.] According to

the government regulations, lieutenant-colonels were to receive 1,200 acres; majors: 1,000 acres; captains: 800 acres; subalterns: 500 acres; sergeant-majors and quarter-master sergeants: 300 acres; sergeants: 200 acres. The vast majority of soldier settlers were privates, and, like their civilian settlers, were given only one hundred acres, making the large farms of the officers all the more obvious. See Haydon, *Pioneer Sketches*, 44–45; and Virginia Howard Lindsay, "The Perth Military Settlement," 24.

19. Angus Cameron and his wife, Euphemia McGregor, settled with their children on Con. 11, lot 6NE, in Drummond Township. Cameron also received Con. 6, lot 3SW, in Leeds Township as part of his land grant. Reverend Bell reported that he had attended Cameron on his deathbed in May 1822, and that John Adamson's wife had left him for a man named Robert Forrest. According to Bell, Adamson himself had died from over-drinking. In 1841 Adamson's Inn was taken over by his son-in-law, William Fraser, husband of his daughter Catherine. See McGill, *Pioneer History*, 53–55, 59; LAC, "Upper Canada Located Settlers (Monthly Returns)," 17, 19. For an account of the contemporary debates concerning taverns in Upper Canada, see Julia Roberts, *In Mixed Company: Taverns and Public Life in Upper Canada* (Vancouver: University of British Columbia Press, 2009).

20. Virginia H. Lindsay did find that single soldiers were more likely to leave their land, but that the rates of departure were comparable for all groups — with the exception of foreign-born British soldiers who left in far greater numbers. Of the 1,176 adult males who had settled in Drummond and Bathurst by 1822, 534 (45 percent) had left the area. Of the 574 British-born soldiers who were awarded land grants, 303 (52 percent) had departed. Among the 459 adult male civilians who settled Drummond and Bathurst, 143 (35 percent) had abandoned their lots. Lindsay, "The Perth Military Settlement," 78, 79, 83–86.

21. Angus McMillan, Donald McGregor, and William Wilson were located in September 1816, on Con. 1, lot 11NE; Con. 5, lot 23SW; and Con. 2, lot 12NE in Drummond. In June 1817 Charles and Alexander Duncan were granted lot 20NE and lot 20SW, on Con. 12 in Bathurst. John Bowie was settled with his wife on Con. 5, lot 23W, in Bathurst. In 1817 he was also given lot 16SW on Con. 2 in Elmsley. David Hogg and Duncan McKenzie each had a young daughter. Hogg's family settled on Con. 2, lot 22NE, in Drummond in November 1816, and McKenzie's was given lot 4SW, Con. 8, in Burgess on August 21, 1817. See LAC, "Upper Canada Located Settlers (Monthly Returns)," 6, 19, 22, 29–30, 33. Hogg would later serve as an ensign in the 1st Regiment of the Lanark Militia. Brown, *Lanark Legacy*, 273.

22. According to the land-settlement records, James McIntosh had one son over twelve years old and this may have encouraged him to take on the pioneer life. Those records also identify him as a sergeant, but his discharge papers indicate that he was a labourer when he joined the army and that he was still a private when he was demobilized at the age of thirty-five. Private Donald Gillis, age thirty-eight, and Sergeant Alexander Cameron, age thirty, both with six years service in the 103rd, and their wives were settled, respectively, on Con. 9, lot 11SW, in Burgess, and Con. 5, lots 12SW, 12NE, in

Bathurst. Ronald McLelland settled with his wife and two young daughters on Con. 7, lot 10SW, in Beckwith, while the single William Robinson was located on Con. 9, lot 10SW, in Bathurst. All five men were given lots that had been abandoned. NA(UK) WO97/189/90, WO97/1070/22 & 65; LAC "Upper Canada Located Settlers (Monthly Returns)," 35, 40, 45; and LAC MG24 I 158, John Forrest Fonds, f.10.

23. Marianne McLean has pointed out that the overwhelming majority of 1815 Highland emigrants chose to settle in Glengarry rather than Lanark County. See her "Achd an Rhigh: A Highland Response to the Assisted Emigration of 1815," *Canadian Papers in Rural History*, Vol. V (1986), 181–97.

24. Henry Goulburn responded that, indeed, veterans' pensions would be paid in Canada, and that while the government had no objection to settlers taking guns with them the nature of Upper Canada ensured that there was no need for them to arm themselves unless war broke out once again. NA(UK) CO 42/165 ff.93–96.

25. List of 1815 Assisted Scottish Emigrants Settled in Lanark County. See Appendix III.

26. John Campbell's notice was first published on February 22, 1815, and is reproduced in Haydon, *Pioneer Sketches*, 16–18. See also NA(UK) CO42/165 f.84, 105, Campbell to Bathurst, February 24, 1815, and Campbell to Goulburn, March 20, 1815. Only a handful of English emigrants actually made the trek to Greenock to depart in the summer of 1815, and no Irish emigrants left from the port with the exception of John Flood, who was of Irish origin but a resident of Anderston in Glasgow. John Oliver, who committed suicide in 1822 after the death of his wife Mary Munn, appears to have been an Englishman who settled in Kilmarnock before emigrating. The emigrants who left England to depart from Greenock in 1815 were from Penkridge, Staffordshire, Charles Barker, a bachelor farmer, and Henry B. Barker, also a farmer with wife and two sons; from Liverpool, Robert Davidson, a labourer, and his wife; from Wakefield, Joseph Holdsworth, a bachelor schoolmaster; and from Spaldington, the farmer William Holderness, with his wife, three sons, and two daughters. They were joined by James Fraser, a Scottish-born joiner from Newcastle and his wife, son, and daughter.

27. NA(UK) CO 42/165 ff.109-10, Pilkington to Campbell, March 20,1815; Campbell to Pilkington, March 24, 1815.

28. John Campbell had also printed a pamphlet containing "some practical advices to settlers," written by a Mr. Stennett, who had travelled in Canada, but this author has not been able to identify Mr. Stennett or locate a copy of his pamphlet. See NA(UK), CO 42/165 f.164, Campbell to Goulburn, July 11, 1815. For Dr. Brewster and the *Edinburgh Encyclopaedia*, see A.D. Morrison-Low, "Brewster, Sir David (1781–1868)," *DNB*. The entry on Canada was prepared with the assistance of William Ellice, MP, a member of a Scottish gentry family heavily involved with the Hudson's Bay Company. See Gordon F. Millar, "Ellice, Edward (1763–1863)," *DNB*. Emigrant advice literature was not generally available in Britain until the 1830s, see Robert D. Grant, *Representations of British Emigration, Colonization and Settlement: Imagining Empire, 1800–1860* (London: Palgrave, 2005).

29. John Campbell managed the accounts of both Alexander and Duncan Campbell and recommended improvements for their estates, even to the point of arranging for Robert Reid, Lord Breadalbane's factor, to do a complete survey of the Barcaldine Argyllshire lands in 1808. NAS GD170/2134/9, John Campbell to Mary Campbell, 1808. Campbell enjoyed some political influence in Perthshire, where he helped to ensure the election of James Drummond, and in Lanark where Lord Lauderdale asked him to intercede on behalf of Lord Archibald Hamilton in the 1803 election. NAS GD112/40/15, Letters of John Campbell, W.S. to Captain Colin Campbell, c.1789; NAS GD112/74/6/9/b Lord Lauderdale to the Earl of Breadalbane, December 29, 1803; NA(UK) CO 42/165 f.61 Colquhoun to Bathurst, February 15, 1815; NA(UK) CO 42/165 ff.84, 89, Campbell to Bathurst, February 24, March 11, 1815.

30. John and Colin Campbell inherited control of the Brochastle farm near Callander when their father died in 1777. Colin Campbell gained fame for his success in the Peninsula War and served as lieutenant governor of Gibraltar, but by the time of John Campbell's appointment as government agent, he had fallen victim to a Mediterranean fever. See SBA UGD 37/1/7, "Memorial of John Campbell Writer to the Signet and Captain Colin Campbell to the Commissioners of the Annexed Estates in Scotland, 1783"; H.M. Stephens, revised, Roger T. Stearn, "Campbell, Colin (1754–1814)," *DNB*; and NA(UK) CO 42/165 f.110 Campbell to Pilkington, March 24, 1815.

    Campbell's other brothers, James and Alexander, also chose military careers and both served in India. Alexander Campbell served in the 26th Native Infantry. See NAS GD170/2333/39&41 Campbell to Duncan Campbell of Barcaldine, November 20, 1818, and January 11, 1818. Apart from enlightening Campbell as to the nature of Britain's overseas dominions, these familial contacts were particularly useful in providing patronage opportunities for the elder brother's clients in the form of posts in the Indian civil and military service. In a letter from Gibraltar written on June 25, 1813, Colin complained to his brother of the frequent impositions that he had to endure on behalf of John's friends and clients. SBA UGD 37/1/17.

31. In 1780 John Campbell held £1900 in stock with the Jamaican trading firm MacLean, McKay and Company, managed the accounts of several other large West Indies merchants, such as the "Tobacco Lord" Henry Riddell, and was insuring goods in New York warehouses. In 1815 he had property in America valued at £170. See SBA UGD37/2/2, "Private Ledger 1761–80," 10, 34. For Henry Riddell and his brother John, who were both prominent in the tobacco trade, see T.M. Devine, *Tobacco Lords: A Study of the Tobacco Merchants of Glasgow and Their Trading Activities* (Edinburgh: John Donald, 1975), 7. For a detailed discussion of Campbell's business interests, see Michael E. Vance, "Emigration and Scottish Society: The Background of Three Assisted Emigrations to Upper Canada, 1815–1821" (University of Guelph: unpublished Ph.D. thesis, 1990), 14–42. For an overview of the cotton mill at New Lanark and its significance for the history of Lowland industrial development, see Ian L. Donnachie and George Hewitt, *Historic New Lanark: The Dale and Owen Industrial Community Since 1785* (Edinburgh: Edinburgh University Press, 1993).

32. It would appear that the Bracaldine estate's difficulties began when John Campbell's sister, Mary, chose to reside in Edinburgh rather than the Argyllshire estate. See Stana Nenadic, *Lairds and Luxury: The Highland Gentry in Eighteenth-Century Scotland* (Edinburgh: John Donald, 2007), 19–21, 73–77, 130–32. For Campbell's property holdings, see SBA UGD37/2/3, "Private Ledger." For the career of John Campbell Sr., see John Sibbald Gibson, "Campbell, John (c. 1703–1777)," *DNB*.

33. John Campbell expressed sympathy with Highland tenants who were experiencing rapid change and increased rents. As a lawyer based in the Lowland capital, he viewed such developments as natural and inevitable, and found himself endorsing Lord Selkirk's earlier argument that in these circumstances emigration could offer some Highlanders "an asylum elsewhere," as their former lands were "improved." He also claimed that his experience as an honourary commander of the Breadalbane Fencibles left him with little doubt that Highlanders would provide a more "stable security" for British North America's colonies than could be expected "from the mixed mass of the low country ... from cities such as Edinburgh and Glasgow." NA(UK) CO 42/165 f.183, Campbell to Bathurst, October 14, 1815.

34. See Vance, *Emigration and Scottish Society*, 28–33. It would appear that William Wilberforce, the leading parliamentary critic of the trade, was the source of the comparison with slavery. The two men corresponded and Campbell paid to have one of Wilberforce's anti-slave trade tracts printed and circulated in Scotland. NA(UK) CO 42/165 f.84, John Campbell to Bathurst, February 24, 1815; NAS GD170/2974, Wilberforce to Campbell, February 16, 1808; SBA UGD37/2/3, Private Ledger, 62. Campbell also employed a black manservant in his home and invested in the Sierra Leone Company, which oversaw the black Loyalists who began settling the West African colony in 1787. For that migration and settlement, see Cassandra Pybus, *Epic Journeys of Freedom: Runaway Slaves of the American Revolution and their Global Quest for Liberty* (Boston: Beacon Press, 2006).

35. List of 1815 Assisted Scottish Emigrants, see Appendix III.

36. In the regular British Army, Scots were outnumbered by their English and, especially, Irish compatriots, but this was not seen as a cause for concern. Only later, when assisted emigration was provided to emigrants arriving directly from Ireland, were efforts made to locate the Irish in separate districts. The men of the de Watteville and de Meuron regiments, two units comprised of soldiers drawn from various locations across Europe, were also settled primarily in Drummond and Bathurst. Ron B. Shaw has compiled a list of soldier locations by regiment, see *www.perthhs.org*. For the de Watteville and de Meuron regiments, see McGill, *Pioneer History*, 18–19.

37. Bell recorded 111 women and 366 children among the "civilians," and 179 women and 287 children in the "military" families. Bell's statistics were published in George F. Playter, "An Account of the Founding of Three Military Settlements in Eastern Ontario: Perth, Lanark and Richmond, 1815–1820," *Ontario Historical Society Papers and Records*, Vol. 20 (1923), 99. Records for the fifty-one Scottish soldiers (accompanied by twenty-four women and forty-eight children) as well as the 121

civilians (with fifty-eight women and 213 children) are found in LAC "Upper Canada Located Settlers (Monthly Returns)," 4–32, 72–80.

38. The majority of the Scottish emigrants who arrived in Lanark County between 1815 and 1818 departed on ships sailing from Greenock. Aside from the *Morningfield* only two other vessels, the *Speculation* from Oban and the *Hibernia* from Stornoway, left from northern ports while seven vessels, in addition to the *Lord Middleton*, left from Leith: the *Rothiemurchus*, *Prompt*, *Alexander*, *Agincourt*, *John*, *Trafalgar*, and *Renown*. A handful of other Scots left on ships departing England or Ireland, while an even smaller number arrived in the settlement via the United States. See Campey, *Scottish Pioneers*, 217–21; and LAC "Upper Canada Located Settlers (Monthly Returns)," 72–100.

39. LAC, Perth Military Settlement, "Upper Canada Located Settlers (Monthly Returns)."

40. *Ibid.*

41. Corporal Daniel McLeod of the Canadian Fencibles was the first Scottish soldier to settle in Beckwith Township. He took up his grant, Con. 4, lot 25SW, on December 19, 1816. He was preceded by Donald McLelland and John MacDonald, both passengers on the *Morningfield*, who were settled on their lots, Con. 7, lot 3NE, and Con. 7, lot 6SW, on November 30, 1816. Lieutenant Ferguson appears to have settled on Con. 4, lot 9NE, in Beckwith, although this is not certain. LAC, "Upper Canada Located Settlers (Monthly Returns)," 25, 77, 92. See also "Lt. Robert Ferguson, Beckwith to John Moir, Kippen, Stirlingshire," LAC MG 55/24 no.199.

Chapter Three: The Breadalbane Immigrants

1. Daniel Wilson tried on several occasions to obtain an academic post in his native land. Among these unsuccessful attempts were applications for the chair in history at St. Andrews in 1861, the chair in English literature at Edinburgh in1863, and historiographer royal of Scotland in 1881. He was knighted for his educational work in Toronto in 1888. Marinell Ash, *et al.*, *Thinking with Both Hands: Sir Daniel Wilson in the Old World and the New* (Toronto: University of Toronto Press, 1999), 274, 286–87. See also Daniel Wilson, "Notice of the Quigrich or Crozier of St. Fillan and of its Hereditary Keepers in a Letter to John Stuart …," *Proceedings of the Society of Antiquaries of Scotland*, Vol. 12 (1876–77), 122–31; Carl Berger, "Wilson, Sir Daniel," *DCB*, XII (1891–1900); and Elizabeth Hulse, "Wilson, Sir Daniel (1816–1892)," *DNB*.

2. Although the medieval sources are vague and at times contradictory, it would appear that St. Fillan was an Irish monk who served as the abbot of Iona in the early eighth century. Earlier, he had been based in northern Perthshire, which is reflected in regional place names such as Strathfillan. W.D. Macray and Reverend Benjamin T. Hudson, "Fáelán Amlabar [St. Fillan] (641\2-724)," *DNB*.

3. As a boy, the well-read Wilson had learned about the Elgin Marbles from the popular educational publication *The Library of Entertaining Knowledge*. Ash, *et al.*, *Thinking with Both Hands*, 7, 274. It was not until 1914, when the Royal Ontario Museum

opened its doors, that an institution comparable to the British Museum was in place in Toronto, although there were early efforts made to collect indigenous artefacts. For this early history and an analysis of the extension of the British Museum model to the empire, see John M. Mackenzie, *Museums and Empire: Natural History, Human Cultures and Colonial Identities* (Manchester: Manchester University Press, 2009).

4. Wilson, "Notice of the Quigrich," 124, 129. See also James Stuart, "Historical Notices of St. Fillan's Crozier, and of the Devotion of King Robert Bruce to St. Fillan," *Proceedings of the Society of Antiquaries of Scotland*, Vol. 12 (1876–1877), 134–82. Wilson's father was from Gaelic-speaking Srachur in Argyllshire. Ash, *et al.*, *Thinking with Both Hands*, 3.

5. *Proceedings of the Society of Antiquaries of Scotland*, Vol. 12 (1876–1877), 122–31.

6. Ash, *et al.*, *Thinking with Both Hands*, 274; Wilson, "Notice of the Quigrich," 127–28. Archibald and his wife, Margaret Ferguson, settled with their young sons, Duncan and Archibald, on Con. 7, lot 25SW, in Beckwith on October 24, 1818. Their adult sons, John and Malcolm Dewar, settled nearby on Con. 7, lot 23SW and lot 25NE. Alexander Dewar followed the family the next year, settling on Con. 9, lot 19SW, and his son, named Archibald after his grandfather, was born in 1826. Malcolm Dewar had married Anne Comrie before emigrating, but Peter Dewar married Janet McEwen after settling in Beckwith. Alexander Dewar married Janet Kennedy after his arrival in Upper Canada. Lockwood, *Beckwith*, 581–82, 586; Carol Bennett McCuaig, *Founding Families of Beckwith Township, 1816–1846* (Renfrew, ON: Juniper Books, 2007), 40–42.

7. Andrew MacKillop, "Highland Estate Change and Tenant Emigration," in T.M. Devine and John R. Young, eds., *Eighteenth Century Scotland: New Perspectives* (Edinburgh: Tuckwell, 1999), 237–58.

8. Three ships carried the 1818 assisted emigrants from Scotland, the *Curlew*, the *Sophia*, and the *Jane*. Lists survive for the first two in the Colonial Office records, and Glenn Lockwood has reconstructed a partial list for the *Jane* based on Beckwith land records. See Lucille H. Campey, *The Scottish Pioneers of Upper Canada, 1784–1855: Glengarry and Beyond* (Toronto: Natural Heritage Books, 2005), Appendix I; Lockwood, *Beckwith*, 585–88. For the 1815 Perthshire settlers on the Scotch Line, see Appendix III.

9. Lieutenant Colin Campbell, who fought with the 78th, was among the original settlers in the Passamaquoddy region of New Brunswick. Campbell maintained a correspondence with the Earl of Breadalbane, in the hopes that the earl would use his political influence to secure the ex-soldier an official appointment in the colony. Lucille H. Campey, *With Axe and Bible: The Scottish Pioneers of New Brunswick, 1784–1874* (Toronto: Natural Heritage Books, 2007), 30–31; NAS GD112/74/9, Campbell to Breadalbane, October 20, 1800. For Perthshire settlers in Nova Scotia after the American Revolution, see Lucille H. Campey, *After the Hector: The Scottish Pioneers of Nova Scotia and Cape Breton, 1773–1852* (Toronto: Natural Heritage Books, 2004), 80, 212–14.

10. Campey, *With Axe and Bible*, 74–85; William A. Spray, "Ferguson, Robert," *DCB*, Vol. VIII (1851–60); Lucille H. Campey, *"A Very Fine Class of Immigrants": Prince Edward Island's Scottish Pioneers, 1770–1850* (Toronto: Natural Heritage Books, 2001), 62–64.

11. NAS GD112/61/1, Letters, October 22, 1802.

12. NAS GD112/41/7 ff.268, 274 McGillewie to Breadalbane, January 17, 1817; McGillewie to Campbell, W.S., January 28, 1817.

13. NA[UK] CO 384/1/f.141, Campbell W.S. to Bathurst, February 11, 1817.

14. The unadvertised 1818 government scheme, operating under the same conditions as in 1815, also included an Irish group from County Tipperary in addition to over three hundred emigrants from the Breadalbane region. Johnston, *British Emigration Policy*, 28–30; Helen Cowan, *British Emigration to British North America* (Toronto: University of Toronto Press, 1961), 44–47; NAS GD112/41/7 f.302, McGillewie to Campbell, W.S., March 12, 1817; NAS GD112/41/7 f.270, McGillewie to Breadalbane, January 17, 1817.

15. NAS GD112/41/7 f.302, McGillewie to Campbell, W.S., March 12, 1817.

16. According to John McGillewie, Duncan Campbell, along with John Robertson and John McDiarmid of Carwhin, also on the north side of the loch, were the principal men involved in gathering signatures for the petition to the Prince Regent, see NAS GD112/41/7 f.268, McGillewie to Breadalbane, January 17, 1817.

 All three men would settle with their families in Beckwith Township. Robertson and his wife, Jannet, along with their children, John, sixteen, and Duncan, fourteen, appear to have settled in Beckwith on Con. 2, lot 27, while McDiarmid, along with his wife and two young children, appears to have settled in the township on Con. 8, lot 17NE. Duncan Campbell and family settled on Con. 4, lot 11NE. Lockwood, *Beckwith*, 578, 582–86, 593.

17. NA(UK) CO384/3 f.403, McEwen (Tombeck Farm) to Bathurst, November 28, 1818.

18. Many of these men subsequently transferred to regular army units. MacKillop, *More Fruitful than the Soil*, 115.

19. NAS GD112/11/7/2/16, Petitions, 1799; NAS GD112/11/7/1/19, Petition, March 20, 1799.

20. For an analysis of the social origin of the Breadalbane Fencible recruits, see MacKillop, *More Fruitful than the Soil*, 119–20. The request of former soldier and crofter Alexander McDougall, to be preferred to a cow-holding, is typical of the petitions received. NAS GD112/11/7/1/14, Petition, March 14, 1799. See also NAS GD112/74/12, Breadalbane's draft letter, January 1804.

21. NAS GD112/11/7/7/6, Duncan Clark Petition, January 2, 1804.

22. McKillop, *More Fruitful than the Soil*, 118, 128.

23. NAS GD112/11/8/8/5, MacEwan to Breadalbane, October 19, 1813.

24. For the early changes on the Breadalbane estate, see M.M. Mcarthur, ed. *Survey of Lochtayside 1769* (Edinburgh: Scottish History Society, 1936); and William A. Gillies, *In Famed Breadalbane* (Perth: Munro Press, 1938), 199. Malcolm Gray noted that the Earls of Breadalbane and the Duke of Argyll were the first Highland magnates to conduct a systematic elimination of the communal farming system known as "runrig" on their estates. Malcolm Gray, *The Highland Economy* (Edinburgh: Oliver and Boyd, 1957), 66–75.

25. NAS GD112/9/2/2/2x, Kennedy to Breadalbane, 1791.

26. NAS GD112/74/19, Removal List, 1795; NAS GD112/41/6, Breadalbane to Kennedy, January 20, 1800. Despite efforts to "improve" the small tenants, it appears that old practices continued in the new settlement at Lix. Early archaeological study of the abandoned community revealed that central open hearths were still in use rather than more "civilized" fireplaces and chimneys at a gable end. Hoarce Fairhurst, "The Deserted Settlement at Lix, West Perthshire," *Proceedings of the Society of Antiquaries of Scotland*, Vol. 100 (1969), 135–69, cited in Chris Dalglish, *Rural Society in the Age of Reason: An Archaeology of the Emergence of Modern Life in the Southern Scottish Highlands* (New York: Kluwer Academic/Plenum Publishers, 2003), 122–23.

27. NAS GD112/41/5, Kennedy to Breadalbane, July 16, 1800.

28. NAS GD112/11/7/2/30, Petition, September 1799.

29. While the precise date of the transition was not established by the archaeologists, it appears likely that the change in building use at Meall Griegh coincided with the practice of letting the traditional communal grazings to a single tenant as part of the estate reorganization. John A. Atkinson, *et al.*, *Ben Lawers Historic Landscape Project: Excavations at Kiltyrie and Meall Geigh — Project 1580* (Glasgow University: GAURD, 2004), available at *www.benlawers.org.uk.*

30. NAS GD112/9/2/2/2x, Kennedy to Breadalbane, 1791.

31. NAS GD112/11/7/5, Patrick and Widow Campbell Petition, June 16, 1802; NAS GD112/9/2/2/17x, Arrears of Rent, 1810.

32. The 1810 arrears list indicated that Duncan and Donald Campbell owed over £78, and a marginalia note "at Law" reveals that the matter had been turned over the sheriff clerk. The previous year the Campbells' possessions had been sequestered, and half the arrears of that year were recovered, but failure to pay in 1810 prompted the earl to enter into the process of removal. By the time of Duncan Campbell's emigration, the factor was still attempting to recover the arrears. NAS GD112/9/2/2/17x; GD112/9/69, Rental Arrears, 1810 and 1818.

33. See NAS GD112/9/2/2/11, GD112/9/67, GD112/9/69, GD112/9/68, Rental Arrears, 1808, 1816, and 1818. An archaeological survey of Shenlarich found traces of ploughing on land that is now fallow, suggesting much more arable farming in the past. It is also indicative of multiple tenant farms. See John A. Atkinson, *et al.*, *Ben Lawers Historic Landscape Project: Shenlarich, Tombreck and Kiltyrie — Survey*

Sampling Season Project 1998 (Glasgow University: GAURD, 2005), available at *www.benlawers.org.uk.*

34. John McGillewie suggested that the reason why the stock farms were in such desperate straits was because the previous factor had been too quick to impound livestock, but his own policies did not improve the levels of debt. See McGillewie to Breadalbane, December 6, 1816, NAS GD112/41/7 ff, 230–31. For the cost of Fencible recruits, see MacKillop, *More Fruitful than the Soil*, 116–18. A detailed account of the economic crisis on the Breadalabane estate can be found in Vance, *Emigration and Scottish Society*, 81–120.

35. McGillewie to Breadalbane, January 31, 1817, and March 27, 1817, NAS GD112/41/7 ff, 281–82, 315.

36. For Breadalbane's political career, see William Anderson, *The Scottish Nation Or the Surnames, Families, Literature, Honours and Biographical History of The People of Scotland*, Vol. I (Edinburgh: A. Fullerton 1877), 377–78; and his obituary in *The Gentleman's Magazine*, 156 (June 1834), 650–51.

37. As early as 1800 the Earl of Breadalbane was obtaining estimates and plans for the work at Taymouth. Three years later £300 was spent on the pleasure gardens alone. NAS GD112/41/6, Breadalbane to Kennedy, January 20,1800; NAS GD112/9/60, Abstract of Rents, 1803.

38. Breadalbane's son, the fifth earl, hosted Queen Victoria at the family seat in 1842. See Willie Orr, *Deer Forests, Landlords and Crofters: The Western Highlands in Victorian and Edwardian Times* (Edinburgh: John Donald, 1982).

39. NAS GD112/41/9, Breadalbane to McGillewie, February and May 1820; NAS GD112/41/7 ff.142, 283, McGillewie to John Campbell, W.S., July 27, 1816; McGillewie to Breadalbane, January 31,1817.

40. NAS GD112/41/7 f.317, McGillewie to Breadalbane, March 27, 1817.

41. John Ramsay, *Letters of John Ramsay of Ochteryre, 1799–1812* (Edinburgh: Scottish History Society, 1966).

42. Niel Gow, *Second Collection of Niel Gow's Reels* (1788), 10; Malcolm MacDonald, *A Second Collection of Strathspey Reels* (c. 1789), 1; *A Fourth Collection of Strathspey Reels* (1797), 2. For a discussion of Breadalbane's patronage of piping, see John G. Gibson, *Old and New World Highland Bagpiping* (Montreal: McGill-Queen's University Press, 2002), 161. For the Earl of Breadalbane's marriage and family, see Gillies, *In Famed Breadalbane*, 196.

43. T.M. Devine, "The Emergence of the New Elite in the Western Highlands and Islands, 1760–1860," in T.M. Devine, ed. *Clearance and Improvement: Land, Power and People in Scotland, 1700–1900* (Edinburgh: John Donald, 2006), 187–210; Nenadic, *Lairds and Luxury*, 159–82; Eric Richards, *Patrick Sellar and the Highland Clearances: Homicide, Eviction, and the Price of Progress* (Edinburgh: Polygon, 1999).

44. Gibson, *Highland Bagpiping*, 162.

45. For the role of the "seer" in Highland society, see Hilda Roderick Ellis Davidson, *The Seer in Celtic and Other Traditions* (Edinburgh: John Donald, 1989). Hugh Robertson's second sight was recalled by a descendant, Neil Robertson, in the early twentieth century. It appears that he may have confused the details, since he mis-identified the number of children in the family of John Robertson, his grandfather and co-author of the 1817 petition. John Robertson, who sailed on the *Curlew* with Duncan Campbell, settled with his wife Jannet and their two children in Beckwith, Con. 2, lot 27. Hugh Robertson settled with his wife and daughter in Drummond, Con. 7, lot 15NE. See McGill, *Pioneer History*, 20; AO MU 1084 Box 2 Env 2 F1015, Alexander Fraser Papers, "A Short Account of Settlers from Perthshire"; LAC Perth Military Settlement R11465-0-3-E, Microfilm Reel C-4651, "Upper Canada Located Settlers (Monthly Returns)," 78; Lockwood, 582, 586. For the request for a Gaelic-speaking minister, see Lockwood, *Beckwith*, 41–44, 176.

46. For the extent of Gaelic in nineteenth-century Scotland, see Charles W. J. Withers, *Gaelic in Scotland, 1698–1981: The Geographical History of a Language* (Edinburgh: John Donald, 1984). James McDairmid settled as a single man in Beckwith Township, Con. 8, lot 16SW. He appears to have corresponded with his brother in Glenlyon from an early date, but he does not seem to have been able to persuade the brother to emigrate. A nephew, John McDairmid, did come to Upper Canada in the 1840s, and in the 1850s Glenlyon farmers at Kerrowmore, Creag Ard, Creag nan Elidaeg, and Innerwick were expressing interest in emigrating to the colony. Lockwood, *Beckwith*, 37–38, 48–49.

Chapter Four: Paisley and the Emigration Societies

1. NA(UK) CO 384/6 f. 796.

2. The "Caffer War" was reported in the *Glasgow Chronicle*, June 15, 1819, and August 12, 1819.

3. Michael E. Vance, "The Politics of Emigration: Scotland and Assisted Emigration, 1815–1826," in T.M. Devine, ed., *Scottish Emigration and Scottish Society* (Edinburgh: John Donald, 1992), 41–42. It appears that just over eight hundred individuals participated in the 1820 assisted emigration. Campey, *Scottish Pioneers of Upper Canada*, 59.

4. Thomas and Janet Bridget along with their four children settled on Con. 11, lot 11W, in Ramsay Township. Thomas Ferguson, his wife Mary Barr, and their six children settled on Con. 3, lot 26, in Dalhousie Township. John Hart and his wife "Hodgert" settled with their five children on Con. 1, lot 26, in Dalhousie Township. The members of all three families had been born in Paisley, although at the time of their emigration Thomas Bridget was weaving in Williamsburg, and Thomas Ferguson and John Hart were working as miners in Johnston. See Paisley Townhead Emigration Society List, NA(UK) CO 42/189 f.538; Carol Bennett, *The Lanark*

Society Settlers (Renfrew, ON: Juniper Books, 1991), 160, 163, 166; LAC, Census of 1851, Canada West, Lanark County, Dalhousie, Subdistrict 177, Schedule A, f.27; and Appendix I.

5. Michael E. Vance, "Advancement, Moral Worth and Freedom: The Meaning of 'Independence' for Early Nineteenth-Century Lowland Emigrants to Upper Canada," in Ned Landsman, ed., *Nation and Province in the First British Empire* (Lewisburg, PA: Bucknell University Press, 2001): 151–80.

6. J.K. Johnson, "'Claims of Equity and Justice': Petitions and Petitioners in Upper Canada 1815–1840," *Histoire Sociale/Social History*, Vol. XXVIII, No. 55 (May 1995), 219–40. For other examples of the charitable appeal, see R.B. Outhwaite, "'Objects of Charity': Petitions to the London Foundling Hospital, 1768–72," *Eighteenth Century Studies*, Vol. 32, No. 4 (1999), 497–510; and David Englander, "From the Abyss: Pauper Petitions and Correspondence in Victorian London," *London Journal*, Vol. 25, No. 1 (2000), 71–83.

7. NA(UK) CO 384/6 f. 796.

8. *Ibid.*

9. Vance, "Advancement, Moral Worth and Freedom," 151–80.

10. A petition signed by six hundred weavers was initially sent to the kirk session, which denied the request for relief. The court session decided against the Paisley weavers in December 1821, on the basis that Scots poor law only allowed for voluntary assessments from property owners. Only one weaver, a man named Richmond, was identified in the court documents. See Rosalind Mitchison, *The Old Poor Law in Scotland: The Experience of Poverty, 1574–1845* (Edinburgh: Edinburgh University Press, 2000), 150–51, and *Process of the Poor Operatives of the Abbey Parish Against the Heritors and Kirk Session of the Said Parish, Paisley* (Paisley: James Mayne,1820), Paisley Pamphlets PC 269, Vol. 10, Paisley Central Library.

11. Petition of the Operative Manufacturers of Paisley, May 1820, see Appendix IV.

12. William Robertson's wife came from Ayr, making them the only couple on both Daniel Murchie's petition and the Townhead Emigration Society list without a Paisley origin for either spouse. Other communities appearing on the society list were Nielston, Bridge of Weir, Kilmarnock, Beith, Houston, Pollockshaws, Crossmyloof, Logie, Bute, and Campbellton. The document also lists the additional vocations of shoemaker, cooper, plasterer, mason, teacher, and smith. Paisley Townhead Emigration Society List, NA(UK) CO 384/6 f.541 and Appendix IV.

13. Alexander Wilson also worked as a weaver in Edinburgh and Queensferry before trying to make a living as a peddler. His father "Saunders" Wilson was born in Campbellton in Argyllshire, but the family was originally from Lochwinnoch in Renfrewshire. Saunders Wilson may also have served as a soldier before he married Alexander's mother, Mary McNabb from Rhu, and he appears to have learned the art of whisky distillation while he was still in Argyllshire. See Clark Hunter, ed.,

The Life and Letters of Alexander Wilson (Philadelphia: American Philosophical Society: 1983), 15–64.

14. In 1755 the population of Paisley stood at 4,290, but by 1791 the number of residents in the town and suburbs had risen to 19,903. In 1791 there were 3,602 looms operating in the district, and by 1818 it was estimated that between 7,000 and 8,000 of Scotland's 78,000 handloom weavers worked in Paisley. As late as 1840 two-thirds of Lowland weavers remained in rural or semi-urban districts. Sir John Sinclair, *Statistical Account of Scotland*, Vol. VII, Lanark and Renfrew (Edinburgh: M. Creech, 1791–1799), 66, 87–88, 91; David Gilmour, *Reminiscences of the Pen-Folk, Paisley Weavers of Other Days, Etc.* (Edinburgh & Paisley: Alex Gardner, 1879), 13; Norman Murray, *The Handloom Weavers 1790-1850: A Social History* (Edinburgh: John Donald, 1978), 4–6, 16–17, 22–26.

15. Several of Wilson's workmates left weaving to become school teachers, as Wilson himself did in the United States before he obtained work as an editor for the Philadelphia publisher Samuel F. Bradford. See Hunter, *Alexander Wilson*, 57, 62–72, 79; and Michael Durey, *Transatlantic Radicals and the Early American Republic* (Lawrence, KA: University of Kansas Press, 1997), 60. The high value placed upon education among weavers is discussed in Murray, *Handloom Weavers*, 161–67.

16. Hunter, *Alexander Wilson*, 48. Alexander Wilson, like many other contemporaries, was inspired by the success of Robert Burns. While he was able to get the Paisley printer John Neilston to publish his work, he was disappointed in his ambition to emulate Burn's success, although he continued to write poetry in the United States. For the town's remarkable number of weaver-poets, see Robert Brown, *Paisley Poets: With Brief Memoirs of Them, and Selections from Their Poetry* (Paisley: J. & J. Cook, 1889–90).

17. Hunter, *Alexander Wilson*, 58–61.

18. Thomas Witherspoon, a weaver and long-standing friend in Seedhill, posted Alexander Wilson's bail in the "Shark" incident, and William Wilson, a weaver in Williamsburgh, did the same for the subsequent "Reform meeting" imprisonment. Hunter, *Alexander Wilson*, 58–61, 412. For the manipulation of elite fears of insurrection in 1820, see Vance, "The Politics of Emigration," 49–50.

19. NA(UK) CO 384/6 f. 796.

20. William Taylor, *The Delights of Benevolence, Exemplified in the Utility of Friendly Society* (Glasgow: Neil Douglas, 1814), Paisley Pamphlets, Paisley Central Library. In the 1790s, Paisley weavers further extended the idea of friendly societies by forming co-operatives to purchase food from local farmers. Murray, *Handloom Weavers*, 144.

21. Five of the eight emigration society presidents whose occupations can be identified were weavers. For the link between "friendly society" and "emigration society" methods of organization, see Murray, *Handloom Weavers*, 144–45; and Vance, *Emigration and Scottish Society*, 196–203, 352–354. See also Campey, *Scottish Pioneers of Upper Canada*, 57–59; NA[UK] CO 384/6 f.253, f. 254, f.540-1.

22. In a follow up petition to Bathurst, Daniel Murchie noted the departure of emigration society members from Glasgow during the summer of 1820 and asked that the same provisions be extended to his group. NA(UK) CO 386/6 f.236.

23. Vance, *Emigration and Scottish Society*, 207–08, 213–17; Brown, *Paisley Poets*, 198–99, 276; Vance, "Advancement, Moral Worth and Freedom," 158, 163.

24. NA(UK) CO 384/6 f. 796.

25. NA[UK] CO 386/6 f. 236; Robert Brown, *The History of Paisley: From the Roman Period Down to 1884*, Vol. II (Paisley: J. & J. Cook, 1886), 168–69. For the membership and activities of the Glasgow Committee on Emigration, see Robert Lamond, *A Narrative of the Rise and Progress of Emigration from the Counties of Lanark and Renfrew, to the New Settlements in Upper Canada* (Glasgow: Chalmers and Collins, 1821) and Vance, *Emigration and Scottish Society*, 152–79.

26. Vance, "The Politics of Emigration," 47–49.

27. John Parkhill spent fourteen months in North America before returning to Paisley when a general amnesty was granted to participants in the "Radical War." Another Paisley reformer and schoolteacher, Alexander Taylor, also fled to Montreal, where he was later murdered. Like Alexander Wilson before them, several others fled to the United States. Brown, *The History of Paisley*, 169–206, *Paisley Poets*, 198–99; John Parkhill, *The History of Paisley* (Paisley: Robert Stewart, 1859), 59–66.

28. As well as monitoring the activities of weaver's groups prior to the "Radical War," Kirkman Finlay played a key role in the suppression a region-wide weavers' strike in 1812. Robert Beath, who was arrested for "illegal combination" during that strike, served as the president of the Kirkfield Bank Emigration Society, but he did not emigrate to Upper Canada. See Vance, "Politics of Emigration," 44–46, 48–49; *Emigration and Scottish Society*, 152–61.

29. *Hansard* 1 (1820), col. 744.

30. *Ibid.*

31. LAC RG 5, A1, Vol.75 ff. 39920. For Captain William Marshall, see McGill, *Pioneer History*, 52, 62–64, 96, 135, 181; and Brown, *Lanark Legacy*, 66, 273. It is possible that Marshall was aiding David Campbell and his wife Ann Sykes of the Milton Dumbartonshire Emigration Society, who had settled with their infant son on Con. 8, lot 13W, in Lanark Township. Campbell was originally from Perthshire, and the 97th was a Highland regiment. Bennett, *Lanark Society Settlers*, 152.

32. For settlement patterns in North Sherbrooke, see Barbara J. Griffith, "Kinship, Religion, Politics and Community in Two Frontier Settlements of Upper Canada: Some Baptists of Lanark and Lambton Counties" (Canadian Baptist Archives: unpublished paper, 2005).

33. In a letter to her sister and brother-in-law, sent in 1823, Mary Stoaks named the Gilmour family from the Lanark society; the Brownlie family from the Hamilton

society; the Twaddle, McDougall, and Smith families from the Parkhead society; and the Sym and Campbell families from the Rutherglen Union Society. Among the other members identified from the Townhead society were the Porter, Wylie, Christilaw, Dunlop, Edwards, Davies, Nisbet, McBryde, Crilly, Eason, Young, Taylor, and Watson families. William Dunlop was also born in Kilmarnock, Duncan McDougall was born in Iverary, and Robert Sym was from Pitlochry. For their settlement locations, see Bennet, *Lanark Society Settlers*. Mary Stoaks letter can be found in A.I. Macinnes, et al., eds., *Scotland and the Americas, c. 1650–c.1939: A Documentary Source Book* (Edinburgh: Scottish History Society, 2002), 221–22.

34. Ebenezer Wilson, his wife Jean, and their three children settled on Con. 1, lot 12W, in North Sherbrooke. Bennett, *Lanark Society Settlers*, 173–74; McGill, *Pioneer History*, 54; Griffith, "Kinship, Religion, Politics and Community," 15, 25, 48; LAC MG 24 I 57 Robert Lyon Papers, "The Duel of 1833"; *Bathurst Courier*, November 21, 1834; AO RG 22 Series 75, Vol. 1, "Quarter Sessions, 1823–1846," September 1827.

35. John Wilson, a pioneer fruit grower in New Annan, just south of Tatamagouche, was born in Kilmarnock and could have been the brother of Ebenezer and Mary Wilson. Israel Longworth, *History of Colchester County, Nova Scotia c. 1886* (Truro, NS: The Book Nook, 1986), 96, 103.

36. John McIntyre was a member of the Anderson and Rutherglen Society. He came with the first group of emigration society settlers in 1820 and settled with his wife and two children on Con. 2, lot 15W, in Dalhousie Township. Bennet, *Lanark Society Settlers*, 49; Johnson, "Claims of Equity and Justice," 235.

37. NA(UK) CO 42/393 ff.227-232, "Memorial of the Society Settlers of Lanark Settlement to Sir John Colborne." Signatories William Gordon and George Waddell were members of the Abercrombie Street society, James Thompson was a member of the Alloa society, and William Barrowman had joined the Bridgeton society. James Donaldson was a member of the Kirkman Finlay society and Dougle Ferguson belonged to the Balfron society. Aside from Robert Craig, the other Townhead society members were William Lambie and John McLaren Sr. Thomas Scott and Charles Ballie were members of the Lesmahagow society. Bennett, *Lanark Society Settlers*, 35, 40, 43, 55, 75, 137, 144, 149, 167, 170. While the author of the document was not identified, it was likely written by Charles Ballie, who had also lobbied William Marshall for support for a settlers' lending library at Watson's Corners. It appears that Ballie was the driving force behind that library, writing to leading figures in both Scotland and Upper Canada requesting donations. In Scotland, Ballie had earlier drafted a petition to the Duke of Hamilton, with a sophisticated argument in favour of plan to create allotments for unemployed weavers. When that scheme failed, he served as president of the Hamilton Emigration Society before eventually emigrating as a member of the Lesmahagow society. He settled with his wife and six children on Con. 4, lot 12E, in Dalhousie Township, but died on July 25, 1831, as the result of injuries sustained from an overturned cart. Vance, *Emigration and Scottish Society*, 136–37, 207–08. For a detailed account of the Dalhousie Library, see Haydon, *Pioneer Sketches*, 166–96.

38. The survey of the townships settled by emigration society members was undertaken by Charles Rankin in 1834. As a consequence of his report, which suggested that the soil was so poor on many of the assigned lots that "settlement should never have been attempted," the imperial government agreed to cancel any outstanding debt in January 1836, granting what Scottish settlers had been petitioning for since 1825. AO, F 1018, "Charles Rankin Fonds"; RG 1 (Shelf 52, no. 20) "Return of Settling (Scotch) Emigrants of 1820-21 ... 31 December, 1834"; Haydon, *Pioneer Sketches*, 117–21.

39. Reid, *Upper Ottawa Valley*, cxi.

40. Paisley weavers may have been predisposed to support the anti-slave trade movement since Peter Burnet, a former slave from Virginia, was a well-regarded member of their community. See Brown, *Paisley Poets*, Vol. 2, 40; and John Parkhill, *Sketch of the Life of Peter Burnet* (Paisley: 1841). For Paisley artisan petitioning, see Iain Whyte, *Scotland and the Abolition of Black Slavery, 1756-1838* (Edinburgh: Edinburgh University Press, 2006) 83, 89, 148; Murray, *Handloom Weavers*, 186, 212, 218, 227–29.

41. "Second Report of Select Committee on Emigration from the United Kingdom," *Parliamentary Papers*, 1826–1827, (88), V:19, 68–70, 182, 500–08.

42. NA(UK) CO 384/7 ff. 387–388 Mure to Bathurst, November 29, 1821; NA(UK) CO 384/7 f.607 Petition to Bathurst, October 20, 1821.

43. Since these groups were also lobbying members of the elite for contributions, they sought to remove any hint of their earlier radicalism. One later Paisley society went as far as insisting that its members must be of "good moral character, unconvicted of crime, and belong to a Protestant church." James M. Cameron, "A Study of the Factors that Assisted and Directed Scottish Emigration to Upper Canada, 1815-55" (University of Glasgow: unpublished Ph.D. thesis, 1970), Chapter Four, fn. 39; Vance, *Emigration and Scottish Society*, 291–92.

Chapter Five: Immigrant Politics and Religion

1. *Bathurst Independent Examiner*, October 23, 1829, LAC; McGill, *Pioneer History*, 142–44; Brown, *Lanark Legacy*, 158–59. The Irish-born John Stewart was a member of Perth's "True Briton's" Orange Lodge, founded at the time he arrived in the community. The Orange Order was conspicuous in its demonstrations of loyalty and this could account for Stewart's use of the Royal Coat of Arms in his paper's masthead. Nevertheless, as several scholars have pointed out, loyalty to the Crown did not rule out criticism of Parliament. Lockwood, *Beckwith*, 100; Michael Gauvreau, "Covenanter Democracy: Scottish Popular Religion, Ethnicity, and the Varieties of Politico-religious Dissent in Upper Canada, 1815-1841," *Histoire Sociale/ Social History*, 36 (May 2003), 68–69; David Mills, *The Idea of Loyalty in Upper Canada, 1784-1850* (Montreal: McGill-Queen's University Press, 1988); Jane Errington, *The Lion, the Eagle, and Upper Canada: A Developing Colonial Ideology* (Montreal: McGill-Queen's University Press, 1987).

2. Jeffrey L. McNairn, *The Capacity to Judge: Public Opinion and Deliberative Democracy in Upper Canada, 1791–1854* (Toronto: University of Toronto Press, 2000).

3. LAC, *Bathurst Independent Examiner*, October 23, 1829, and October 30, 1829. The October 30th article lists the petitioners as follows: Wm. Morris, Esq. Perth; Mr. Charles Bailey [Ballie], Dalhousie; Mr. A. Craig, Innkeeper, Lanark; Mr. E. Wilson, North Sherbrooke; Mr. Samuel Boulton, Bathurst Mills; Mr. John Richey, Ferguson's Falls; Mr. Robert Ball, Murphy's [Morphy's] Falls; Mr. John Gemmel, Shipman's Mills; Mr. John Blowson, Innkeeper; Mr. Patrick Newlan [Nowlan], Beckwith; Mr. Andrew Hill, Richmond; Mr. John Adamson, Bytown; Mr. John Toschach [Toshack], Ramsay; Louis Rendt, Esq., Bathurst; Mr. John Gray, Bathurst; and Mr. Joshua Adams, Bathurst.

4. H.J. Bridgman, "Morris, William (1786–1858)," *DCB*, VIII (1851–1860).

5. John Toshack (1780–1862), a Bridgeton millwright, settled with his wife, Isabella Wilson, and their nine children on Con. 8, lot 24W, in Ramsay Township in 1821. William Moir, a Lanarkshire Emigration Society member who had settled with his wife, Janet King, and four children on lot 20E of the same Ramsay concession, claimed that Toshack "was not honoured with many hearers." Nevertheless, Robert Forrest, a Lesmahagow society member who settled with his wife, Nelly, and six children on Con. 8, lot 21E, in Lanark Township, appeared grateful for the lay preacher's sermons given in the township once every four weeks. Bennett, *Lanark Society Settlers*, 139–40, 147, 186; LAC, MG24 Vol: 158, ff.9–11, Forrest Letters; Brown, *Lanark Legacy*, 32.

6. Other Scots charged with collecting signatures were John Gemmell (Gemmill), merchant in Ramsay; Robert Bell, son of Reverend Bell and merchant in Murphy (Morphy's) Fall(s); John Gray, who had settled with his wife on lot Con. 2, lot 4NE, in Bathurst Township in 1817; and Charles Bailey (Ballie), the Lesmahagow Emigration Society settler who had authored petitions in both Scotland and Upper Canada. A. Craig, listed as an innkeeper in Lanark, could be another Scot, since an Alexander Craig appears to have been a member Robert Craig's family who emigrated with the Camlachie society and settled in the township. Another possibility is Adam Craig, who was a cooper and arrived in the township in 1821. See Brown, *Lanark Legacy*, 132; Courtney C.J. Bond, "Bell, Robert," *DCB*, IX (1891–1900); Perth Military Settlement, LAC MG9-D8-27, Microfilm Reel C-4651, "Upper Canada Located Settlers (Monthly Returns)," 74; Bennett, *Lanark Society Settlers*, 95, 144, 213; Patrick Nowlan, an Irish Anglican, ran the government store in Franktown and was the first tavern keeper in Beckwith. Lockwood, *Beckwith*, 20, 22, 64.

7. William Lyon Mackenzie's petitioning campaign was also influenced by the contemporary efforts in Britain made by local Political Unions to have the Reform Bill adopted, and campaigns in the imperial homeland also influenced Robert Gourlay. Michael E. Vance and Mark D. Stephen, "Grits, Rebels and Radicals: Anti-Privilege Politics and the Pre-History of 1849 in Canada West," in Derek Pollard and Ged Martin, eds., *Canada 1849* (University of Edinburgh: Centre for Canadian Studies, 2001), 186, 191–92. For a detailed discussion of the involvement of Gourlay and

Mackenzie in political petitioning in Upper Canada, see Carol Wilton, *Popular Politics and Political Culture in Upper Canada, 1800–1850* (Montreal: McGill-Queen's University Press, 2000), 27–38, 42–43, 46–47, 61–64.

8. McNairn, *The Capacity to Judge*, 150–51; Roberts, *In Mixed Company*, 56–76. Alexander Snedden's coal-mining father, James, a veteran of both the Revolutionary and Napoleonic Wars, was born in Camlachie and emigrated with the Rutherglen Union Society. Alexander had married Mary Whyte in 1817. Mary's sister Agnes married David Snedden, while her brother James married Janet Snedden. See Marilyn Snedden, *The Snedden Saga: From Lanarkshire to Lanark County* (Burnstown, ON: General Store Publishing, 1994), 15–17, 35–40; Bennett, *Lanark Society Settlers*, 184–85.

9. LAC, *Bathurst Courier*, June 24, 1836.

10. Margaret Coleman, "Cameron, Malcolm (1808–1876)," *DCB*, X (1871–1880); Reid, *Upper Ottawa Valley*, cxi–cxiii, 267; Brown, *Lanark Legacy*, 58, 106, 278; McGill, *Pioneer History*, 157–61.

11. Bridgman, "Morris, William," *DCB*. For "loyal" petitions, see Haydon, *Pioneer Sketches*, 74–75; and Wilton, *Popular Politics and Political Culture*, 177–78. An account of Morris's lawsuit against Cameron can be found in Haydon, 215–18.

12. Bridgman, "Morris, William," *DCB*.

13. Skelton, *A Man Austere*, 56–64; H.J. Bridgman, "Bell, William (1780–1857)," *DCB*, VIII (1851–1860).

14. Clarence Halliday, *John Halliday: A Forthright Man* (Coburg, ON: C. Halliday, 1962), 57–63. For background on the Cameronians, see Nigel M. de S. Cameron, *et al.*, *Dictionary of Scottish Church History & Theology* (Downers Grove, IL: InterVarsity Press, 1993).

15. Both Alexander McMillan and Roderick Matheson had illegitimate children with their servants. According to Reverend Bell, McMillan flew into a rage when the clergyman refused to baptize the baby girl he had with Janet McGregor. In 1832 Bell recorded in his journal that McMillan's daughter, then eleven, was living with her mother in Ramsay Township, but that she had an arm amputated after a sugar bush accident. Barbara J. Griffith, "Kinship, Religion, Politics and Community," 28–29, 79. Michael Gauvreau suggests that Bell's objection to the Church of Scotland was based on his anti-aristocratic world view, and that his marriage to Mary Black, who was a Seceder, precipitated his break with the established church. In Upper Canada, Bell supported the effort led by William Morris to unify the various Presbyterian churches. Gauvreau, "Covenanter Democracy," 65–66; Bridgman, "Bell, William," *DCB*; and "Morris, William," *DCB*.

16. Reverend Bell's First Presbyterian Church was located on the corner of Drummond and Halton Streets, while Reverend Wilson's St. Andrews Church, completed in 1833, stood on the corner of Drummond and Craig Streets. Wilson remained in Perth until 1844, when he returned to Scotland. Elizabeth Ann Kerr McDougall and John Moir,

eds., *Selected Correspondence of the Glasgow Colonial Society* (Toronto: Champlain Society, 1994), 34–35. Halliday left Wilson's church in 1835 as a consequence of the minister's "reading of sermons," which he denounced as a "popish" practice, and join the congregation of the Reformed Presbyterian Church run on Cameronian principles. Halliday, *A Forthright Man*, 62–63.

17. Lockwood, *Beckwith*, 172–76, 178.

18. James Hall (1768–1833), a native of Dollar, Alloa, was one of the first settlers in Lanark village. Although he does not appear to have been a member of an emigration society, he left Scotland at the same time — travelling on the *Commerce* in 1820 with his wife, Jean Russell, and their six children. Bennett, *Lanark Society Settlers*, 204–05. See NAS, Lennoxlove Muniments, TD 89/33 bundle 1003, James Hall to the Duke of Hamilton, March 20, 1823.

19. Reverend Dr. John Gemmill (1760–1844) was born in Dunlop, Ayrshire. He emigrated with his wife, Elizabeth (1791–1850), and their seven children, and settled in Lanark village, where he also served as a medical doctor. Bennett, *Lanark Society Settlers*, 122. See also McDougall and Moir, *Glasgow Colonial Society*, xi–xv, xxxi–xxxiv, 9–11, 15–19, 34–36.

20. McDougall and Moir, *Glasgow Colonial Society*, 10–11.

21. *Ibid.*, 75–76.

22. Vance, *Emigration and Scottish Society*, 57–61; Lockwood, *Beckwith*, 44, 126, 176, 188; Among the original members of the Baptist Community in North Sherbrooke were the families of Andrew McAlpine (1775–1848), a Paisley-born weaver, and his wife, Janet Mills (c.1779–1827), born in Kilmarnock, of the Barrowfield and Anderston society; Robert Sym, a ploughman from Pitlochry, of the Rutherglen Union Society; and Josiah Davis (1773–1834), a Paisley mason, and his wife, Gaff Caird (1779–1830). The Paisley Townhead Society members were David Wylie, a Paisley weaver, and his wife, born in Dalry; Arthur Stoaks (1771–1860), a Paisley weaver, and his wife, Mary Wilson, born in Kilmarnock; William Dunlop, a Kilmarnock wright, and his wife; and George Watson (1790–1871), a millwright born "near Dundee," and his wife, Catherine Walker (1792–1839). In 1834 Daniel Ritchie (1780–1848) and his wife, Margaret [Ewing?] (?–1859), moved their family to a farm near Marcy, Oneida County, New York. Griffith, "Kinship, Religion, Politics and Community," 11–20, 22–23, 41–42.

23. Ebenezer Wilson's son David was also a Baptist, as was his daughter Margaret. Wilson also became a member of the North Sherbrooke Temperance Society in 1841. Josiah Davies Jr. also worked as a "stone cutter" in Perth. Robert Sym would be a leading figure in the Sarnia Township Reform Association and shared his Perthshire origins with Malcolm Cameron's mother. Griffith, "Kinship, Religion, Politics and Community," 15, 32–33, 51–52.

24. James Wilkie senior settled on Con. 9, lot 16W, in Ramsay Township with his wife, Janet Thompson (1790–1870), and their two children. Bennett, *Lanark Society Settlers*, 93.

25. The McMillan-Thom duel, fought in 1833, was called off when Thom was slightly injured in the leg after the first shots were exchanged. Griffith, "Kinship, Religion, Politics and Community," 15, 27–29; Brown, *Lanark Legacy*, 90–94. PCA, "Records of the Kirk Session of St. Andrews Church, Perth," 21 July, 1833, f.15.

"Chivari" or "charivari" was a form of popular protest that originated in Europe. The celebrants often targeted couples for inappropriate or unconventional marriages. For the practice in North America, see Brian Palmer, "Discordant Music: Charivaris and Whitecapping in North America," *Labour-La Travial*, Vol. 3 (1978), 5–62.

26. The Irish-born Jane Quigley was the wife of Robert Love's neighbour, John McConnell, a native of Kilbridge, Lanarkshire, who had served with the 19th Regiment of Foot in India and Ceylon. John arrived in North Sherbrooke, with his army pension, in 1825 in order to join his parents, James McConnell and Agnes McClarkin, who had also emigrated with the Camlachie Emigration Society. John McConnell farmed his brother Richard's land grant, Con. 3, lot 3W, North Sherbrooke. NA(UK) WO 97/387/9; LAC, Barbara J. Griffith and Iva M. Headrick, *The Love Family of Lanark County* (Ottawa: B.J. Griffith, 2007), 9–10, 22; Bennett, *Lanark Society Settlers*, 96–97.

27. Lockwood, *Beckwith*, 96–114. For the township locations of the Cork settlers, see Carol Bennett, *Peter Robinson's Settlers, 1823-1825* (Renfrew, ON: Juniper Books, 1987).

28. For early anti-Catholicism in the west of Scotland, see Elaine McFarland, *Protestants First: Orangeism in 19th Century Scotland* (Edinburgh: Edinburgh University Press, 1990), 49–61. In 1829 artisan petitions were drawn up in Glasgow, opposing the extension of Catholic political rights with the Catholic Emancipation Bill. Ian A. Muirhead, "Catholic Emancipation: Scottish Reactions in 1829," *Innes Review*, XXIV (1973), 26–42.

29. For the argument linking Protestantism with Britishness, see Linda Colley, *Britons: The Forging of a Nation, 1707-1837*, revised edition (New Haven, CT: Princeton University Press, 2009). Scholars have noted that Colley's argument largely ignores the Irish experience of "Britishness." For the exercise of church discipline in Lanark County, see Duff Willis Crerar, "Church and Community: The Presbyterian Kirk Session in the District of Bathurst, Upper Canada" (University of Western Ontario: unpublished M.A. thesis, 1979); and Lockwood, *Beckwith*, 178–82.

30. Ramsay Township was divided into five districts. William McQueen, a member of the Bridgeton Transatlantic Society who settled with his family on Con. 9, lot 20E, was given responsibility for Con. 5–7 from lot 15 up. John Hutchison, a passenger on *Earl of Buckingham* who settled with his wife and son on Con. 7, lot 10W, was to look after Con. 4–8 up to lot 14. John Lochart, a member of the Lesmahagow society who settled with his wife, Jane McMillan, and three daughters on Con. 12, lot 4W, took care of Con. 8–12 up to lot 12. Alexander Erskine was responsible for Con. 8–12 from lot 15, and Thomas Kennedy looked after Con. 1–4 from lot 12. UCA, "Ramsay Kirk Session Minutes," July 24, 1834; Bennett, *Lanark Society Settlers*, 83, 151, 205. Leah Leneman and Rosalind Mitchison, "Girls in Trouble: The Social and Geographical Setting of Illegitimacy in Early Modern Scotland," *Journal of Social History*, Vol. 21, No. 3 (Spring 1988), 483–97.

31. Bennie's Corners in Ramsay Township was named after the family. They settled on Con. 8, lot 25W. John Bennie married Helen Carswell in 1834. UCA, "Ramsay Kirk Session Minutes," May 16, 1835; November 12, 1835. Bennett, *Lanark Society Settlers*, 182.

32. Selected Entries from "Auld Kirk" Session Minutes, Ramsay Township, see Appendix V.

33. PCA, "Records of the Kirk Session of St. Andrews Church, Perth," November 20, 1836; January 25, August 27, 1837; July 28, August 25, September 8, October 7, November 24, 1838. In 1829, Reverend Bell's public denunciations of sabbath-breaking resulted in a conflict with James Stewart, who brought a libel charge against him. According to Bell, the jury was packed with Stewart's fellow Orangemen, who awarded the newspaper proprietor £5 in damages. McGill, *Pioneer History*, 143; Gauvreau, "Covenanter Democracy," 68–69.

34. In Scotland there were four types of sabbath breach offences (non-attendance, idling, working, or immoral behavior). Leah Leneman, "Profaning the Lord's Day: Sabbath Breach in Early Modern Scotland," *History*, Vol. 74, No. 241 (June 1989), 217–31.

35. UCA, "Ramsay Kirk Session Minutes," May 28, 1838. The Gilmour and Bowes families were members of the Glasgow Trongate Society. James Bowes, although born in Manchester, was farming the family's ancestral lands in Glamis before emigrating to Canada. He had eloped with Lady Margaret Monteith, whose family objected to a union with a social inferior. William Bowes (b. 1810) was their twelfth child. The family settled on Con. 5, lot 21E, in Ramsay. Several Gilmour families in the Trongate society settled in the township; Allan Gilmour was likely the son of Allan and Margaret Gilmour, who settled on Con. 8, lot 15E. James Hart from the Paisley Townhead society settled in Ramsay, but Janet Hart was more likely the daughter of John Hart, an original signatory to Daniel Murchie's petition, since the Paisley Townhead Society records indicate that he had a seven-year-old daughter (making her twenty-seven in 1841). The two families may have been related. Bennett, *Lanark Society Settlers*, 119, 122–23,166; NA(UK) CO 42/189 f.538. See also Appendix V.

36. Lockwood, *Beckwith*, 178–80.

37. See Appendix V. In 1826 the kirk session of Reverend Bell's First Presbyterian Church admonished Besty Little for being pregnant with an illegitimate child. William Halliday, one of John Halliday's sons, was named as the father and this may have contributed to the ill feeling between the two men. PCA, "Session Book, Presbyterian Congregation, Perth," June 10, July 9, August 6, December 3, 1826. It is possible that John Paterson was the son of James Paterson, a Srathaven and Kilbride Emigration Society member who settled with his wife and five children on Con. 2, lot 17W, in Ramsay. Janet McGregor, wife of J. David Fumerton, the son of Paisley Townhead Emigration Society member John Fumerton, was also rebuked for antenuptial fornication by the Ramsay kirk session, UCA, "Ramsay Kirk Session Minutes," May 13, 1840; September 2, 1840. Bennett, *Lanark Society Settlers*, 165, 195. For the Scottish church's concern with "irregular marriages," see Leah Leneman and Rosalind Mitchison, *Sin in the City: Sexuality and Social Control in Urban Scotland, 1660–1780* (Edinburgh: Scottish Cultural Press, 1998), 128–44.

38. John MacTaggart, *Three Years in Canada: An Account of the Actual State of the Country in 1826-7-8*, Vol. I (London: Henry Colburn, 1829), 201–02. The popular custom of "trial" marriages persisted among the labouring population in many parts of Scotland, despite church efforts to stamp out the practice. The working people of the southwest of Scotland, where many of the assisted emigrants had originated, were particularly notorious for resisting church discipline and for high illegitimacy rates in the early nineteenth century. Leah Leneman and Rosalind Mitchison, *Girls in Trouble: Sexuality and Social Control in Rural Scotland* (Edinburgh: Scottish Cultural Press, 1998), 83–85, 106–08.

39. See Appendix V. Alexander Duncan had his church privileges restored on June 27, 1840, but there was no mention of his wife in that entry. The family occupied Con. 11, lot 6W, in Ramsay. UCA, "Ramsay Kirk Session Minutes," December 16, 1836; Bennett, *Lanark Society Settlers*, 162.

40. James Dunlop could be one of the sons of John Dunlop, a member of the Abercrombie Emigration Society who settled with his wife and two sons on Con. 6, lot 12W, in Ramsay Township. Bennett, *Lanark Society Settlers*, 29.

41. Robert Carswell (1778-1872), who was born in Hillhead, Glasgow, appears to have studied medicine as a young man. He married Helen Russell, daughter of the Glasgow merchant Robert Russell, in 1804. The couple and their three daughters settled on Con. 8, lot 22E, in Ramsay Township. Bennett, *Lanark Society Settlers*, 89; UCA, "Ramsay Kirk Session Minutes," November 12, November 23, December 7, December 17, December 31, 1837; September 24, 1838. While the extent of domestic violence is hard to measure, there was a violent death recorded in 1828, when Thomas Easby killed his wife, Ann, and four of his children before burning down their house on Con. 9 in Drummond. The four-year-old son, Joseph, was adopted by the neighbouring Richardson family, and his version of events help to convict Easby, who was hanged for his crime. John Tullis, a neighbouring farmer and member of the Hamilton Emigration Society, was one of the chief crown witnesses at the trial. *Perth Courier*, June 18, 1964. John C. Ebbs, *A History of Drummond Township* (Burnstown, ON.; General Store Publishing House, 1999), 12–13. See also Elizabeth Jane Errington, *Wives and Mothers, Schoolmistresses and Scullery Maids: Working Women in Upper Canada, 1790-1840* (Montreal: McGill-Queen's University Press, 1995), 38–42, 46–52, 269, fn. 82. For an imaginative recreation of events based on the surviving sources, see Susan Code, *A Matter of Honour: And Other Tales of Early Perth* (Burnstown, ON: General Store Publishing, 1996), 62–71.

42. *Paisley Advertizer*, December 10, 1825.

43. Leneman and Mitchison, *Sin in the City*, 17, 33–36.

44. PCA, "Records of the Kirk Session of St. Andrews Church, Perth," June 30, July 14, August 24, November 3, December 7, 1839. According to the 1851 Census, Alexander Ferguson (b. 1796) and his wife, Elizabeth (b. 1799), occupied Con. 6, lot 1, in Drummond. The house that the Paton's occupied was in the southwest corner

of the lot. LAC, Census of 1851, Canada West, Lanark County, Drummond, Part 2, Con. 5, 6, 7, 8, Sch. A, p. 65, line 40, Sch. B, p. 81, line 41. Adam Paton's origins are not clear, but from the testimony given before the kirk session it appears that Margaret may have been related a MacDonald family in the township. The Paton's joined the Ramsay Church in April 1842. UCA, "Roll Book for the Communicants in the Ramsay Church." See also Appendix V.

45. Lynn Marks, "No Double Standard? Leisure, Sex, and Sin in Upper Canadian Church Discipline Records, 1800–1860," in Kathryn McPherson, *et al*, eds., *Gendered Pasts: Historical Essays in Femininity and Masculinity in Canada* (Don Mills, ON: Oxford University Press Canada, 1999), 48–64.

Chapter Six: Pioneer Patriarchs

1. AO MU 7424, Series 1-1. John Gemmill Sr. Correspondence, James Gemmill, Irvine, Scotland to John Gemmill, Merchant, Ramsay Township, Upper Canada, July 31, 1829.

2. Margaret Muirhead (1790–1854), John Gemmill's second wife, was born in "St. Ninian's Parish." The couple's first child was born in 1830. The Gemmill family settled on Con. 9, lot 15W, in Ramsay Township. Bennett, *Lanark Society Settlers*, 120.

3. For a discussion of the strengths and weaknesses of emigrant letters as historical sources, see David A. Gerber, *Authors of their Lives: The Personal Correspondence of British Immigrants to North America in the Nineteenth Century* (New York: New York University Press, 2006); David Fitzpatrick, *Oceans of Consolation: Personal Accounts of Irish Migration to Australia* (Cork: Cork University Press, 1994); Bruce S. Elliott *et al.*, eds., *Letters Across Borders: The Epistolary Practices of International Migrants* (New York: Palgrave Macmillan, 2006); and Elizabeth Jane Errington, *Emigrant Worlds and Transatlantic Communities: Migration to Upper Canada in the First Half of the Nineteenth Century* (Montreal: McGill-Queen's University Press, 2007), 167–76. For an illustration of how the challenges of recovering women's experience in the Ottawa Valley can be overcome, see Carol Bennett McCuaig, *Invisible Women* (Renfrew, ON: Juniper Books, 1999).

4. AO MU 7424, Series 1-1. John Gemmill Sr. Correspondence, Alexander Adam, Saltcoats, Scotland to John Gemmill, "Ramsay by Perth," April 9, 1827; and James Hendry, Rochsoles (a Glenmavis farm north of Airdrie) to John Gemmill, August 11, 1829. There were a number of John Gemmills in the emigration societies, but their relationship to each other is unclear. Another John Gemmill in the Glasgow Trongate Society, who was married to Ann Weir and settled with his family on Con. 8, lot 13W, in Lanark Township, is sometimes confused with John Gemmill of Almonte, since their wives shared first names. For an analysis of the letters written by John Gemmill in Lanark, see Errington, *Emigrant Worlds*, 29–31, 141–51. See also Carol Bennett, *Lanark Society Settlers*, 121, 126–27.

5. NAS GD 1/814/5, Colquhoun and MacArthur Family Papers, Ebenezer Wilson to Mr and Mrs. John Colquhoun, July 16, 1836.

6. NAS GD 1/814/5, Colquhoun and MacArthur Family Papers, Mary Stoaks (née Wilson) to family in Scotland, January 6, 1829. In his letter of July 16, 1836, Ebenezer Wilson communicated the tragic news that Betty Stoaks and her infant daughter had died in January of that year.

7. Barbara J. Griffith, "Kinship, Religion, Politics and Community,"13; Bennett, *Lanark Society Settlers*, 185–86, 215.

8. Macinnes *et al.*, *Scotland and the Americas*, 221–22; Lockwood, *Beckwith*, 90.

9. LAC MG24 I158, f.6, John Forrest Fonds, copy of a letter from William Davie to his sons and daughters in Scotland, November 25, 1821; Bennett, *Lanark Society Settlers*, 175.

10. AO MU 7424, Series 1-1. John Gemmill Sr. Correspondence, Alexander Adam, Saltcoats, Scotland to John Gemmill, "Ramsay by Perth," April 9, 1827.

11. LAC MG24 I158, ff. 9, 14, John Forrest Fonds, Robert Forrest to John Forrest, n.d.; Robert Forrest to his parents, May 23, 1824.

12. Bennett, *Lanark Society Settlers*, 132–33, 147. The Gardner family settled Con. 5, lot 6E, in Dalhousie Township. Robert Gardner was born in Houston and his wife Margaret Calinder [*sic*] was born near Falkirk and the couple married in Glasgow. Their son Archibald became an influential Mormon. See Brigham Young University, Special Collections, "Archibald Gardner Journal, 1814–1857," typescript 1944. The journal is posted online at *archibaldgardnerjournal.blogspot.com*.

13. LAC MG24 I158, f.15, John Forrest Fonds, Robert Forrest to his parents, May 23, 1824.

14. It has been suggested that the anonymous author may have been Stephen Young, but James Aikenhead of the Strathaven and Kilbride society appears to be a more likely candidate. The author of the 1861 *Perth Courier* article identified his Ramsay holding as Con. 2, lot 20. Aikenhead was first settled on Con. 3, lot 20W, but soon moved to Con. 2, lot 19E. His family consisted of three boys and three girls from his marriage to Janet Croumbie. It is not certain if Janet or James's second wife, Ann, emigrated with the family in 1821. Bennett, *Lanark Society Settlers*, 13, 193.

15. Bennett, *Lanark Society Settlers*, 137. For the New York canal, see Janet Larkin, "The Oswego Canal: A Connecting Link Between the United States and Canada," *Ontario History*, CIII, 1 (Spring 2011), 20–41. For working conditions, see Peter Wry, *Common Labour: Workers and the Digging of North American Canals, 1780–1860* (Cambridge: Cambridge University Press, 1993).

16. Quoted in Bennett, *Lanark Society Settlers*, 53.

17. Recounted by James Black in the *Almonte Gazette*, 1897, and quoted in Bennett, *Lanark Society Settlers*, 103. The family settled on Con. 7, lot 21W, in Ramsay.

18. Macinnes *et al.*, *Scotland and the Americas*, 222.

19. *Ibid.*

20. NAS GD 1/814/5, Colquhoun and MacArthur Family Papers, Mary Stoaks to family in Scotland, January 6, 1829.

21. Bell, *Hints to Emigrants*, 154.

22. QUA, Bell Papers, Vol. 1, ff. 165–67, Reverend Bell to Mary Bell, Ford, Midlothian, February 3, 1817.

23. McGill, *Pioneer History*, 185–86. For the role of emigrant reading in maintaining the link with Scotland, see Bill Bell, "Print Culture in Exile: the Scottish Emigrant Reader in the Nineteenth Century," *Papers of the Bibliographical Society of Canada*, Vol. 36, No. 2 (1998), 87–106. Arthur Lang, while listed as a member of the Paisley Townhead Emigration Society, was not recorded on the *Earl of Buckingham*'s ship list. He was thirty-one at the time of his emigration and his wife was twenty-seven. Their family consisted of two boys, at eight and seven years old, and four girls, at twelve, ten, two, and, the youngest, less than a year old. The family settled on Con. 1, lot 14W, in Ramsay. NA(UK) CO 384/6 f.541; Bennett, *Lanark Society Settlers*, 166–67.

24. Leprince de Beaumont (1711–80), who worked as a governess in England while composing her *Magazine*, also popularized many French tales, including *Beauty and the Beast*. See Sonya Stephens, *A History of Women's Writing in France* (Cambridge: Cambridge University Press, 2000), 89. The full title of her book was *The Young Misses' Magazine: Containing dialogues between a governess and several young ladies of quality, her scholars: In which each lady is made to speak according to her particular genius, temper, and inclination: their several faults are pointed out, and the easy way to mend them, as well*. A two-volume translation was published in Glasgow in 1800. A Glasgow edition of Reverend Wilson's *Afflicted Man's Companion, or, A directory for families and persons afflicted with sickness or any other distress* was published in 1811, and a two-volume edition Daniel Fenning's *New System of Geography*, with a corrected entry for North America, was published in London in 1780.

25. QUA, Bell Papers, Vol.2, f. 175.

26. For a discussion of the separate spheres ideology and women's actual experience in Upper Canada, see Elizabeth Jane Errington, "Suitable Diversions: Women, Gentility and Entertainment in an Imperial Outpost," *Ontario History*, CII, 2 (Autumn 2010), 175–96, and *Wives and Mothers, Schoolmistresses and Scullery Maids*, 20–27; as well as Roberts, *In Mixed Company*, 138–64.

27. NLS, L.C.Fol.73(094), "Copy of a very Curious Letter from a Cotton Spinner in Canada," available online at *digital.nls.uk/broadsides/broadside.cfm/id/16583*.

28. *Ibid.*

29. John Nielson's own letters were written in Standard English. He and his wife, Ann Wilson, and their infant son, James, were granted Con. 12, lot 6W, in Ramsay Township. McGill, *Pioneer History*, 185; Bennett, *Lanark Society Settlers*, 171–72.

30. Anna Clark, *The Struggle for the Breeches: Gender and the Making of the British Working Class* (Berkeley: University of California Press, 1995), 7.

31. *Ibid.*, 70, 76.

32. *Ibid.*, 58, 63–87.

33. The long-standing tradition of textile families' marriages being based on an ideal of "patriarchal co-operation" — that is, the husband, although insisting on control, recognizing the economic value of his wife and children — appears to have been adapted in the 1820s to the cotton-spinning industry. Perhaps knowledge of this led the author of the Upper Canada "letter" to emphasize mill lasses. Clark, *Struggle for the Breeches*, 132, 136–38.

34. John C. Holley, "The Two Family Economies of Industrialism: Factory Workers in Victorian Scotland," *Journal of Family History*, Vol. 6 (1981), 57–69, cited in Clark, *Struggle for the Breeches*, 255.

35. Single men were only allowed to take one sister with them and widows, with or without families, were not to offered any assistance under the 1815 terms. NA(UK) CO 42/165 ff. 93–96.

36. NA(UK) CO 384/6 f.725, Margaret Tait to Earl Bathurst, July 12, 1820.

37. NA(UK) CO 384/8 f.295, Sarah Neilson to Earl Bathurst, June 1822. The letter is transcribed in Bennett, *Lanark Society Settlers*, 208. Several families were split during the assisted emigrations. The provisions of the 1815 scheme had made allowances for the practice, and by 1819 the authorities in Quebec were decrying it. An 1822 petition from the relatives of individuals who had departed with the 1821 assisted emigration demonstrated that family division was a popular strategy with several members of the Glasgow Emigration Societies [NA(UK) CO 384/8 ff.436-37]. The petitioners argued that it was the hope of another season of assisted emigration that encouraged them "to part with those to whom they are bound by closest ties of kindred and affection." Endorsement of the petition by Robert Lamond, William McGavin, Thomas Chalmers, and a host of Glasgow ministers, ensured that the government provided a passage for the majority of signatories. Sarah Neilson later became aware of this petition and may have used it as a model for her own letter to Bathurst. The Colonial Office records do not mention passage being provided for Sarah and her family, and Carol Bennett found no trace of her husband in the Ottawa Valley land records.

38. In a second letter sent to his uncle sent from Lanark on April 10, 1822, John Dick's younger brother James reported that his fifteen-year-old sister was working as a domestic servant about a mile out of Perth, "where she gets about two dollars a month." Twelve-year-old Agnes was with the Perth storekeeper, Mr. Ferguson, and her twin sister was with her eight-year-old brother, Robert, at Mr. Adams, three miles outside Perth. Finally, six-year-old Catherine had been taken in by Mr. and Mrs. Brice from West Calder. John Dick had two older sisters, Janet and Margaret, who were excluded from obtaining land grants in Upper Canada. Both of John and James' letters have been transcribed by Carol Billingham and posted on the Lanark County Genealogical Society webpage: *www.globalgeneaology.com/LCGS/articles/A-DICKT.*

HTM. The family farm was located on Con. 9, lot 13W, in Lanark Township. Further details on the Dick family can be found in Bennett, *Lanark Society Settlers*, 135–36.

39. James Craig's grant was Con. 8, lot 18W, in Ramsay Township. His adult son, Thomas, occupied, Con. 7, lot 18E, but appears not to have been able to assist his mother-in-law, Grizel Wallace. One of her daughters, Jean, married Busteed Green, a Peter Robinson settler, but the fate of Grizel and her other daughter is unclear. Bennett, *Lanark Society Settlers*, 85–86.

40. The letters reprinted in Robert Lamond's *Narrative* were selected in order to put the Glasgow Committee on Emigration in the best possible light, and need to be treated with caution. As is often the case with published letters, the original no longer appears to exist. As a consequence, there is no means to corroborate its authenticity or to determine if it had been edited prior to publication. Nevertheless, the reference to Mrs. Graham was clearly a causal aside in a letter that focused on praising the benevolence of government and was, therefore, unlikely to have been altered. It has been suggested that the woman in question was the wife of John Graham, who had been assigned Con. 8, lot 6E, in Lanark Township, a lot that had been reallocated to Edward Bennett at an early date, perhaps as a consequence of Graham's death. Graham and his wife had emigrated with the Glasgow Emigration Society in 1820, and would have arrived in Upper Canada at the same time as Toshack. They could have met in Lanark, where the letter had been composed. Lamond, *Narrative of the Rise and Progress of Emigration from the Counties of Lanark and Renfrew*, 105–06; Bennett, *Lanark Society Settlers*, 109. For the problems associated with published emigrant letters, see Terry McDonald, "'Come to Canada While You Have a Chance': A Cautionary Tale of English Emigrant Letters in Upper Canada," *Ontario History*, Vol. 91, No. 2 (Autumn 1999), 111–30.

41. Andrew and Mary Boag emigrated with the Anderston and Rutherglen Emigration Society and settled on Con. 6, lot 11E, in Lanark Township. Their son John was born in 1821, and while he was unable to inherit until he reached the age of nineteen, under Canadian regulations Mary could maintain the property in his name. This is in contrast to Grizel "Grace" Wallace, who had two daughters but no son to inherit the family property. Bennett, *Lanark Society Settlers*, 52.

42. Bennett, *Lanark Society Settlers*, 75.

43. According to Lamond, the state of the country "as to money matters" had prevented Janet Bulloch from selling the farm, and, as a consequence, she required government assistance to rejoin her husband and family in Upper Canada. Rather condescendingly, Lamond described her as "an intelligent woman who has seen better days." NAS GD 45/3/64-85 f.217, Lamond to Dalhousie, August 27, 1821. In Scottish law both husband and wife retained independent rights to family property brought into a marriage. For women's legal rights in Scotland, see R.A. Houston, "Women in the Economy and Society of Scotland, 1500–1800," in R.A. Houston and I.D. Whyte, eds., *Scottish Society, 1500–1800* (Cambridge: Cambridge University Press, 1989), 118–47.

44. Duncan and Catherine Kippen are listed among St. Andrews communicants in 1833, and Duncan is named with Catherine in the 1838 minutes reporting the ball held in their house. Duncan, however, does not appear in the subsequent minutes. One can assume that either he had died or that he had left Perth looking for wage labour. In any event, it is clear that Mrs. Kippen was on her own in 1839. PCA, "Records of the Kirk Session of St. Andrews Church, Perth," September 1, 1833; February 24, 1838; January 13, March 2, August 24, September 7, 1839.

45. Thomas Radenhurst had acted as McMillan's "second" and Henry Boulton also had his own associations with duelling. John Wilson served as a Tory MPP until 1849, when he switched to the Reform Party. Malcolm Cameron was one of the pallbearers at his funeral in 1869. For a thorough discussion of the surviving evidence and subsequent career of the participants in the Wilson-Lyon duel, which, despite claims to the contrary, was not the "last" in Canada, see Edward Shortt, *The Memorable Duel at Perth* (Perth, ON: The Perth Museum, 1970). See also Cecilia Morgan, "'In Search of the Phantom Misnamed Honour': Duelling in Upper Canada," *Canadian Historical Review*, Vol. 76, No. 4 (December 1995), 529–62.

46. Shortt, *Memorable Duel*, 51.

47. UCA, "Ramsay Kirk Session Minutes," April 10, 14, 17; May 8, 14. The Galbraith family settled on Con. 5, lot 10W, and the Smith family settled beside them on Con. 5, lot 10E, in Ramsay Township. Daniel Galbraith served as warden of Lanark and Renfrew Counties, as well as a member of Parliament for North Lanark. Bennett, *Lanark Society Settlers*, 105, 107; Brown, *Lanark Legacy*, 278–80.

48. For separate spheres ideology in England and Scotland, see John Tosh, *A Man's Place: Masculinity and the Middle Class Home in Victorian England* (New Haven, CT: Yale University Press, 1999); Clark, *Struggle for the Breeches*, 247–63; Deborah Simonton, "Work, Trade and Commerce," in Lynn Abrams *et al.*, *Gender in Scottish History Since 1700* (Edinburgh: Edinburgh University Press, 2006); and Lesley A. Orr MacDonald, *A Unique and Glorious Mission: Women and Presbyterianism in Scotland, 1830–1930* (Edinburgh: John Donald, 2000), 23–34.

Chapter Seven: Recalling and Retelling

1. Feminist scholars have been the most attune to the strengths and weaknesses of diaries as historical sources. See Kathryn Carter, ed., *The Small Details of Life: Twenty Diaries by Women in Canada, 1830–1996* (Toronto: University of Toronto Press, 2002), 3–29.

2. QUA, Bell Papers, Vol. II, ff.134–135, Sunday, February 1, 1824, and Vol. III, ff. 87–90.

3. John Robson is also erased in the retelling where he appears only as "a young man." QUA, Bell Papers, Vol. III, ff. 87–90.

4. QUA, Bell Papers, Vol. III, ff. 20–21.

5. LAC MG24 I 158 f.13, "John Forrest Fonds," Robert Forrest to his parents, May 23, 1824.

6. Both snakes and bears are mentioned by John McDonald. *Narrative of a Voyage to Quebec, And Journey from Thence to New Lanark in Upper Canada* (Edinburgh: Andrew Jack, 1823), 13, 19.

7. McDonald included himself among the "society" emigrants, but he is not on any of the lists. A Malcolm McDonald was a member of the Glasgow Trongate Society and may have been a relative. McDonald could have accompanied that group as an independent settler since he refers to the death of the society president, William Purdie, at Prescott. McDonald appears to have also travelled widely and certainly visited Montreal on occasion, which also suggests that he had some capital. *Narrative of a Voyage*, 8.

8. [LAC] *Perth Courier*, December 23, 1892, "The Story of Dalhousie's Settlement — By One of the Pioneers."

9. [LAC] *Carleton Place Herald*, February 9, 1938, "Sketch of the Life of William Lang." A transcript of Arthur Lang's diary detailing the journey to Upper Canada was published in the *Carleton Place Herald* on Febrary 2, 1938. The location of the original is not known to this author. The family settled on Lot 14W, Con.1, in Ramsay Township. Carol Bennett, *The Lanark Society Settlers* (Renfrew, ON.: Juniper Books, 1991), 166–67; Howard M. Brown, *Lanark Legacy: Nineteenth-Century Glimpses of an Ontario County* (Perth, ON: County of Lanark, 1984), 33–42.

10. *The Daily Citizen* [Ottawa], Monday, November 5, 1877.

11. [LAC] *Perth Courier*, June 30, 1905, "The Early History of Balderson's Corners."

12. [LAC] *Perth Courier*, June 30 and May 19, 1905, "History of Old Perth and the Perth District," by J.M. Walker, Gananoque, and "Letter to the editor, Apr. 25, 1905," by J.W.D. Although "Old Girls" were mentioned in the reunion accounts, they do not appear to have organized any of their own events before 1958, but were treated instead as secondary to the "Old Boys" — reflecting the patriarchal attitudes of the early settlers. See John C. Walsh, "Performing Public Memory and Re-Placing Home in the Ottawa Valley, 1900-1958," in James Opp and John C. Walsh, eds., *Placing Memory and Remembering Place in Canada* (Vancouver: University British Columbia Press, 2010), 25–56, fn.6. (I am grateful to Dr. Renée Hulan for this reference.)

13. The original typescript of J.G. Harvey's talk is held by the Perth Museum.

14. [LAC] *Perth Courier*, December 22, 1916. This article also reprinted an edited version of the 1877 *Daily Citizen* article.

15. The Pembroke Pageant program is quoted in Walsh, "Performing Public Memory," 37.

16. For an analysis of a "captivity" tale from Grey County, Ontario, see William Wye Smith, Scott McLean and Michael E. Vance, eds., *William Wye Smith: Recollections of a Nineteenth Century Scottish Canadian* (Toronto: Natural Heritage Books, 2008), 216, 382, fn.18.

17. [LAC] *Carleton Place Herald*, February 9, 1938, "Sketch of the Life of William Lang." It has been suggested that John Steel[e] was the son of Alexander Steel, a member of the Camlachie society who settled with his wife, Isabella, on Con. 7, lot 22E, in Ramsay Township. John would have been a nine-year-old boy at the time. Bennett, *Lanark Society Settlers*, 97–98.

18. [LAC] Hilda Geddes, *Historical sketch of McDonalds Corners, Snow Road and Elphin* (s.l.: s.n., 1975), 61–62, and *The Canadian Mississippi River* (Snow Road Station, ON.: H. Geddes, 1988), 102. (I am grateful to Barbara J. Griffith for these references.)

   The "Indian Lot," now known as the Lett farm, is located at 4263 Elphin-Maberly Road. Elizabeth Miller (née Smith) was born in Paisley in 1818 and had settled with her family in North Sherbrooke. Her father, Robert Smith, was a member of the Parkhead Emigration Society. Beryl Scott and Barbara J. Griffith, *Inside North Sherbrooke*, Vol. I (McDonalds Corners, ON: North Sherbrooke Historical Society, 2008), 105–06.

19. Barbara J. Griffith, personal communication, May 18, 2000.

20. Solomon Benedict's brother ran a drugstore in Windsor, Ontario, where he sold Native remedies. The Benedict farm was on Con. 2, lot 10, in Palmerston Township. Scott and Griffith, *Inside North Sherbrooke*, 79–83. According to their marriage record, on April 16, 1890, Annie's father and mother, Andrew McInnis and Rachel Leckie, also resided in Palmerston.

BIBLIOGRAPHY

A. Newspapers
Bathurst Courier
Bathurst Independent Examiner
Carleton Place Herald
The Daily Citizen (Ottawa)
Glasgow Chronicle
Paisley Advertizer
Perth Courier [Ontario]

B. Nineteenth-Century Publications
Beattie, William. *Scotland Illustrated*. London: George Virtue, 1838.

Bell, Reverend William. *Hints to Emigrants; in a Series of Letters from Upper Canada*. Edinburgh: Waugh and Innes, 1824.

Brown, Robert. *Paisley Poets: With Brief Memoirs of Them, and Selections from Their Poetry*. Paisley: J. & J. Cook, 1889–90.

_____ . *The History of Paisley: from the Roman Period down to 1884*. Vol. II. Paisley: J. & J. Cook, 1886.

Gilmour, David. *Reminiscences of the Pen-Folk, Paisley Weavers of Other Days, Etc.* Edinburgh & Paisley: Alex Gardner, 1879.

Indian Treaties and Surrenders from 1680 to 1890. Vol. I. Ottawa: Queen's Printer, 1891. Facsimile edition, Coles Pub. Co, 1971.

Lamond, Robert. *A Narrative of the Rise and Progress of Emigration from the Counties of Lanark and Renfrew, to the New Settlements in Upper Canada*. Glasgow: Chalmers and Collins, 1821. Facsimile Edition, Ottawa: Canadian Heritage Publications, 1978.

MacTaggart, John. *Three Years in Canada: An Account of the Actual State of the Country in 1826-7-8*. London: Henry Colburn, 1829.

McDonald, John. *Narrative of a Voyage to Quebec, and Journey from Thence to New Lanark in Upper Canada.* Edinburgh: Andrew Jack, 1823.

Parkhill, John. *The History of Paisley.* Paisley: Robert Stewart, 1859.

Sinclair, Sir John. *Statistical Account of Scotland.* Edinburgh: M. Creech, 1791–1799.

Stuart, James. "Historical Notices of St. Fillan's Crozier, and of the Devotion of King Robert Bruce to St. Fillan." *Proceedings of the Society of Antiquaries of Scotland.* Vol. 12 (1876–1877), 134–82.

Willis, Nathaniel Parker. *Canadian Scenery Illustrated.* London: George Virtue, 1842.

Wilson, Daniel. "Notice of the Quigrich or Crozier of St. Fillan and of its Hereditary Keepers in a Letter to John Stuart...." *Proceedings of the Society of Antiquaries of Scotland.* Vol. 12 (1876–1877), 122–31.

C. Books and Articles

Ash, Marinell, *et al. Thinking with Both Hands: Sir Daniel Wilson in the Old World and the New.* Toronto: University of Toronto Press, 1999.

Bennett, Carol. *The Lanark Society Settlers.* Renfrew, ON: Juniper Books, 1991.

_____. *Peter Robinson's Settlers.* Renfrew, ON: Juniper Books, 1987.

Bennett McCuaig, Carol. *Founding Families of Beckwith Township, 1816–1846.* Renfrew, ON: Juniper Books, 2007.

_____. *Invisible Women.* Renfrew, ON: Juniper Books, 1999.

Brown, Howard M. *Lanark Legacy: Nineteenth-Century Glimpses of an Ontario County.* Perth, ON: County of Lanark, 1984.

Buckley, Roger Norman. *The British Army in the West Indies: Society and the Military in the Revolutionary Age.* Gainesville: University Press of Florida, 1998.

Cameron, James M. "A Study of the Factors that Assisted and Directed Scottish Emigration to Upper Canada, 1815–55." University of Glasgow: unpublished Ph.D. Thesis, 1970.

Campey, Lucille H. *"A Very Fine Class of Immigrants": Prince Edward Island's Scottish Pioneers, 1770-1850*. Toronto: Natural Heritage Books, 2001.

_____. *After the Hector: The Scottish Pioneers of Nova Scotia and Cape Breton, 1773-1852*. Toronto: Natural Heritage Books, 2004.

_____. *The Scottish Pioneers of Upper Canada, 1784-1855: Glengarry and Beyond*. Toronto: Natural Heritage Books, 2005.

_____. *The Silver Chief: Lord Selkirk and the Scottish Pioneers of Belfast, Baldoon and Red River*. Toronto: Natural Heritage Books, 2003.

_____ . *With Axe and Bible: The Scottish Pioneers of New Brunswick, 1784-1874*. Toronto: Natural Heritage Books, 2007.

Carter, Kathryn, ed. *The Small Details of Life: Twenty Diaries by Women in Canada, 1830-1996*. Toronto: University of Toronto Press, 2002.

Clark, Anna. *The Struggle for the Breeches: Gender and the Making of the British Working Class*. Berkeley: University of California Press, 1995.

Colley, Linda. *Britons: The Forging of a Nation, 1707-1837*. New Haven: Princeton University Press, 2009. Revised edition.

Cookson, J.E. "Early Nineteenth-Century Scottish Military Pensioners as Homecoming Soldiers." *The Historical Journal*. Vol. 52, No. 2 (2009), 319-41.

_____. *The British Armed Nation, 1793-1815*. Oxford: Clarendon Press, 1997.

Cowan, Helen. *British Emigration to British North America*. Toronto: University of Toronto Press, 1961.

Devine, T.M. *Scotland's Empire, 1600-1815*. London: Allen Lane, 2003.

Devine, T.M., ed. *Clearance and Improvement: Land, Power and People in Scotland, 1700-1900*. Edinburgh: John Donald, 2006.

_____. *Scottish Emigration and Scottish Society: Proceedings of the University of Strathclyde Scottish Historical Studies Seminar 1990-91*. Edinburgh: John Donald, 1992.

Devine, T.M., and John R. Young, eds. *Eighteenth Century Scotland: New Perspectives*. Edinburgh: Tuckwell, 1999.

Dickason, Olive Patricia. *Canada's First Nations: A History of Founding Peoples from the Earliest Times*. Oxford: Oxford University Press, 1997. Second edition.

Durey, Michael. *Transatlantic Radicals and the Early American Republic*. Lawrence, KS: University of Kansas Press, 1997.

Elliott, Bruce S. *Irish Migrants in the Canadas: A New Approach*. Montreal: McGill-Queens University Press, 1988.

Elliott, Bruce S., *et al*, eds. *Letters Across Borders: The Epistolary Practices of International Migrants*. New York: Palgrave Macmillan, 2006.

Errington, Elizabeth Jane. *Emigrant Worlds and Transatlantic Communities: Migration to Upper Canada in the First Half of the Nineteenth Century*. Montreal: McGill-Queen's University Press, 2007.

_____. *The Lion, the Eagle, and Upper Canada: A Developing Colonial Ideology*. Montreal: McGill-Queen's University Press, 1987.

_____. "Suitable Diversions: Women, Gentility and Entertainment in an Imperial Outpost." *Ontario History*. CII, 2 (Autumn 2010), 175–96.

_____. *Wives and Mothers, Schoolmistresses and Scullery Maids: Working Women in Upper Canada, 1790–1840*. Montreal: McGill-Queen's University Press, 1995.

Fitzpatrick, David. *Oceans of Consolation: Personal Accounts of Irish Migration to Australia*. Cork: Cork University Press, 1994.

Gates, Lillian F. *Land Policies of Upper Canada*. Toronto: University of Toronto Press, 1968.

Gauvreau, Michael. "Covenanter Democracy: Scottish Popular Religion, Ethnicity, and the Varieties of Politico-religious Dissent in Upper Canada, 1815–1841." *Histoire Sociale/Social History*. No. 36 (May 2003), 55–83.

Gerber, David A. *Authors of their Lives: The Personal Correspondence of British Immigrants to North America in the Nineteenth Century*. New York: New York University Press, 2006.

Gibson, John G. *Old and New World Highland Bagpiping*. Montreal: McGill-Queen's University Press, 2002.

Godlewska, A., and N. Smith, eds. *Geography and Empire*. Oxford: Blackwell Publishing, 1994.

Grant, Robert D. *Representations of British Emigration, Colonization and Settlement: Imagining Empire, 1800–1860*. London: Palgrave, 2005.

Graves, Donald E. "The Redcoats are Coming!: British Troop Movements to North America in 1814." *Journal of the War of 1812*. Vol. VI, No. 3 (Summer 2001), 12–18.

Griffith, Barbara J. "Kinship, Religion, Politics and Community in Two Frontier Settlements of Upper Canada: Some Baptists of Lanark and Lambton Counties." Canadian Baptist Archives: unpublished paper, 2005.

Halliday, Clarence. *John Halliday: A Forthright Man*. Cobourg, ON: C. Halliday, 1962.

Harley, J.B. *The New Nature of Maps: Essays in the History of Cartography*. Baltimore: Johns Hopkins University Press, 2001.

Harris, R. Cole. *The Reluctant Land: Society, Space, and Environment in Canada Before Confederation*. Vancouver: University of British Columbia Press, 2008.

Haydon, Andrew. *Pioneer Sketches in the District of Bathurst*. Toronto: Ryerson Press, 1925.

Hessel, Peter. *The Algonkin Nation, the Algonkins of the Ottawa Valley: An Historical Outline*. Arnprior, ON: Kichesippi Books, 1993. Revised edition.

Hunter, Clark, ed. *The Life and Letters of Alexander Wilson*. Philadelphia: American Philosophical Society, 1983.

Jarvis, Eric. "Military Land Granting in Upper Canada following the War of 1812." *Ontario History*. Vol. LXVII, No. 3 (September 1975), 121–34.

Johnson, J.K. "'Claims of Equity and Justice': Petitions and Petitioners in Upper Canada 1815–1840." *Histoire sociale/Social History.* Vol. XXVIII, No. 55 (May 1995), 219–40.

Johnston, H. Winston. *The Glengarry Light Infantry, 1812–1816: Who Were They and What Did They Do in the War?* Charlottetown: Benson Publishing, 1998.

Johnston, H.J.M. *British Emigration Policy 1815–1830.* Oxford: Clarendon Press, 1972.

Legget, Robert. *Ottawa River Canals and the Defence of British North America.* Toronto: University of Toronto Press, 1988.

Leneman, Leah. "Profaning The Lord's Day: Sabbath Breach in Early Modern Scotland." *History.* Vol. 74, No. 241 (June 1989), 217–31.

Leneman, Leah, and Rosalind Mitchison. *Girls in Trouble: Sexuality and Social Control in Rural Scotland.* Edinburgh: Scottish Cultural Press, 1998.

_____. "Girls in Trouble: The Social and Geographical Setting of Illegitimacy in Early Modern Scotland." *Journal of Social History.* Vol. 21, No. 3 (Spring 1988), 483–97.

_____. *Sin in the City: Sexuality and Social Control in Urban Scotland, 1660–1780.* Edinburgh: Scottish Cultural Press, 1998.

Lockwood, Glenn J. *Beckwith: Irish and Scottish Identities in a Canadian Community.* Carleton Place, ON: Township of Beckwith, 1991.

_____. *Montague: A Social History of an Irish Township, 1783–1980.* Smith Falls, ON: Township of Montague, 1980.

_____. "The Pattern of Settlement in Eastern Ontario, 1784–1875." *Families.* Vol. 30, No. 4 (1991), 235–57.

Macinnes, Allan I. *et al.,* eds. *Scotland and the Americas, c.1650– c.1939: A Documentary Source Book.* Edinburgh: Scottish History Society, 2002.

Marks, Lynn. "No Double Standard? Leisure, Sex, and Sin in Upper Canadian Church Discipline Records, 1800–1860." Kathryn

McPherson, *et al.*, eds. *Gendered Pasts: Historical Essays in Femininity and Masculinity in Canada.* Don Mills, ON: Oxford University Press Canada, 1999, 48–64.

McDonald, Terry. "'Come to Canada While You Have a Chance': A Cautionary Tale of English Emigrant Letters in Upper Canada." *Ontario History.* Vol. 91, No. 2 (Autumn 1999), 111–30.

McDougall, Elizabeth Ann Kerr, and John Moir. *Selected Correspondence of the Glasgow Colonial Society.* Toronto: Champlain Society, 1994.

McFarland, Elaine. *Protestants First: Orangeism in 19th Century Scotland.* Edinburgh: Edinburgh University Press, 1990.

McGill, Jean S. *A Pioneer History of the County of Lanark.* Toronto: Self-published, 1968. Reprint edition, Clay Publishing, 1979.

McLean, Marianne. *The People of Glengarry: Highlanders in Transition, 1745–1820.* Montreal: McGill-Queen's University Press, 1991.

McNairn, Jeffrey L. *The Capacity to Judge: Public Opinion and Deliberative Democracy in Upper Canada, 1791–1854.* Toronto: University of Toronto Press, 2000.

Morgan, Cecilia. "'In Search of the Phantom Misnamed Honour': Duelling in Upper Canada." *Canadian Historical Review.* Vol. 76, No. 4 (December 1995), 529–62.

Murray, Norman. *The Handloom Weavers 1790–1850: A Social History.* Edinburgh: John Donald, 1978.

Nenadic, Stana. *Lairds and Luxury: The Highland Gentry in Eighteenth-Century Scotland.* Edinburgh: John Donald, 2007.

Reid, Richard, ed. *The Upper Ottawa Valley to 1855: A Collection of Documents.* Toronto: The Champlain Society, 1990.

Richards, Eric. *Patrick Sellar and the Highland Clearances: Homicide, Eviction, and the Price of Progress.* Edinburgh: Polygon, 1999.

Rider, Peter E., and Heather McNabb, eds. *A Kingdom of the Mind: How the Scots Helped Make Canada.* Montreal: McGill-Queen's University Press, 2006.

Roberts, Julia. *In Mixed Company: Taverns and Public Life in Upper Canada.* Vancouver: University of British Columbia Press, 2009.

Schmalz, Peter S. *The Objibwa of Southern Ontario.* Toronto: University of Toronto Press, 1991.

Scott, Beryl, and Barbara J. Griffith. *Inside North Sherbrooke.* Vol. I. McDonalds Corners, ON: North Sherbrooke Historical Society, 2008.

Shortt, Edward. *The Memorable Duel at Perth.* Perth, ON: The Perth Museum, 1970.

Skelton, Isabel. *A Man Austere: William Bell, Parson and Pioneer.* Toronto: Ryerson Press, 1947.

Smith, Donald, *et al. Aboriginal Ontario: Historical Perspectives on the First Nations.* Toronto: Dundurn Press, 1994.

Surtees, Robert J. *Indian Land Surrenders in Ontario, 1763–1867.* Ottawa: Department of Indian Affairs and Northern Development, 1984.

Swinson, Arthur, ed. *A Register of the Regiments and Corps of the British Army.* London: The Archive Press, 1972.

Turner, Larry. *Perth: Tradition & Style in Eastern Ontario.* Toronto: Natural Heritage Books, 1992.

Vance, Michael E. "Advancement, Moral Worth and Freedom; the Meaning of 'Independence' for Early Nineteenth-Century Lowland Emigrants to Upper Canada." Ned Landsman, ed. *Nation and Province in the First British Empire: Scotland and the Americas, 1600–1800.* Lewisburg, PA: Bucknell University Press, 2001, 151–80.

_____. "Emigration and Scottish Society: The Background of Three Government Assisted Emigrations to Upper Canada 1815–1821." University of Guelph: unpublished Ph.D. thesis, 1990.

_____. "The Politics of Emigration: Scotland and Assisted Emigration, 1815–1826." T.M. Devine, ed. *Scottish Emigration and Scottish Society: Proceedings of the University of Strathclyde Scottish Historical Studies Seminar 1990–91.* Edinburgh: John Donald, 1992, 37–60.

Walsh, John C. "Performing Public Memory and Re-Placing Home in the Ottawa Valley, 1900–1958." James Opp and John C. Walsh, eds. *Placing Memory and Remembering Place in Canada.* Vancouver: University British Columbia Press, 2010, 25–56.

Wilton, Carol. *Popular Politics and Political Culture in Upper Canada, 1800–1850.* Montreal: McGill-Queen's University Press, 2000.

Withers, Charles W. J. *Gaelic in Scotland, 1698–1981: The Geographical History of a Language.* Edinburgh: John Donald, 1984.

D. Useful Internet Resources

Dictionary of Canadian Biography, *www.biographi.ca/index-e.html*

First Nations Profiles, *fnpim-cippn.inac-ainc.gc.ca/index-eng.asp*

First Nations Treaties, *atlas.nrcan.gc.ca/site/english/maps/historical/indian treaties*

Lanark County Genealogical Society, *globalgenealogy.com/LCGS/index. htm*

Maps of Scotland, *maps.nls.uk*

Perth Historical Society, *www.perthhs.org*

The War of 1812 Website, *www.warof1812.ca*

INDEX

Michael E. Vance is a professor of history at Saint Mary's University in Halifax, Nova Scotia. His research focuses on early nineteenth-century Scottish emigration, and he also has an interest in the nature of Scottish overseas identity. His previous publication with Natural Heritage Books, undertaken with co-editor Scott A. McLean, *William Wye Smith: Recollections of a Nineteenth Century Scottish Canadian*, is an annotated edition of the unpublished memoir of a Scottish-born poet, newspaperman, and Congregational minister. Michael lives in Halifax.

BY THE SAME AUTHOR

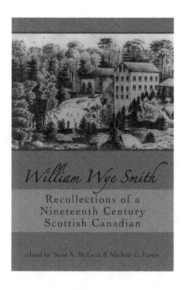

William Wye Smith
Recollections of a Nineteenth Century Scottish Canadian
Scott A. McLean and Michael E. Vance, eds.

978-1-550028041
$25.99

Many writers of the late nineteenth and early twentieth centuries emphasized the virtues of early rural pioneers and life on the land as a general criticism of what they perceived to be the negative, alienating influence of Ontario's rapid urban and industrial expansion. Such work often highlighted the difficulties the recent emigrant faced: the clearing of forest and the breaking of new ground, the isolation and long Canadian winters; however they in turn celebrated the progress demonstrated in the pioneer's domination over nature, the establishment of thriving communities and the extension of transportation networks. William Wye Smith, a popular nineteenth century Upper Canadian poet, was no exception.

Smith prepared his Canadian Reminiscences, a hand-written compilation of anecdotes collected during his lifetime that relate to his experience as journalist, clergyman and son of Scottish settlers, to provide his own unique perspective of pioneer life. This fully annotated version of Smith's unpublished manuscript highlights Smith's unwitting testimony to the social life of the province, his relationship to the construction and maintenance of Scottish and Canadian identity, as well as his position in literary history.

Available at your favourite bookseller.

DUNDURN
www.dundurn.com

VISIT US AT
Dundurn.com
Definingcanada.ca
@dundurnpress
Facebook.com/dundurnpress